Introduction to Finance

Introduction to Finance

STANLEY B. BLOCK
Texas American Bank/Ft. Worth
Chair of Finance
Texas Christian University

GEOFFREY A. HIRT
Associate Professor of Finance
DePauw University

Second Edition • 1985

AMERICAN INSTITUTE FOR
PROPERTY AND LIABILITY UNDERWRITERS
720 Providence Road, Malvern, Pennsylvania 19355-0770

The contents of this text originally appeared in the following work. This adaptation has been made with the permission of the original publisher.

Stanley B. Block and Geoffrey A. Hirt, *Foundations of Financial Management*, Copyright 1984 by Richard D. Irwin, Inc.

First Printing • December 1985

Library of Congress Catalog Number 85-51845
International Standard Book Number 0-89463-046-6

Printed in the United States of America

Foreword

The American Institute for Property and Liability Underwriters and the Insurance Institute of America are companion, nonprofit, educational organizations supported by the property-liability insurance industry. Their purpose is to provide quality continuing education programs for insurance personnel.

The Insurance Institute of America offers programs leading to the Certificate in General Insurance, the Associate in Claims (AIC) designation, the Associate in Management (AIM) designation, the Associate in Risk Management (ARM) designation, the Associate in Underwriting (AU) designation, the Associate in Loss Control Management (ALCM) designation, the Associate in Premium Auditing (APA) designation, the Accredited Adviser in Insurance (AAI) designation, the Associate in Research and Planning (ARP) designation, the Associate in Insurance Accounting and Finance (AIAF) designation, the Introduction to Property and Liability Insurance (INTRO) certificate, and the Supervisory Management (SM) certificate. The American Institute develops, maintains, and administers the educational program leading to the Chartered Property Casualty Underwriter (CPCU) professional designation.

This text, originally entitled *Foundations of Financial Management* by Stanley B. Block and Geoffrey A. Hirt, which is published by the American Institute through an agreement with the book's original publisher, Richard D. Irwin, Inc., was selected by the Institute to be one of three texts used in CPCU 8—Accounting and Finance. The text was selected because of its clarity and usefulness. Further, the Institute has modified the text so that it now contains only those sections which are most directly relevant for CPCU candidates. Finally, the Institute has tailored the text for CPCU candidates through the development of the CPCU 8 Course Guide.

All Institute textbooks—including those not specifically written for the Institute—have been and will continue to be subjected to an extensive review process. Reviewers are drawn from both industry and academic ranks. In addition, it has been necessary to rely on the knowledge and skill of Institute staff members in the preparation of Institute texts. No member of the Institute's staff, however, receives any royalty from the sale of our texts. Text development is seen as an integral part of the duties of these Institute staff members. We have proceeded in this way in order to avoid any possibility of conflict of interests. We invite and will welcome any and all criticisms of our publications. It is only with such comments that we can hope to provide high quality educational texts, materials, and programs.

Edwin S. Overman, Ph.D., CPCU
President

Table of Contents

1 | Financial Forecasting

The old notion of the corporate treasurer burning the midnight oil in order to find new avenues of financing before dawn is no longer in vogue. If there is one element that is essential to the financial manager, it is the ability to plan ahead and to make necessary adjustments before actual events occur. Quite likely, we could construct the same set of external events for two corporations (inflation, recession, severe new competition, etc.), and one would survive, while the other would not. The outcome might be a function not only of their risk-taking desires, but also of their ability to hedge against risk with careful planning.

While we might assume that no growth or a decline in volume is the primary cause for a shortage of funds, this is not necessarily the case. A rapidly growing firm may witness a significant increase in accounts receivable, inventory, and plant and equipment that cannot be financed in the normal course of business. Assume that sales go from $100,000 to $200,000 in one year for a firm that has a 5 percent profit margin on sales. At the same time, assume that assets represent 50 percent of sales and go from $50,000 to $100,000 as sales double. The $10,000 of profit (5 percent × $200,000) will hardly be adequate to finance the $50,000 asset growth. The remaining $40,000 must come from our suppliers, the bank, and perhaps our stockholders. The student should recognize that profit alone is generally inadequate to finance significant growth and that a comprehensive financing plan must be developed. All too often, the small businessman (and sometimes the large one as well) is mystified by an increase in sales and profits, but less cash in the till.

Constructing Pro Forma Statements

The most comprehensive means of financial forecasting is to go through the process of developing a series of pro forma, or projected, financial statements. We will give particular attention to the *pro forma income statement*, the *cash budget*, and the *pro forma balance sheet*. Based on the projected statements, the firm is able to judge its future level of receivables, inventory, payables, and other corporate accounts as well as its anticipated profits and borrowing

Figure 1–1

Development of pro forma statements

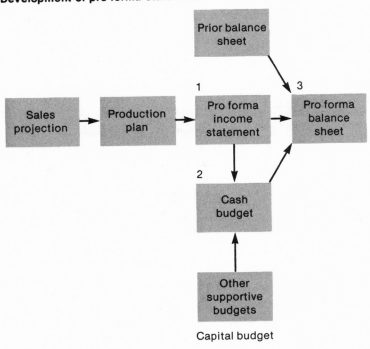

Capital budget

requirements. The financial officer can then carefully track actual events against the plan and make necessary adjustments. Furthermore, the statements are often required by bankers and other lenders as a guide for the future.

A systems approach is necessary for the development of pro forma statements. We first construct a pro forma income statement based on sales projections and the production plan, then translate this material into a cash budget, and finally assimilate all previously developing pro forma financial statements is depicted in Figure 1—1. We will use a six-month time frame to facilitate the analysis, though the same procedures could be extended to one year or longer.

Pro Forma Income Statement

Assume that the Goldman Corporation has been requested by its bank to provide pro forma financial statements for midyear 1984. The pro forma income statement will provide a projection of how much profit the firm anticipates making over the ensuing time period. In developing the pro forma income statement, we will follow four important steps.

1. Establish a sales projection.
2. Determine a production schedule and the associated use of new material, direct labor, and overhead to arrive at gross profit.
3. Compute other expenses.
4. Determine profit by completing the actual pro forma statement.

Establish a sales projection

For purposes of analysis, we shall assume that the Goldman Corporation has two primary products: wheels and casters. Our sales projection calls for the sale of 1,000 wheels and 2,000 casters at a price of $30 and $35, respectively. As indicated in Table 1—1, we anticipate total sales of $100,000.

Table 1–1

Projected wheel and caster sales (first six months, 1981)

	Wheels	Casters
Quantity	1,000	2,000
Sales price	$30	$35
Sales revenue	$30,000	$70,000
Total		$100,000

It is assumed that the sales projections were derived from both an external and internal viewpoint. Using the former, we analyze our prospective sales in light of economic conditions affecting our industry and our company. Statistical techniques such as regression and time series analysis may be employed in the process. Internal analysis calls for surveying our own salespeople within their territories. Ideally, we would proceed along each of those paths in isolation of the other and then assimilate the results into one meaningful projection.

Determine a production schedule and the gross profit

Based on anticipated sales, we determine the necessary production plan for the six-month period. The number of units produced will depend on the beginning inventory of wheels and casters, our sales projection, and the desired level of ending inventory. Assume that on January 1, 1984, the Goldman Corporation has in stock the items shown in Table 1—2.

Table 1–2

Stock of beginning inventory

	Wheels	Casters
Quantity	85	180
Cost	$16	$20
Total value	$1,360	$3,600
Total $4,960		

We will add the projected quantity of unit sales for the next six months to our desired ending inventory and subtract our stock of beginning inventory (in units) to determine our production requirements.

Units
+ Projected sales
+ Desired ending inventory
− *Beginning* inventory
  Production requirements

In Table 1—3, we see a required production level of 1,015 wheels and 2,020 casters.

Table 1–3

Production requirements for six months

	Wheels	Casters
Projected unit sales (Table 1—1)	+1,000	+2,000
Desired ending inventory (assumed to represent 10% of unit sales for the time period)	+100	+200
Beginning inventory (Table 1—2)	−85	−180
Units to be produced	1,015	2,020

We must now determine the cost to produce these units. In Table 1—2, we saw that the cost of units in stock was $16 for wheels and $20 for casters. However, we shall assume that the price of materials, labor, and overhead going into the products is now $18 for wheels and $22 for casters, as indicated in Table 1—4.

Table 1–4

Unit costs

	Wheels	Casters
Materials	$10	$12
Labor	5	6
Overhead	3	4
Total	$18	$22

The *total cost* to produce the required items for the next six months is shown in Table 1—5.

Table 1–5

Total production costs

	Wheels	Casters	
Units to be produced (Table 1—3)	1,015	2,020	
Cost per unit (Table 1—4)	$18	$22	
Total cost	$18,270	$44,440	$62,710

Cost of goods sold The main consideration in constructing a pro forma income statement is the costs specifically associated with units sold during the time period. Note that in the case of wheels we anticipate sales of 1,000 units, as indicated in Table 1—1 but are producing 1,015, as indicated in Table 1—5, to increase our inventory level by 15 units. For profit measurement purposes, we will *not* charge these extra 15 units against current sales.[1] Furthermore,

---

[1] Later on in the analysis we will show the effect that these extra units have on the cash budget and the balance sheet.

in determining the cost of the 1,000 units sold during the current time period, we will *not* assume that all of the items sold represent inventory manufactured in this period. In the case of the Goldman Corporation, we shall assume that it uses FIFO (first-in, first-out) accounting and that it will first allocate the cost of current sales to beginning inventory and then to goods manufactured during the period.

Table 1–6

Allocation of manufacturing cost and determination of gross profits

		Wheels	Casters	Combined
Quantity sold (Table 1—1)		1,000	2,000	3,000
Sales price		$30	$35	
Sales revenue		$30,000	$70,000	$100,000
Cost of goods sold:				
Old inventory (Table 1—2)				
Quantity (units)	85		180	
Cost per unit	$16		$20	
Total		$ 1,360	$ 3,600	
New Inventory (the remainder)				
Quantity (units)	915		1,820	
Cost per unit (Table 1—1)	$18		$22	
Total		16,470	40,040	
Total cost of goods sold . .		17,830	43,640	$ 61,470
Gross profit		$12,170	$26,360	$ 38,530

In Table 1—6, we look at the revenue, associated cost of goods sold, and gross profit for both products. For example, 1,000 units of wheels are to be sold at a total revenue of $30,000. Of the 1,000 units, 85 units are from beginning inventory at a $16 cost (Table 1—2) and the balance of 915 units are from current production at an $18 cost. The total cost of goods sold for wheels is $17,830, yielding a gross profit of $12,170. The same general pattern exists for casters, with sales of $70,000, cost of goods sold of $43,640, and gross profit of $26,360. The combined sales for the two products are $100,000, with cost of goods sold of $61,470 and gross profit of $38,530.

At this point, we also compute the value of ending inventory for later use in constructing financial statements. As indicated in Table 1—7, ending inventory will be $6,200.

Table 1–7

Value of ending inventory

+ Beginning inventory (Table 1—2)	$ 4,960
+ Total production costs (Table 1—5)	62,710
Total inventory available for sales	67,670
– Cost of goods sold (Table 1—6)	61,470
Ending inventory	$ 6,200

Other expense items

Having computed total revenue, cost of goods sold and gross profits, we must now subtract other expense items to arrive at a net profit figure. We deduct general and administrative expenses as well as interest expenses from gross profit to arrive at earnings before taxes, then subtract taxes to determine aftertax income, and finally deduct dividends to ascertain the contribution to retained earnings. For the Goldman Corporation, we shall assume that general and administrative expenses are $12,000, interest expense is $1,500, and dividends are $1,500.

Actual pro forma income statement

Combining the gross profit in Table 1—6, with our assumptions on other expense items, we arrive at the pro forma income statement

Table 1–8

Pro Forma Income Statement
June 30, 1984

Sales revenue	$100,000
Cost of goods sold	61,470
Gross profit	38,530
General and administrative expense	12,000
Operating profit (EBIT)	26,530
Interest expense	1,500
Earnings before taxes (EBT)	25,030
Taxes (20%)*	5,006
Earnings after taxes (EAT)	20,024
Common stock dividends	1,500
Increase in retained earnings	$ 18,524

*Though profit before taxes is slightly over $25,000, a convenient rate of 20 percent is applied to the full amount. The corporate rate is currently 15 percent on the first $25,000, 18 percent on the next $25,000, and so on.

presented in Table 1—8. We anticipate earnings after taxes of $20,024, dividends of $1,500, and an increase in retained earnings of $18,524.

Cash Budget

As previously indicated, the generation of sales and profits does not necessarily ensure that there will be adequate cash on hand to meet financial obligations as they come due. A profitable sale may generate accounts receivables in the short run, but no immediate cash to meet maturing obligations. For this reason, we must translate the pro forma income statement into cash flows. In this process we divide the longer-term pro forma income statement into smaller and more precise time frames in order to appreciate the seasonal and monthly patterns of cash inflows and outflows. Some months may represent particularly high or low sales volume or may require dividends, taxes, or capital expenditures.

Cash receipts

In the case of the Goldman Corporation, we break down the pro forma income statement for the first half of 1984 into a series of monthly cash budgets. In Table 1—1, we showed anticipated sales of $100,000 over this time period; we shall now assume that these sales can be divided into monthly projections, as indicated in Table 1—9.

Table 1–9

Monthly sales pattern

Jan.	Feb.	March	April	May	June
$15,000	$10,000	$15,000	$25,000	$15,000	$20,000

A careful analysis of past sales and collection records indicates that 20 percent of sales are collected in the month of sales and 80 percent in the following month. The cash receipt pattern related to monthly sales is shown in Table 1—10. It is assumed that sales for December 1983 were $12,000.

The cash inflows will vary between $11,000 and $23,000, with the high point in receipts coming in May. We now examine the monthly outflows.

Table 1–10

Monthly cash receipts

	Dec.	Jan.	Feb.	March	April	May	June
Sales	$12,000	$15,000	$10,000	$15,000	$25,000	$15,000	$20,000
Collections (20% of current sales) . . .		$ 3,000	$ 2,000	$ 3,000	$ 5,000	$ 3,000	$ 4,000
Collections (80% of previous month's sales)		9,600	12,000	8,000	12,000	20,000	12,000
Total cash receipts . . .		$12,600	$14,000	$11,000	$17,000	$23,000	$16,000

Cash payments

The primary considerations for cash payments are monthly costs associated with inventory manufactured during the period (material, labor, and overhead), as well as disbursements for general and administrative expenses, interest payments, taxes, and dividends. We must also consider cash payments for any new plant and equipment, an item that does not show up on our pro forma income statement.

Costs associated with units manufactured during the period may . be taken from the data provided in Table 1—5, Total Production Costs. In Table 1—11, we simply recast these data in terms of material, labor, and overhead.

Table 1–11

Component costs of manufactured goods

	Wheels			Casters			
	Units produced	Cost per unit	Total cost	Units produced	Cost per unit	Total cost	Combined cost
Materials	1,015	$10	$10,150	2,020	$12	$24,240	$34,390
Labor	1,015	5	5,075	2,020	6	12,120	17,195
Overhead	1,015	3	3,045	2,020	4	8,080	11,125
							$62,710

We see that the total costs for components in the two products are material, $34,390; labor, $17,195; and overhead $11,125. We shall assume that all of these costs are incurred on an equal monthly basis over the six-month period. Even though the sales volume varies from month to month, we assume that we are employing level monthly production to ensure maximum efficiency in the use of

Table 1-12

Average monthly manufacturing costs

	Total costs	Time frame	Average monthly cost
Material	$34,390	6 months	$5,732
Labor	17,195	6 months	2,866
Overhead	11,125	6 months	1,854

various productive resources. Average monthly costs for material, labor, and overhead are as shown in Table 1—12.

We shall pay for materials one month after the purchase has been made. Labor and overhead represent direct monthly cash outlays, as is true of interest, taxes, dividends, and assumed purchases of $8,000 in new equipment in February and $10,000 in June. We summarize all of our cash payments in Table 1—13. Past records indicate that $4,500 in materials was purchased in December.

Table 1-13

Summary of all monthly cash payments

	Dec.	Jan.	Feb.	March	April	May	June
From Table 1—12:							
Monthly material purchase . . .	$4,500	$ 5,732	$ 5,732	$ 5,732	$ 5,732	$ 5,732	$ 5,732
Payment for material (prior month's purchase) . . .		$ 4,500	$ 5,732	$ 5,732	$ 5,732	$ 5,732	$ 5,732
Monthly labor cost		2,866	2,866	2,866	2,866	2,866	2,866
Monthly overhead		1,854	1,854	1,854	1,854	1,854	1,854
From Table 1—8:							
General and administrative expense ($12,000 over 6 months)		2,000	2,000	2,000	2,000	2,000	2,000
Interest expense							1,500
Taxes (two equal payments)				2,503			2,503
Cash dividend							1,500
Also:							
New equipment purchases . . .			8,000				10,000
Total payments		$11,220	$20,452	$14,955	$12,452	$12,452	$27,953

Actual budget

We are now in a position to bring together our monthly cash receipts and payments into a cash flow statement, as illustrated in Table 1—14. The difference between monthly receipts and payments is net cash flow for the month.

? assignment 5
Discussion #3

Table 1–14

Monthly cash flow

	Jan.	Feb.	March	April	May	June
Total receipts (Table 1—10) . .	$12,600	$14,000	$11,000	$17,000	$23,000	$16,000
Total payments (Table 1—13) . .	11,220	20,452	14,955	12,452	12,452	27,953
Net cash flow . . .	$ 1,380	($ 6,452)	($ 3,955)	$ 4,548	$10,548	($11,953)

The primary purpose of the cash budget is to allow the firm to anticipate the need for outside funding at the end of each month. In the present case, we shall assume that the Goldman Corporation wishes to have a minimum cash balance of $5,000 at all times. If it goes below this amount, the firm will borrow funds from the bank, and if it goes above $5,000 and the firm has a loan outstanding, it will use the excess funds to reduce the loan. This pattern of financing is demonstrated in Table 1—15: a fully developed cash budget with borrowing and repayment provisions.

Table 1–15

Cash budget with borrowing and repayment

	Jan.	Feb.	March	April	May	June
1. Net cash flow	$1,380	($6,452)	($3,955)	$4,548	$10,548	($11,953)
2. Beginning cash balance	5,000*	6,380	5,000	5,000	5,000	11,069
3. Cumulative cash balance	6,380	(72)	1,045	9,548	15,548	(884)
4. Monthly loan or (repayment)	—	5,072	3,955	(4,548)	(4,479)	5,884
5. Cumulative loan balance	—	5,072	9,027	4,479	—	5,884
6. Ending cash balance	6,380	5,000	5,000	5,000	11,069	5,000

*We assume that the Goldman Corporation has a beginning cash balance of $5,000 on January 1, 1984, and that it desires a minimum monthly ending cash balance of $5,000.

The first line in Table 1—15 shows our net cash flow, which is added to the beginning cash balance to arrive at the cumulative cash balance. The fourth entry indicates the additional monthly loan or loan repayment, if any, that is required in order to maintain a minimum cash balance of $5,000. In order to keep track of our loan balance, the fifth entry presents cumulative loans outstanding for all months. Finally, we show the cash balance at the end of the month, which becomes the beginning cash balance for the next month.

At the end of January the firm has $6,380 in cash, but by the end of February the cumulative cash position of the firm is negative, necessitating a loan of $5,072 to maintain a $5,000 cash balance. The firm has a loan on the books until May, at which time there is an ending cash balance of $11,069. During the months of April and May the cumulative cash balance is greater than the required minimum cash balance of $5,000, so loan repayments of $4,548 and $4,479 are made to retire the loans completely in May. In June, the firm is once again required to borrow $5,884 in order to maintain a $5,000 cash balance.

Pro Forma Balance Sheet

Now that we have developed a pro forma income statement and a cash budget, it is a relatively simple matter to integrate all of these items into a pro forma balance sheet. Because the balance sheet represents the cumulative changes in the corporation over time, we must first examine the prior period's balance sheet and then translate these items through time to represent June 30, 1984.

Table 1–16

Balance Sheet
December 31, 1983

Assets

Current assets:	
Cash	$ 5,000
Marketable securities	3,200
Accounts receivable	9,600
Inventory	4,960
Total current assets	22,760
Plant and equipment	27,740
Total assets	$50,500

Liabilities and Stockholders' Equity

Accounts payable	$ 4,500
Notes payable	0
Long-term debt	15,000
Common stock	10,500
Retained earnings	20,500
Total liabilities and stockholders' equity	$50,500

The last balance sheet, dated December 31, 1983, is presented in Table 1—16.

In constructing our pro forma balance sheet for June 30, 1984, some of the accounts from the old balance sheet will remain unchanged, while others will take on new values, as indicated by the pro forma income statement and cash budget. The process is depicted in Figure 1—2 on page 14.

We present the new pro forma balance sheet as of June 30, 1984, in Table 1—17 on page 14.

Explanation of pro forma balance sheets Each item in Table 1—17 can be explained on the basis of a prior calculation or assumption.

1. Cash ($5,000)—minimum cash balance as shown in Table 1—15.
2. Marketable securities ($3,200)—remains unchanged from prior period's value in Table 1—16.
3. Accounts receivable ($16,000)—based on June sales of $20,000 in Table 1—10. Twenty percent will be collected that month, while 80 percent will become accounts receivable at the end of the month.

        $20,000 sales
          80% receivables
        $16,000

4. Inventory ($6,200)—ending inventory as shown in Table 1—7.
5. Plant and equipment ($45,740).

        Initial value (Table 1—16)   . . $27,740
        Purchases* (Table 1—13) . .   18,000
        Plant and equipment $45,740

            *For simplicity, depreciation is not explicitly considered.

6. Accounts payable ($5,732)—based on June purchases in Table 1—13. They will not be paid until July, and thus are accounts payable.
7. Notes payable ($5,884)—the amount we must borrow to maintain our cash balance of $5,000, as shown in Table 1—15.

Figure 1–2

Development of a pro forma balance sheet

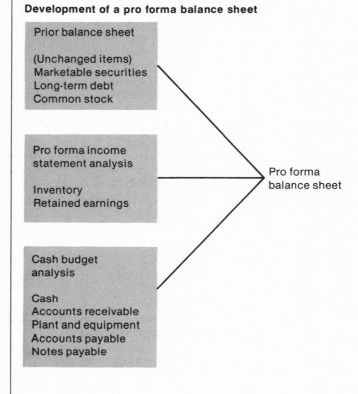

Table 1–17

Pro Forma Balance Sheet
June 30, 1984

Assets

Current assets:
1. Cash . . . . $ 5,000
2. Marketable securities 3,200
3. Accounts receivable 16,000
4. Inventory 6,200

      Total current assets 30,400
5. Plant and equipment 45,740

Total assets $76,140

Liabilities and Stockholders' Equity

6. Accounts payable . . . . $ 5,732
7. Notes payable 5,884
8. Long-term debt 15,000
9. Common stock 10,500
10. Retained earnings 39,024

Total liabilities and stockholders' equity $76,140

8. Long-term debt ($15,000)—remains unchanged from prior period's value in Table 1—16.
9. Common stock ($10,500)—remains unchanged from prior period's value in Table 1—16.
10. Retained earnings ($39,024)

Initial value (Table 1—16)	$20,500
Transfer of pro forma income to retained earnings (Table 1—8)	18,524
Retained earnings	$39,024

Analysis of pro forma statement

In comparing the pro forma balance sheet (Table 1—17) to the prior balance sheet (Table 1—16), we note that assets are up by $25,640.

Total assets (June 30, 1984)	$76,140
Total assets (Dec. 31, 1983)	50,500
Increase	$25,640

The growth must be financed by accounts payable, notes payable, and profit (as reflected by the increase in retained earnings). Though the company will enjoy a high degree of profitability, it must still look to bank financing of $5,884 to support the increase in assets.

Percent-of-Sales Method

An alternative to going through the process of tracing cash and accounting flows to determine financial needs is to assume that accounts on the balance sheet will maintain a given percentage relationship to sales. We then indicate a change in the sales level and ascertain our related financing needs. This is known as the *percent-of-sales method*. For example, for the Howard Corporation, introduced in Table 1—18, we show the following balance sheet accounts in dollars and their percent of sales, based on a sales volume of $200,000.

We observe that cash of $5,000 represents 2.5 percent of sales of $200,000; receivables of $40,000 is 20 percent of sales; and so on. No percentages are computed for notes payable, common stock, and

Table 1–18

HOWARD CORPORATION
Balance Sheet and Percent-of-Sales Table

Assets		Liabilities and Stockholders's Equity	
Cash	$ 5,000	Accounts payable	$ 40,000
Accounts receivable	40,000	Accrued expenses	10,000
Inventory	25,000	Notes payable	15,000
		Common stock	10,000
Total current assets	$ 70,000	Retained earnings	45,000
Equipment	50,000		
Total assets	$120,000	Total liabilities and stockholders' equity	$120,000

$200,000 sales

Percent of Sales

Cash	2.5%	Accounts payable	20.0%
Accounts receivable	20.0	Accrued expenses	5.0
Inventory	12.5		25.0%
Total current assets	35.0		
Equipment	25.0		
	60.0%		

retained earnings because they are not assumed to maintain a direct relationship with sales volume. Note that any dollar increase in sales will necessitate a 60 percent increase in assets,[2] of which 25 percent will be spontaneously or automatically financed through accounts payable and accrued expenses, leaving 35 percent to be financed by profit or additional outside sources of financing. We will assume that the Howard Corporation has an aftertax return of 6 percent on the sales dollar and that 50 percent of profits are paid out as dividends.[3]

If sales increase from $200,000 to $300,000, the $100,000 increase in sales will necessitate $35,000 (35 percent) in additional financing. Since we will earn 6 percent on total sales of $300,000, we will show a profit of $18,000. With a 50 percent dividend pay-

---

[2] We are assuming equipment increases in proportion to sales. In certain cases, there may be excess capacity, and equipment (or plant and equipment) will not increase.

[3] Some may wish to add back depreciation under the percent-of-sales method. Most, however, choose the assumption that funds generated through depreciation (in the sources and uses of funds sense) must be used to replace the fixed assets to which depreciation is applied.

out, $9,000 will remain for internal financing. This means that $26,000 out of the $35,000 must be financed from outside sources. Our formula to determine the need for new funds is:

$$\text{Required new funds (RNF)} = \frac{A}{S}(\Delta S) - \frac{L}{S}(\Delta S) - PS_2(1-D) \quad (1-1)$$

where

$\dfrac{A}{S}$ = Percentage relationship of variable assets to sales [60%]

ΔS = Change in sales [$100,000]

$\dfrac{L}{S}$ = Percentage relationship of variable liabilities to sales [25%]

P = Profit margin [6%]

S_2 = New sales level [$300,000]

D = Dividend payout ratio

Plugging in the values we show:

60% ($100,000) − 25% ($100,000) − 6% ($300,000) (1 − 0.5) =
$60,000 − $25,000 − $18,000 (0.5) =
$35,000 − $9,000 =
$26,000 required sources of new funds

Presumably, the $26,000 can be financed at the bank or through some other appropriate source.

The student will observe that using the percent-of-sales method is a much easier task than tracing through the various cash flows to arrive at the pro forma statements. Nevertheless, the output is much less meaningful and we do not get a month-to-month break-down of the data. The percent-of-sales method is a "broad brush" approach, while the development of pro forma statements is a more exacting approach. Of course whatever method we use, the results are only as meaningful or reliable as the assumptions about sales and production that went into the numbers.

Summary

The process of financial forecasting allows the financial manager to anticipate events before they occur, particularly the need for raising funds externally. An important consideration is that growth itself may call for additional sources of financing because profit is often inadequate to cover the net buildup in receivables, inventory, and other asset accounts.

We develop pro forma financial statements from an overall corporate systems viewpoint. The time perspective is usually six months to a year in the future. In developing a pro forma income statement, we begin by making sales projections, then we construct a production plan, and finally we consider all other expenses. From the pro forma income statement, we proceed to a cash budget in which the monthly or quarterly cash inflows and outflows related to sales, expenditures, and capital outlays are portrayed. All of this information can be assimilated into a pro forma balance sheet in which asset, liability and stockholders' equity accounts are shown. Any shortage of funds is assumed to be financed through notes payable (bank loans).

We may take a shortcut to financial forecasting through the use of the percent-of-sales method. Under this approach, selected balance sheet accounts are assumed to maintain a constant percentage relationship to sales, and thus for any given sales amount we can ascertain balance sheet values. Once again a shortage of funds is assumed to be financed through notes payable.

2 | Operating and Financial Leverage

In the physical sciences as well as politics, the term *leverage* has been popularized to mean the use of special force and effects to produce more than normal results from a given course of action. In business, the same concept is applied, with the emphasis on the employment of "fixed cost" items in anticipation of magnifying returns at high levels of operation. The student should recognize that leverage is a two-edged sword—producing highly favorable results when things go well, and quite the opposite under negative conditions.

Leverage in a Business

Assume that you are approached with an opportunity to start your own business. You are to manufacture and market industrial parts, such as ball bearings, wheels, and casters. You are faced with two primary decisions.

First, you must determine the amount of fixed-cost plant and equipment that you wish to use in the production process. By installing modern, sophisticated equipment, you can virtually eliminate labor in the production of inventory. At high volume, you will do quite well, as most of your costs are fixed. At low volume, however, you could face difficulty in making your fixed payments for plant and equipment. If you decide to use expensive labor rather than machinery, you will lessen your opportunity for profit, but at the same time you will lower your exposure to risk (you can lay off part of the work force).

Second, you must determine how you will finance the business. If you rely on debt financing and the business is successful, you will generate substantial profits as an owner, paying only the fixed costs of debt. Of course, if the business starts off poorly, the contractual obligations related to debt could mean bankruptcy. As an alternative, you might decide to sell equity rather than borrow, a step that will lower your own profit potential (you must share with others) but minimize your risk exposure.

In both decisions, you are making very explicit decisions about the use of leverage. To the extent that you go with a heavy commitment to fixed costs in the operation of the firm, you are employing operating leverage. To the extent that you utilize debt in the financing of the firm, you are engaging in financial leverage. We shall carefully examine each type of leverage and then show the combined effect of both.

Operating Leverage

Operating leverage reflects the extent to which fixed assets and associated fixed costs are utilized in the business firm. As indicated in Table 2—1, a firm's operational costs may be classifed as fixed, variable, or semivariable.

For purposes of analysis, variable and semivariable costs will be combined. In order to evaluate the implications of heavy fixed asset use, we employ the technique of break-even analysis.

Table 2–1

Classification of costs

Fixed	Variable	Semivariable
Rental	Raw material	Utilities
Depreciation	Factory labor	Repairs and maintenance
Executive salaries	Sales commissions	
Property taxes		

Break-even analysis

How much will changes in volume affect cost and profit? At what point does the firm break even? What is the most efficient level of fixed assets to employ in the firm? A break-even chart is presented in Figure 2—1 to answer some of these questions. The number of units produced and sold are shown along the horizontal axis, and revenue and costs are shown along the vertical axis.

Note, first of all, that our fixed costs are $60,000, regardless of volume, and that our variable costs (at $0.80 per unit) are added to

Figure 2–1

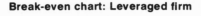
Break-even chart: Leveraged firm

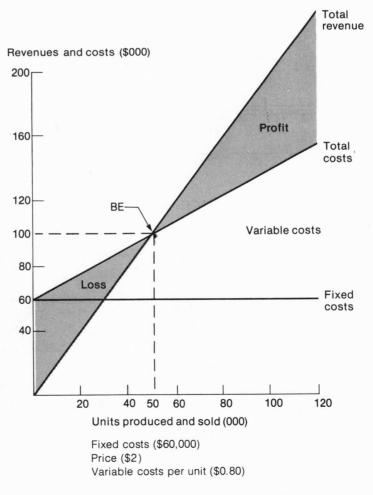

Revenues and costs ($000)

Fixed costs ($60,000)
Price ($2)
Variable costs per unit ($0.80)

fixed costs to determine total costs at any point. The total revenue line is determined by multiplying price ($2) times volume.

Of particular interest is the break-even (BE) point at 50,000 units, where the total costs and total revenue lines intersect. The numbers are as follows:

		Units = 50,000		
Total variable costs (TVC)	Fixed costs (FC)	Total costs (TC)	Total revenue (TR)	Operating income (loss)
(50,000 × $0.80) $40,000	$60,000	$100,000	(50,000 × $2) $100,000	-0-

The break-even point for the company may also be determined by use of a simple formula—in which we divide fixed costs by the contribution margin on each unit sold, with the contribution margin defined as price minus variable cost per unit.

$$BE = \frac{\text{Fixed costs}}{\text{Contribution margin}} = \frac{\text{Fixed costs}}{\text{Price} - \text{variable costs per unit}} = \frac{FC}{P - VC} \quad (2\text{—}1)$$

$$\frac{\$60,000}{\$2.00 - \$0.80} = \frac{\$60,000}{\$1.20} = 50,000 \text{ units}$$

Since we are getting a $1.20 contribution toward covering fixed costs from each unit sold, minimum sales of 50,000 units will allow us to cover our fixed costs (50,000 units × $1.20 = $60,000 fixed costs). Beyond this point, we move into a highly profitable range in which each unit of sales brings a profit of $1.20 to the company. As sales increase from 50,000 to 60,000 units, operating profits increase by $12,000 as indicated in Table 2—2; as sales increase from 60,000 to 80,000 units, profits increase by another $24,000; and so on. As further indicated in Table 2—2, at low volumes such as 40,000 or 20,000 units our losses are substantial ($12,000 and $36,000 in the red).

It is assumed that the firm depicted in Figure 2—1 is operating with a high degree of leverage. The situation is analogous to that of an airline which must carry a certain number of people on board to break even, but beyond that point is in a very profitable range.

Table 2–2

Volume-cost-profit analysis: Leveraged firm

Units sold	Total variable costs	Fixed costs	Total costs	Total revenue	Operating income (loss)
-0-	-0-	$60,000	$ 60,000	-0-	$(60,000)
20,000	$16,000	60,000	76,000	$ 40,000	(36,000)
40,000	32,000	60,000	92,000	80,000	(12,000)
50,000	40,000	60,000	100,000	100,000	-0-
60,000	48,000	60,000	108,000	120,000	12,000
80,000	64,000	60,000	124,000	160,000	36,000
100,000	80,000	60,000	140,000	200,000	60,000

A more conservative approach

Not all firms would choose to operate at the high degree of operating leverage exhibited in Figure 2—1. Fear of not reaching the 50,000-unit break-even level may discourage some companies from heavy utilization of fixed assets. More expensive variable costs may be substituted for automated plant and equipment. Assume that fixed costs for a more conservative firm can be reduced to $12,000— but that variable costs will go from $0.80 to $1.60. If the same price assumption of $2 per unit is employed, the break-even level is 30,000 units.

$$BE = \frac{\text{Fixed costs}}{\text{Price} - \text{variable costs per unit}} = \frac{FC}{P - VC} = \frac{\$12,000}{\$2 - \$1.60} = \frac{\$12,000}{\$0.40}$$
$$= 30,000 \text{ units}$$

With fixed costs reduced from $60,000 to $12,000, the loss potential is small. Furthermore, the break-even level of operations is a comparatively low 30,000 units. Nevertheless, the use of a virtually unlevered approach has cut into the potential profitability of the more conservative firm, as indicated in Figure 2—2.

Even at high levels of operation, the potential profit is rather small. As indicated in Table 2—3, at a 100,000-unit volume, operating income is only $28,000—some $32,000 less than that for the "leveraged" firm previously analyzed in Table 2—2.

The risk factor

Whether management follows the path of the leveraged firm or the more conservative firm depends on its perceptions about the

Figure 2–2

Break-even chart: Conservative firm

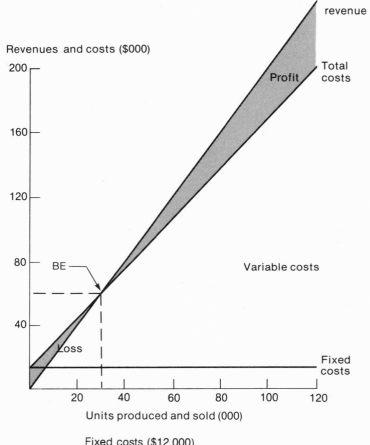

Fixed costs ($12,000)
Price ($2)
Variable costs per unit ($1.60)

Table 2–3

Volume-cost-profit analysis: Conservative firm

Units sold	Total variable costs	Fixed costs	Total costs	Total revenue	Operating income (loss)
-0-	-0-	$12,000	$ 12,000	-0-	$(12,000)
20,000	$ 32,000	12,000	44,000	$ 40,000	(4,000)
30,000	48,000	12,000	60,000	60,000	-0-
40,000	64,000	12,000	76,000	80,000	4,000
60,000	96,000	12,000	108,000	120,000	12,000
80,000	128,000	12,000	140,000	160,000	20,000
100,000	160,000	12,000	172,000	200,000	28,000

future. If the vice president of finance is apprehensive about economic conditions, the conservative plan may be undertaken. For a growing business, in times of relative prosperity, management might maintain a more aggressive, leveraged position. To a certain extent, management should tailor the use of leverage to meet its own risk-taking desires. Those who are risk averse (prefer less risk to more risk) should anticipate a particularly high return before contracting for heavy fixed costs. Others, less averse to risk, may be willing to leverage under more normal conditions. Simply taking risks is not a virtue—our prisons are full of risk takers. The important idea, which is stressed throughout the text, is to match an acceptable return with the desired level of risk.

Cash break-even analysis

Our discussion to this point has dealt with break-even analysis in terms of accounting flows rather than cash flows. For example, depreciation has been implicitly included in fixed expenses, but it represents an accounting entry rather than an explicit expenditure of funds. To the extent that we were doing break-even analysis on a strictly cash basis, depreciation would be excluded from fixed expenses. In the example of the leveraged firm in Formula 2—1, if we eliminate $20,000 of "assumed" depreciation from fixed costs, the break-even level is reduced to 33,333 units.

$$\frac{FC}{P - VC} = \frac{(\$60,000 - \$20,000)}{\$2.00 - \$0.80} = \frac{\$40,000}{\$1.20} = 33,333 \text{ units}$$

Other adjustments could also be made for noncash items. For example, sales may initially take the form of accounts receivable rather than cash, and the same can be said for the purchase of materials and accounts payable. An actual weekly or monthly cash budget would be necessary to isolate these items.

While cash break-even analysis is helpful in analyzing the short-term outlook of the firm, particularly when it may be in trouble, most break-even analysis is conducted on the basis of accounting flows rather than strictly cash flows. Most of the assumptions throughout the chapter are based on concepts broader than pure cash flows.

Degree of operating leverage

Degree of operating leverage (*DOL*) may be defined as the percentage change in operating income that takes place as a result of a percentage change in units sold.

$$DOL = \frac{\text{Percent change in operating income}}{\text{Percent change in unit volume}} \qquad (2\text{---}2)$$

Highly leveraged firms, such as those in the auto or construction industry, are likely to enjoy a rather substantial increase in income as volume expands, while more conservative firms will participate to a lesser extent. Degree of operating leverage (DOL) should only be computed over a profitable range of operations. However, the closer DOL is computed to the company break-even point, the higher the number will be due to a large percentage increase in operating income.[1]

Let us apply the formula to the leveraged and conservative firms previously discussed. Their income or losses at various levels of operation are summarized in Table 2—4.

Table 2–4

Operating income or loss

Units	Leveraged firm (Table 2—2)	Conservative firm (Table 2—3)
-0-	$(60,000)	$(12,000)
20,000	(36,000)	(4,000)
40,000	(12,000)	4,000
60,000	12,000	12,000
80,000	36,000	20,000
100,000	60,000	28,000

We will now consider what happens to operating income as volume moves from 80,000 to 100,000 units.

---

[1]While the value of DOL varies at each level of output, the beginning level of volume determines the DOL regardless of the location of the end point.

Leveraged firm

$$DOL = \frac{\text{Percent change in operating income}}{\text{Percent change in unit volume}} = \frac{\dfrac{\$24,000}{\$36,000} \times 100}{\dfrac{20,000}{80,000} \times 100}$$

$$= \frac{67\%}{25\%} = 2.7$$

Conservative firm

$$DOL = \frac{\text{Percent change in operating income}}{\text{Percent change in unit volume}} = \frac{\dfrac{\$8,000}{\$20,000} \times 100}{\dfrac{20,000}{80,000} \times 100}$$

$$= \frac{40\%}{25\%} = 1.6$$

We see the *DOL* is much greater for the leveraged firm, indicating at 80,000 units, a 1 percent increase in volume will produce a 2.7 percent change in operating income versus a 1.6 percent increase for the conservative firm.

The formula for degree of operating leverage (*DOL*) may be algebraically manipulated to read:

$$DOL = \frac{Q(P - VC)}{Q(P - VC) - FC} \qquad (2\text{—}3)$$

where

Q = Quantity at which *DOL* is computed
P = Price per unit
VC = Variable costs per unit
FC = Fixed costs

Using the newly stated formula for the first firm at $Q = 80,000$, with $P = \$2$, $VC = \$0.80$, and $FC = \$60,000$:

$$DOL = \frac{80,000\ (\$2.00 - \$0.80)}{80,000\ (\$2.00 - \$0.80) - \$60,000}$$

$$= \frac{80,000\ (\$1.20)}{80,000\ (\$1.20) - 60,000} = \frac{96,000}{96,000 - 60,000}$$

$$= 2.7$$

We once again derive an answer of 2.7.[2] The same type of calculation could be performed for the conservative firm.

Limitations of analysis

Throughout our analysis of operating leverage, we have assumed that a constant or linear function exists for revenues and costs as volume changes. For example, we have used $2 as the hypothetical sales price at all levels of operation. In the "real world," however, we may face price weakness as we attempt to capture an increasing market, or we may face cost overruns as we move beyond an optimum-size operation. Relationships are not so fixed as we have assumed.

Nevertheless, the basic patterns we have studied are reasonably valid for most firms over an extended operating range (in our example that might be between 20,000 and 100,000 units). It is only at the extreme levels that linear assumptions break down, as indicated in Figure 2—3.

---

[2] The formula for DOL may also be rewritten as:

$$DOL = \frac{Q(P - VC)}{Q(P - VC) - FC} = \frac{QP - QVC}{QP - QVC - FC}$$

We can rewrite the second terms as:

QP = S, or Sales (Quantity × Price)
QVC = TVC, or Total variable costs (Quantity × Variable costs per unit)
FC = Total fixed costs (remains the same term)

We then have:

$$DOL = \frac{S - TVC}{S - TVC - FC}, \text{ or } \frac{\$160,000 - \$64,000}{\$160,000 - \$64,000 - \$60,000} = \frac{\$96,000}{\$36,000} = 2.7$$

Figure 2–3

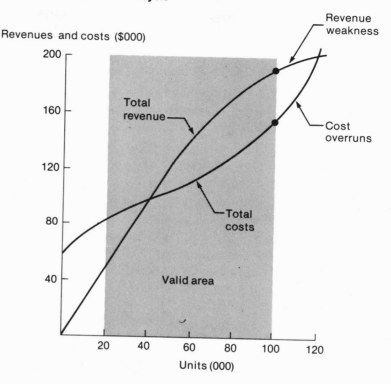

Nonlinear break-even analysis

**Financial
Leverage**

Having discussed the effect of fixed costs on the operations of the firm (operating leverage), we now turn to the second form of leverage. Financial leverage reflects the amount of debt used in the capital structure of the firm. Because debt carries a fixed obligation of interest payments, we have the opportunity to greatly magnify our results at various levels of operation. You may have heard of the real estate developer who borrows 100 percent of the costs of his project and will enjoy an infinite return on his zero investment if all goes well.

It is helpful to think of *operating leverage* as primarily affecting the left-hand side of the balance sheet and *financial* leverage as affecting the right-hand side.

Balance Sheet

Assets	Liabilities and Net Worth
Operating leverage	Financial leverage

Whereas operating leverage influences the mix of plant and equipment, financial leverage determines how the operation is to be financed. It is entirely possible for two firms to have equal operating capabilities and yet show widely different results because of the use of financial leverage.

Impact on earnings

In studying the impact of financial leverage, we shall examine two financial plans for a firm, each employing a significantly different amount of debt in the capital structure. Financing totaling $200,000 is required to carry the assets of the firm.

	Total assets—$200,000	
	Plan A (leveraged)	Plan B (conservative)
Debt (8% interest) . . .	$150,000 ($12,000 interest)	$ 50,000 ($4,000 interest)
Common stock	50,000 (8,000 shares at $6.25)	150,000 (24,000 shares at $6.25)
Total financing . .	$200,000	$200,000

Under *leveraged* Plan A we will borrow $150,000 and sell 8,000 shares of stock at $6.25 to raise an additional $50,000, whereas *conservative* Plan B calls for borrowing only $50,000 and acquiring an additional $150,000 in stock with 24,000 shares.

In Table 2—5, we compute earnings per share for the two plans at various levels of "earnings before interest and taxes" (*EBIT*). These earnings represent the operating income of the firm—before deductions have been made for financial charges or taxes. We assume *EBIT* levels of 0, $12,000, $36,000, and $60,000.

The impact of the two financing plans is dramatic. Although both plans assume the same operating income, or *EBIT*, for comparative purposes at each level (say $36,000 in calculation 3) the reported income per share is vastly different ($1.50 versus $0.67). It is also evident that the conservative plan will produce better results at low income levels—but that the leveraged plan will generate much better earnings per share as operating income, or *EBIT*, goes up. The firm would be indifferent between the two plans at an *EBIT* level of $16,000 as indicated on the bottom of page 31.

Table 2-5

Impact of financing plan on earnings per share

	Plan A (leveraged)	Plan B (conservative)
1. EBIT—0		
Earnings before interest and taxes (EBIT)	-0-	-0-
— Interest (I)	$(12,000)	$(4,000)
Earnings before taxes (EBT)	(12,000)	(4,000)
— Taxes (T)*	(6,000)	(2,000)
Earnings after taxes (EAT)	$(6,000)	$(2,000)
Shares	8,000	24,000
Earnings per share (EPS)	$(0.75)	$(0.08)
2. EBIT—$12,000		
Earnings before interest and taxes (EBIT)	$12,000	$12,000
— Interest (I)	12,000	4,000
Earnings before taxes (EBT)	-0-	8,000
— Taxes (T)	-0-	4,000
Earnings after taxes (EAT)	$ -0-	$4,000
Shares	8,000	24,000
Earnings per share (EPS)	-0-	$0.17
3. EBIT—$36,000		
Earnings before interest and taxes (EBIT)	$36,000	$36,000
— Interest (I)	12,000	4,000
Earnings before taxes (EBT)	24,000	32,000
— Taxes (T)	12,000	16,000
Earnings after taxes (EAT)	$12,000	$16,000
Shares	8,000	24,000
Earnings per share (EPS)	$1.50	$0.67
4. EBIT—$60,000		
Earnings before interest and taxes (EBIT)	$60,000	$60,000
— Interest (I)	12,000	4,000
Earnings before taxes (EBT)	48,000	56,000
— Taxes (T)	24,000	28,000
Earnings after taxes (EAT)	$24,000	$28,000
Shares	8,000	24,000
Earnings per share (EPS)	$3.00	$1.17

*The assumption is that large losses can be written off against other income, perhaps in other years, thus providing the firm with a tax savings benefit. The tax rate is 50 percent.

	Plan A (leveraged)	Plan B (conservative)
Earnings before interest and taxes (EBIT)	$16,000	$16,000
— Interest (I)	12,000	4,000
Earnings before taxes (EBT)	4,000	12,000
— Taxes (T)	2,000	6,000
Earnings after taxes (EAT)	$ 2,000	$ 6,000
Shares	8,000	24,000
Earnings per share (EPS)	$0.25	$0.25

Figure 2–4

Financing plans and earnings per share

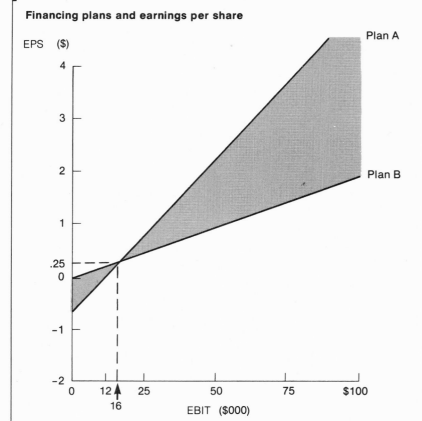

In Figure 2—4, we graphically demonstrate the effect of the two financing plans on earnings per share.

With an *EBIT* of $16,000, we are earning *8 percent* on total assets of $200,000—precisely the percentage cost of borrowed funds to the firm. The use or nonuse of debt does not influence the answer. Beyond $16,000, Plan A, employing heavy financial leverage, really goes to work, allowing the firm to greatly expand earnings per share as a result of a change in *EBIT*. For example, at the *EBIT* level of $36,000, an 18 percent return on assets of $200,000 takes place—and financial leverage is clearly working to our benefit as earnings greatly expand.

Degree of financial leverage

As was true of operating leverage, degree of financial leverage measures the effect of a change in one variable on another variable.

Degree of financial leverage (DFL) may be defined as the percentage change in earnings (EPS) that takes place as a result of a percentage change in earnings before interest and taxes (EBIT).

$$DFL = \frac{\text{Percent change in } EPS}{\text{Percent change in } EBIT} \qquad (2\text{---}4)$$

For purposes of computation, the formula for DFL may be conveniently restated as:

$$DFL = \frac{EBIT}{EBIT - I} \qquad (2\text{---}5)$$

Let's compute the degree of financial leverage for Plan A and Plan B, presented in Table 2—5, at an EBIT level of $36,000. Plan A calls for $12,000 of interest at all levels of financing, and Plan B requires $4,000.

Plan A (leveraged)

$$DFL = \frac{EBIT}{EBIT - I} = \frac{\$36,000}{\$36,000 - \$12,000} = \frac{\$36,000}{\$24,000} = 1.5$$

Plan B (conservative)

$$DFL = \frac{EBIT}{EBIT - I} = \frac{\$36,000}{\$36,000 - \$4,000} = \frac{\$36,000}{\$32,000} = 1.1$$

As expected, Plan A has a much higher degree of financial leverage. At an EBIT level of $36,000, a 1 percent increase in earnings will produce a 1.5 percent increase in earnings per share under Plan A but only a 1.1 percent increase under Plan B. DFL may be computed for any level of operation, and it will change from point to point, but Plan A will always exceed Plan B.

Limitations to use of financial leverage

The alert student may quickly observe that if debt is such a good thing, why sell any stock at all? (Perhaps one share to yourself.) With exclusive debt financing at an EBIT level of $36,000, we would have a degree of financial leverage factor (DFL) of 1.8.

$$DFL = \frac{EBIT}{EBIT - I} = \frac{\$36,000}{\$36,000 - \$16,000} = \frac{\$36,000}{\$20,000} = 1.8$$

(With no stock, we would borrow the full $200,000.)

($8\% \times \$200,000 = \$16,000$ interest)

As stressed throughout the text, debt financing and financial leverage offer unique advantages, but only up to a point—beyond that point, debt financing may be detrimental to the firm. For example, as we expand the use of debt in our capital structure, lenders will perceive a greater financial risk for the firm. For that reason, they may raise the average interest rate we pay and they may demand that certain restrictions be placed on the corporation. Furthermore, concerned common stockholders may drive down the price of our stock—forcing us away from our *objective of maximizing our overall value* in the market. The impact of financial leverage must be carefully weighed.

This is not to say that financial leverage does not work to the benefit of the firm—it very definitely does if properly used. Further discussion of appropriate debt-equity mixes is covered in Chapter 8, "Valuation and the Cost of Capital." For now, we accept the virtues of financial leverage, knowing that all good things must be used in moderation. For firms in industries that offer some degree of stability, are in a positive stage of growth, and are operating in favorable economic conditions, the use of debt is recommended.

Summary

Leverage may be defined as the use of fixed cost items to magnify returns at high levels of operation. Operating leverage primarily affects fixed versus variable cost utilization in the operation of the firm. An important concept—degree of operating leverage (DOL)—measures the percentage change in operating income as a result of a percentage change in volume. The heavier the utilization of fixed cost assets, the higher DOL is likely to be.

Financial leverage reflects the extent to which debt is used in the capital structure of the firm. Substantial use of debt will place a great burden on the firm at low levels of profitability, but it will help to magnify earnings per share as volume or operating income increases.

Because leverage is a two-edged sword, management must be sure that the level of risk assumed is in accord with its desires for risk and its perceptions of the future. High operating leverage may be balanced off against lower financial leverage if this is deemed desirable, and vice versa.

Introduction

Working capital policy involves the management of the current assets of the firm and the acquisition of the appropriate financing for those assets. While a firm may be able to sustain a decrease in sales or profitability for some period of time, the need for current assets and the associated financing is now.

Typical working capital decisions involve a determination of the appropriate level of cash, accounts receivable, and inventory that the firm should maintain. On the financing side, we must determine whether to carry these assets through credit extension from our supplier, short-term bank loans, or longer term credit arrangements. The smaller firm usually has a limited number of options.

As we shall see, one of the unfortunate choices of terms in the vernacular of finance and accounting is the phrase "current asset." The normal definition of a current asset is a short-term asset that can be converted to cash within one year or within the normal operating cycle of the firm. Regrettably, as a business begins to grow, some current assets become more "permanent" in nature—perhaps a portion of inventory is not liquidated and a growing volume of receivables, in aggregate, remains on the books. All too often, firms think of current assets as being temporary, when, in fact, a rather sizable portion require longer term financing. The lesson about the true nature of current assets is well taught every three or four years, as the U.S. economy finds itself in a credit crunch and financing cannot be found for "permanent" current assets.

In the initial chapter on working capital, Chapter 3, we examine some of the basic conceptual items related to working capital and the financing decision with an eye toward the various risk-return alternatives that are available to the financial manager. We also look at the effects of various production policies on the financing requirements of the firm. In Chapter 4, we look at specific techniques for the management of cash, marketable securities, accounts receivable, and inventory. Credit instruments arising in international trade are also considered.

Finally, in Chapter 5, we examine the various sources of short-term financing that are available to the firm. The emphasis is on trade credit, bank financing, and the use of secured loans through the pledging of receivables or inventory as collateral. The relative costs, advantages, and disadvantages of these financing outlets are considered. Also, at the end of the chapter, we examine how the financial futures market can be used to hedge the firm's exposure to changing interest rates.

3 | Working Capital and the Financing Decision

The rapid growth of business firms in the post–World War II period has challenged the ingenuity of financial managers to provide adequate financing. Rapidly expanding sales may cause intense pressure for inventory and receivables buildup—draining the cash resources of the firm. As indicated in Chapter 1, "Financial Forecasting," a large sales increase creates an expansion of current assets, especially acounts receivable and inventory. Some of the increased current assets can be financed by the firm's retained earnings, but in most cases internal funds will not provide enough financing and some external sources of funds must be found. In fact, the faster the growth in sales, the more likely it is that an increasing percentage of financing will be external to the firm. These funds could come from the sale of common stock, preferred stock, long-term bonds, short-term securities, and bank loans, or from a combination of short- and long-term sources of funds.

Working capital management involves the financing and management of the current assets of the firm. The financial executive probably devotes more time to working capital management than to any other activity. Current assets, by their very nature, are changing daily, if not hourly, and managerial decisions must be made. "How much inventory is to be carried, and how do we get the funds to pay for it?" Unlike long-term decisions, there can be no deferral of action. While long-term decisions, involving plant and equipment or market strategy, may well determine the eventual success of the firm, short-term decisions on working capital determine whether the firm gets to the long term.

The high interest-rate and tight-money periods over the last 10 years have added an extra dimension to working capital management. The question, at times, is not only what are the firm's needs and requirements—but will any funds *at all* be available, and at what price? For firms in certain industries, such as mobile homes and land development, the well has gone completely dry at times—while firms in other industries have paid exorbitant rates of interest.

In this chapter, we examine the nature of asset growth, the process of matching sales and production, financial aspects of working capital management and finally, the factors that go into the development of an optimum policy.

The Nature of Asset Growth

Any company that produces and sells a product, whether the product is consumer or manufacturer oriented, will have current assets and fixed assets. If a firm grows, those assets are likely to increase over time. The key to current asset planning is the ability of management to forecast sales accurately and then to match the production schedules with the sales forecast. Whenever actual sales are different from forecasted sales, unexpected buildups or reductions in inventory will occur that will eventually affect receivables and cash flow.

In the simplest case, stage one, all of the firm's current assets will be self-liquidating (sold off at the end of a specified time period). Assume that at the start of the summer you buy 100 tires to be disposed of by September. It is your intention that all tires will be sold, receivables collected, and bills paid over this time period. In this case, your working capital (current asset) needs are truly short term.

Now let us begin to expand the business. In stage two, you add radios, seat covers, and batteries to your operation. Some of your inventory will again be completely liquidated, while other items will form the basic stock for your operation. In order to stay in business, you must maintain floor displays and multiple items for selection. Furthermore, not all items will sell. As you eventually grow to more than one store, this "permanent" aggregate stock of current assets will continue to increase. Problems of inadequate financing arrangements are often the result of the businessperson's failure to realize that the firm is carrying not only self-liquidating inventory—but also the anomaly of "permanent" current assets.

The movement from stage one to stage two growth for a typical business is depicted in Figure 3—1. In Panel A, the buildup in current assets is temporary—while in Panel B, part of the growth in current assets is temporary and part is permanent. (Fixed assets are

Figure 3–1

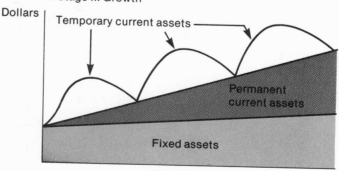

The nature of asset growth

A. Stage I: Limited or no growth

B. Stage II: Growth

included in the illustrations, but they are not directly related to the present discussion.)

Controlling Assets—Matching Sales and Production

In most firms, fixed assets grow slowly as productive capacity is increased and old equipment is replaced, but current assets fluctuate in the short run, depending on the level of production versus the level of sales. When the firm produces more than it sells, inventory rises. When sales rise faster than production, inventory declines and receivables rise.

As discussed in the treatment of the cash budgeting process in Chapter 1, some firms employ level production methods to smooth production schedules and use manpower and equipment efficiently at a lower cost. One consequence of level production is that current assets go up and down when sales and production are not equal. Other firms may try to match sales and production as closely as possible in the short run. This allows current assets to increase or decrease with the level of sales and eliminates the large seasonal bulges or sharp reductions in current assets that occur under level production.

Many retail-oriented firms have been more successful in matching sales and production in recent years because of new, computerized inventory control systems linked to on-line point-of-sales terminals. These point-of-sales terminals either allow digital input or use optical scanners to record the inventory code numbers and the amount of each item sold. At the end of the day, managers are able to examine sales and inventory levels item by item and, if need be, to adjust orders or production schedules. The predictability of the market will influence the speed with which the manager reacts to this information, while the length and complexity of the production process will dictate just how fast production levels can be changed.

Temporary assets under level production—an example

In order to get a better understanding of how current assets fluctuate, let us use the example of the Yawakuzi Motorcycle Company, which manufactures and sells in the snowy U.S. midwest. Not too many people will be buying motorcycles during October through

March, but sales will pick up in early spring and summer and will trail off during the fall. Because of the fixed assets and the skilled labor involved in the production process, Yawakuzi decides that level production is the least expensive and the most efficient production method. The marketing department provides a sales forecast for October through September (Table 3—1).

Table 3–1

Yawakuzi sales forecast (in units)

1st quarter		2d quarter		3d quarter		4th quarter	
October . . .	300	January . .	-0-	April . .	1,000	July	2,000
November . .	150	February . .	-0-	May . .	2,000	August . . .	1,000
December . .	50	March . . .	600	June . .	2,000	September . .	500

Total sales of 9,600 units at $3,000 each = $28,800,000 in sales.

After reviewing the sales forecast, Yawakuzi decides to produce 800 motorcycles per month, or one year's production of 9,600 divided by 12. A look at Table 3—2 shows how level production and seasonal sales combine to create fluctuating inventory. Assume that October's beginning inventory is one month's production of 800 units. The production cost per unit is $2,000.

Table 3–2

Yawakuzi's production schedule and inventory

	Beginning inventory	+	Production (level production)	−	Sales	=	Ending inventory	Inventory (at cost of $2,000 per unit)
October	800		800		300		1,300	$2,600,000
November	1,300		800		150		1,950	3,900,000
December	1,950		800		50		2,700	5,400,000
January	2,700		800		-0-		3,500	7,000,000
February	3,500		800		-0-		4,300	8,600,000
March	4,300		800		600		4,500	9,000,000
April	4,500		800		1,000		4,300	8,600,000
May	4,300		800		2,000		3,100	6,200,000
June	3,100		800		2,000		1,900	3,800,000
July	1,900		800		2,000		700	1,400,000
August	700		800		1,000		500	1,000,000
September	500		800		500		800	1,600,000

The inventory level at cost fluctuates from a high of $9 million in March, the last consecutive month in which production is greater than sales, to a low of $1 million in August, the last month in which

Table 3–3

Sales forecast, cash receipts and payments, and cash budget

	Oct.	Nov.	Dec.	Jan.	Feb.	March	April	May	June	July	Aug.	Sept.
				Sales forecast ($ millions)								
Sales (units) per unit price ($3,000)	300	150	50	-0-	-0-	600	1,000	2,000	2,000	2,000	1,000	500
Sales ($ millions)	$0.9	$0.45	$0.15	$ 0	$ 0	$1.8	$3.0	$6.0	$6.0	$6.0	$3.0	$1.5
				Cash receipts schedule ($ millions)								
50% cash	$0.45	$0.225	$0.075	$ 0	$ 0	$0.9	$1.5	$3.0	$3.0	$3.0	$1.5	$0.75
50% from prior month's sales	0.75*	0.450	0.225	0.075	0	0	0.9	1.5	3.0	3.0	3.0	1.50
Total cash receipts	$1.20	$0.675	$0.300	$0.075	0	$0.9	$2.4	$4.5	$6.0	$6.0	$4.5	$2.25

*Assumes September sales of $1.5 million.

	Oct.	Nov.	Dec.	Jan.	Feb.	March	April	May	June	July	Aug.	Sept.
				Cash payments schedule ($ millions)								
Constant production of 800 units/month—per unit cost: $2,000	$1.6	$1.6	$1.6	$1.6	$1.6	$1.6	$1.6	$1.6	$1.6	$1.6	$1.6	$1.6
Overhead	0.4	0.4	0.4	0.4	0.4	0.4	0.4	0.4	0.4	0.4	0.4	0.4
Dividends and interest	—	—	—	—	—	—	—	—	—	—	1.0	—
Taxes	0.3	—	—	0.3	—	—	0.3	—	—	0.3	—	—
Total cash payments	$2.3	$2.0	$2.0	$2.3	$2.0	$2.0	$2.3	$2.0	$2.0	$2.3	$3.0	$2.0

	Oct.	Nov.	Dec.	Jan.	Feb.	March	April	May	June	July	Aug.	Sept.
			Cash budget ($ millions; required minimum balance is $0.25 million)									
Cash flow	$(1.1)	$(1.325)	$(1.7)	$(2.225)	$(2.0)	$(1.1)	$0.1	$2.5	$4.0	$3.7	$1.5	$0.25
Beginning cash	0.25*	0.25	0.25	0.250	0.25	0.25	0.25	0.25	0.25	0.25	1.1	2.60
Cumulative cash balance	$(0.85)	$(1.075)	$(1.45)	$(1.975)	$(1.75)	$(0.85)	$0.35	$2.75	$4.25	$3.95	$2.6	$2.85
Monthly loan or (repayment)	1.1	1.325	1.7	2.225	2.0	1.1	(0.1)	(2.5)	(4.0)	(2.85)	0	0
Cumulative loan	1.1	2.425	4.125	6.350	8.350	9.45	9.35	6.85	2.85	0	0	0
Ending cash balance	0.25	0.25	0.25	0.25	0.25	0.25	0.25	0.25	0.25	1.1	2.6	2.85

*Assumes cash balance of $0.25 million at the beginning of October and that this is the desired minimum cash balance.

sales are greater than production. Table 3—3 combines a sales forecast, a cash receipts schedule, a cash payments schedule, and a brief
cash budget in order to examine the buildup in accounts receivable
and cash.

In Table 3—3, the *sales forecast* is based on assumptions in Table
3—1. The unit volume of sales is multiplied by a sales price of
$3,000 to get sales dollars in millions. Next *cash receipts* represent
50 percent collected in cash during the month of sale and 50 percent
from the prior month's sales. For example, in October this would
represent $0.45 million from the current month plus $0.75 million
from the prior month's sales.

Cash payments in Table 3—3 are based on an assumption of level
production of 800 units per month at $2,000 per unit or $1.6 million
plus payments for overhead, dividends, interest and taxes.

Finally the *cash budget* in Table 3—3 represents a comparison of
the cash receipts and cash payments schedules to determine cash
flow. We further assume that the firm desires a minimum cash balance of $0.25 million. Thus in October, a negative cash flow of $1.1
million brings the cumulative cash balance to a negative $0.85 mil-
lion and $1.1 million must be borrowed to provide an ending cash
balance of $0.25 million. Similar negative cash flows in subsequent
months necessitate expanding the bank loan. For example, in November there is a negative cash flow of $1.325 million. This brings
the cumulative cash balance to $ – 1.075 million, requiring addi-
tional borrowings of $1.325 million to insure a minimum cash bal-
ance of $0.25 million. The cumulative loan through November
(October and November borrowings) now adds up to $2.425 million.
Our cumulative bank loan is highest in the month of March.

We now wish to ascertain our total current asset buildup as a
result of level production and fluctuating sales for October through
September. The analysis is presented in Table 3—4. The cash figures
come directly from the last line of Table 3—3. The accounts receivable balance is based on the assumption that accounts receivable
represent 50 percent of sales in a given month, as the other 50 percent is paid for in cash. Thus, the accounts receivable figure in Table
3—4 represents 50 percent of the sales figure from the third line in
Table 3—3. Finally, the inventory figure is taken directly from the
last column of Table 3—2, which presented the production schedule
and inventory data.

Table 3-4

Total current assets, first year ($ millions)

	Cash	Accounts receivable	Inventory	Total current assets
October	$0.25	$0.45	$2.6	$ 3.3
November	0.25	0.225	3.9	4.375
December	0.25	0.075	5.4	5.725
January	0.25	0.000	7.0	7.25
February	0.25	0.000	8.6	8.85
March	0.25	0.90	9.0	10.15
April	0.25	1.50	8.6	10.35
May	0.25	3.00	6.2	9.45
June	0.25	3.00	3.8	7.05
July	1.10	3.00	1.4	5.50
August	2.60	1.50	1.0	5.10
September . . .	2.85	0.75	1.6	5.20

Total current assets start at $3.3 million in October and rise to $10.35 million in the peak month of April. From April through August, sales are larger than production and inventory falls to its low of $1.0 million in August, but accounts receivables peak at $3.0 million in the highest sales months of May, June, and July. The cash budget in Table 3—3 explains the cash flows and external funds borrowed to finance asset accumulation. From October to March, Yawakuzi borrows more and more money to finance the inventory buildup, but from April to July it eliminates all borrowing as inventory is liquidated and cash balances rise to complete the cycle. In October the cycle starts all over again; but now the firm has accumulated cash which it can use to finance next year's asset accumulation, pay a larger dividend, replace old equipment, or—if growth in sales is anticipated—invest in new equipment to increase productive capacity. Table 3—5 presents the cash budget and total current assets for the second year. Under a simplified no-growth assumption, the monthly cash flow is the same as that of the first year, but beginning cash in October is much higher from the first year's ending cash balance and this lowers the borrowing requirement and increases the ending cash balance and total current assets at year-end. Higher current assets are present in spite of the fact accounts receivable and inventory do not change.

Figure 3—2 is a graphic presentation of the current asset cycle. It includes the two years covered in Tables 3—4 and 3—5 assuming level production and no sales growth.

Table 3–5   Cash budget and assets for second year with no growth in sales ($ millions)

	End of first year Sept.	Second year Oct.	Nov.	Dec.	Jan.	Feb.	March	April	May	June	July	Aug.	Sept.
Cash flow	$0.25	$(1.1)	$(1.325)	$(1.7)	$(2.225)	$(2.0)	$(1.1)	$0.1	$2.5	$4.0	$3.7	$1.5	$0.25
Beginning cash	2.60	2.85	1.750	0.425	0.25	0.25	0.25	0.25	0.25	0.25	0.25	3.7	5.2
Cumulative cash balance		1.75	0.425	(1.275)	(1.975)	(1.75)	(0.85)	0.35	2.75	4.25	3.95	5.2	5.45
Monthly loan or (repayment)		—	—	1.525	2.225	2.0	1.1	(0.1)	(2.5)	(4.0)	(0.25)	—	—
Cumulative loan		—	—	1.525	3.750	5.75	6.85	6.75	4.25	0.25	0	—	—
Ending cash balance	$2.85	$1.75	$0.425	$0.25	$0.25	$0.25	$0.25	$0.25	$0.25	$0.25	$3.70	$5.2	$5.45
Total current assets													
Ending cash balance	$2.85	$1.75	$0.425	$0.25	$0.25	$0.25	$0.25	$0.25	$0.25	$0.25	$3.70	$5.2	$5.45
Accounts receivable	0.75	0.45	0.225	0.075	0	0	0.90	1.50	3.0	3.0	3.0	1.5	0.75
Inventory	1.6	2.6	3.9	5.4	7.0	8.6	9.0	8.6	6.2	3.8	1.4	1.0	1.60
Total current assets	$5.2	$4.8	$4.55	$5.725	$7.25	$8.85	$10.15	$10.35	$9.45	$7.05	$8.1	$7.7	$7.80

Figure 3–2

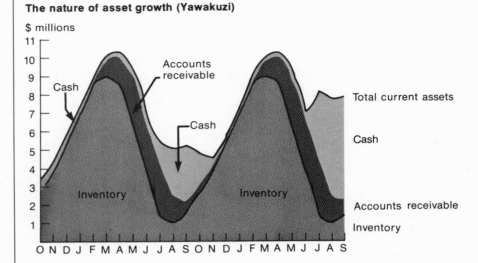

The nature of asset growth (Yawakuzi)

Patterns of Financing

The financial manager's selection of external sources of funds may be one of the firm's most important decisions. The axiom that all current assets should be financed by current liabilities (accounts payable, bank loans, commercial paper, etc.) is subject to challenge when one sees the permanent buildup that can take place in current assets. In the Yawakuzi example, the buildup in inventory was substantial, at $9.0 million. The example had a logical conclusion in that the motorcycles were sold, cash was generated, and current assets became very liquid. What if a much smaller level of sales had occurred? Yawakuzi would be sitting on a large inventory which needed to be financed and would be generating no cash. Theoretically, the firm could be declared technically insolvent (bankrupt) if short-term sources of funds were used but were unable to be renewed when they came due. How would the interest and principal be paid without cash flow from inventory liquidation? The most appropriate financing pattern would be one in which asset buildup and length of financing terms are perfectly matched, as indicated in Figure 3—3.

In the upper part of Figure 3—3, we see that the temporary buildup in current assets is financed by short-term funds. More important, however, permanent current assets, as well as fixed assets,

Figure 3-3

Matching long-term and short-term needs

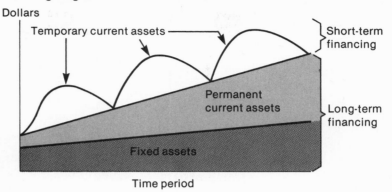

Dollars

Temporary current assets

Short-term financing

Permanent current assets

Long-term financing

Fixed assets

Time period

are financed with long-term funds from the sale of stock, the issuance of bonds, or retention of earnings.

Alternative plans

Only a financial manager with unusual insight and timing could construct a financial plan for working capital that adhered perfectly to the design in Figure 3—3. The difficulty rests in precisely determining what part of current assets is temporary and what part is permanent. Even if dollar amounts could be ascertained, the exact timing of asset liquidation is a difficult matter. To compound the problem, we are never quite sure how much short-term or long-term financing is available at a given point in time. While the precise synchronization of temporary current assets and short-term financing depicted in Figure 3—3 may be the most desirable and logical plan, other alternatives must be considered.

Long-term financing

To protect against the danger of not being able to provide adequate short-term financing in tight money periods, the financial manager may rely on long-term funds to cover some short-term needs. As indicated in Figure 3—4, long-term capital is now being used to finance fixed assets, permanent current assets, and part of *temporary current assets.*

Figure 3–4

Using long-term financing for part of short-term needs

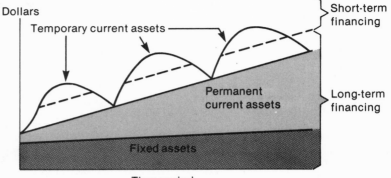

By borrowing on a long-term basis to cover short-term needs, the firm virtually assures itself of having adequate capital at all times. The firm may prefer to borrow a million dollars for ten years—rather than attempt to borrow a million dollars at the beginning of each year for ten years and paying it back at the end of each year.

Short-term financing (opposite approach)

This is not to say that all financial managers utilize long-term financing on a large scale. In order to acquire long-term funds, the firm must generally go to the capital markets with a bond or stock offering or must privately place longer term obligations with insurance companies, wealthy individuals, and so forth. Many small businesses do not have access to such long-term capital and are forced to rely heavily on short-term bank and trade credit. In the capital shortage era of the 1970s and early 1980s, even some large businesses were forced to operate with short-term funds.

Furthermore, short-term financing does offer some advantages over more extended financial arrangements. As a general rule, the interest rate on short-term funds is lower than that on long-term funds. We might surmise then that a firm could develop a working capital financing plan in which short-term funds are used to finance not only temporary current assets but also part of the permanent working capital needs of the firm. As depicted in Figure 3—5, bank and trade credit as well as other sources of short-term financ-

Figure 3–5

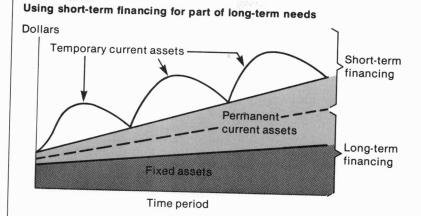

Using short-term financing for part of long-term needs

Dollars

Temporary current assets

Short-term financing

Permanent—— current assets

Long-term financing

Fixed assets

Time period

ing are now supporting part of the permanent current asset needs of the firm.

The Financing Decision

Some corporations are more flexible than others because they are not locked into a few available sources of funds. Corporations would like many financing alternatives in order to minimize their cost of funds at any point in time. Unfortunately, not many firms are in this enviable position through the duration of a business cycle. During an economic boom period, a shortage of low-cost alternatives exists and firms often minimize their financing costs by raising funds in advance of forecasted asset needs.

Not only does the financial manager encounter a timing problem, but he also needs to select the right type of financing. Even for companies having many alternative sources of funds, there may be only one or two decisions that will look good in retrospect. At the time the financing decision is made, the financial manager is never sure it is the right one. Should the financing be long-term or short-term, debt or equity, and so on? Figure 3—6 is a decision tree diagram which shows many of the financing decisions that can be made. At each point a decision is made until a final financing method is reached. In most cases a corporation will use a combination of these financing methods. At all times the financial manager will balance short-term versus long-term considerations against the composition of the firm's assets and the firm's willingness to

Figure 3–6

Decision tree of the financing decision

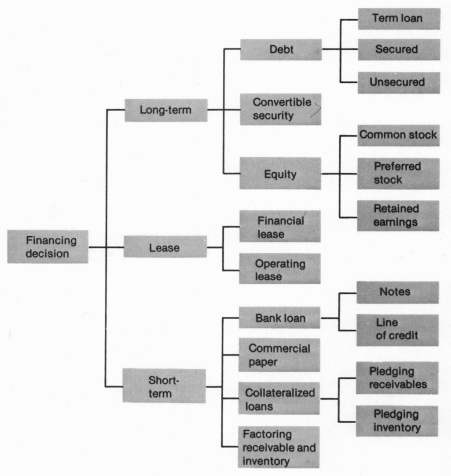

accept risk. The ratio of long-term financing to short-term financing at any point in time will be greatly influenced by the term structure of interest rates.

Term structure of interest rates

The term structure of interest rates is often referred to as a yield curve. It shows the interest rate at a specific point in time for all securities having equal risk but different maturity dates. Generally

U.S. government securities are used to construct yield curves because they have many maturities and each of the securities has an equally low risk of default. Corporate securities will move in the same direction as government securities but will have higher interest rates because of their greater financial risk. Yield curves for both corporations and government securities change daily to reflect current competitive conditions in the money and capital markets, expected inflation, and changes in economic conditions.

Figures 3—7, 3—8, and 3—9 depict three term structures over the last decade indicating the cyclical nature and changing levels of interest rates. Figure 3—7 shows five yield curves in a period of falling interest rates—from August 1974 to November 1976.

Each yield curve has a different shape. The August 1974 curve is called downward sloping or inverted because short-term rates are higher than long-term rates. This shape is usually present at peak periods in economic expansions and sometimes well into economic recessions. The September 1975 curve is called a humped curve because the intermediate rates are higher than both the short- and long-term rates. The other three yield curves are all upward slop-

Figure 3–7

Yield curves: Yields on U.S. government securities

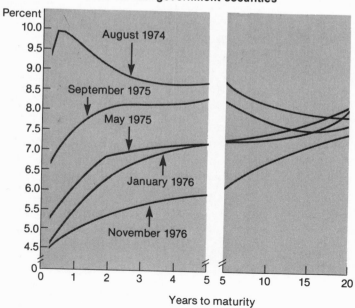

Years to maturity

Figure 3–8

Yield curves: Yield on U.S. government securities

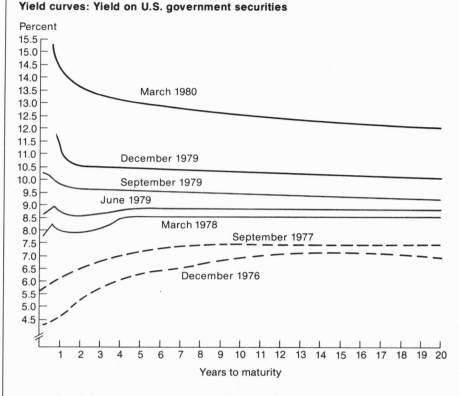

Percent

March 1980

December 1979

September 1979

June 1979

March 1978

September 1977

December 1976

Years to maturity

ing, which is the normal case. The yield curves pictured in Figure 3—8 represent a period of rising interest rates—from December 1976 to March 1980. The shape of the curves changes from the normal upward-sloping position in late 1976 (bottom of chart) to the inverted downward-sloping curves in 1979-80.

Figure 3—9 continues the period of rising interest rates from Figure 3—8. The rates finally peaked out and started declining after September 1981, fostered by an economic recession. Short-term rates on U.S. Treasury bills reached historic levels in September of 1981 as the Federal Reserve Bank maintained high interest rates during this period in an attempt to break the back of inflation even though the economy was quite weak.[1] Subsequently, interest rates did begin coming down as the last three curves in Figure 3—9 indicate.

Interest rates are influenced by many variables, but in recent years

[1]The prime interest rate on bank loans reached the 20 percent level during this time period.

Figure 3–9

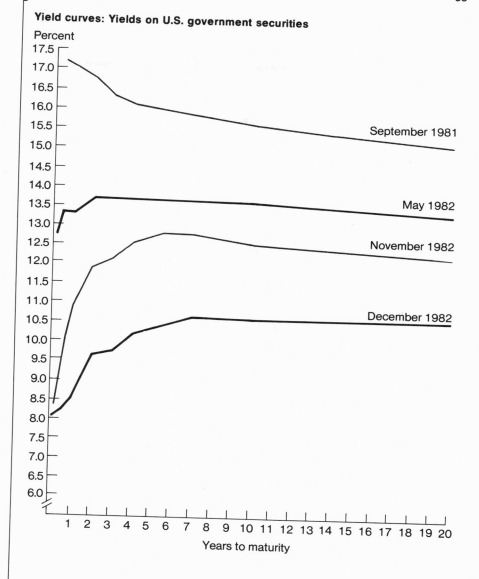

Yield curves: Yields on U.S. government securities

Percent

September 1981

May 1982

November 1982

December 1982

Years to maturity

inflation has had a large effect in boosting interest rates to record levels. As inflation increases, lenders charge a premium for the lost purchasing power that they will have when their loan is repaid in inflated dollars. Short-term rates are influenced more by current demands for money than by inflation, but long-term rates are greatly affected by expected inflation. The shift in the yield curves from August 1974 to November 1976 can be partly attributed to a decline in the rate of inflation, while the increased interest rates in the 1976–81 period are directly linked to a spiraling rate of inflation and soaring government deficits. Eventually Fed policy did reduce the wholesale price index for 1982 to an increase of only 3.5 percent, the lowest rate since 1971. If inflation continues to be repressed, interest rates may find new levels below those reached in 1980–81. Not until mid-1982 did the Federal Reserve ease up on credit and allow a significant reduction in interest rates, which normally stimulates economic activity and reduces unemployment over time. No doubt the interaction of inflation (and disinflation), government deficits, and political considerations will have much to do with the future level of interest rates through the 1980s.

In designing working capital policy, the astute financial manager is interested not only in the term structure of interest rates, but also in the relative volatility and the historical level of short-term and long-term rates. Figure 3—10 uses long-term AAA-rated corporate bonds and short-term commercial paper to provide insight into interest rate volatility over a long period of time.

Figure 3–10

Long- and short-term interest rates (annually)

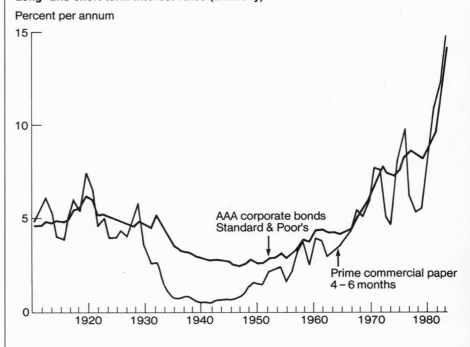

The period between 1970 and 1982 demonstrates the large historical differences in relative volatility, with short-term rates being much more volatile than long-term rates. As a general rule short-term rates have been lower than long-term rates, with a few exceptions of course. For example, as indicated in Figure 3—10, in the period before 1930 and after 1971, short-term rates fluctuated around long-term rates quite a bit even though long-term AAA corporate bond yields soared to dramatic historical highs in the later period. Notice that both long-term and short-term rates have been increasing since about 1953 and that the major increase in rates began in 1965, which is defined by some economists as the beginning of a long inflationary spiral.

How should the financial manager respond to fluctuating interest rates and changing term structures? When interest rates are high, the financial manager generally tries to borrow short term (if funds are available). As rates decline, the chief financial officer will try to lock in the lower rates with heavy long-term borrowing. Some of these long-term funds will be used to reduce short-term debt and the rest will be available for future expansion of plant and equipment and working capital if necessary.

A Decision Process

Assume that we are comparing alternative financing plans for working capital. As indicated in Table 3—6, $500,000 of working capital (current assets) must be financed for the Edwards Corporation. Under Plan A, we will finance all our current asset needs with short-term funds, while under Plan B we will finance only a relatively small portion of working capital with short-term money—relying heavily on long-term funds. In either case, we will carry $100,000 of fixed assets with long-term financing commitments. As indicated in part 3 of Table 3—6, under Plan A we will finance total needs of $600,000 with $500,000 short-term and $100,000 long-term financing, whereas with Plan B we will finance $150,000 short term and $450,000 long term.

Plan A carries the lower cost of financing, with interest of 6 percent on $500,000 of the $600,000 required. We show the impact of both plans on bottom-line earnings in Table 3—7.[2] Assuming that

---

[2]Common stock is eliminated from the example to simplify analysis. If it were included, all of the basic patterns would still hold.

Table 3–6

Alternative financing plans

EDWARDS CORPORATION

	Plan A	Plan B
Part 1. Current assets		
Temporary	$250,000	$250,000
Permanent	250,000	250,000
Total current assets	500,000	500,000
Short-term financing (6%)	500,000	150,000
Long-term financing (10%)	0	350,000
	$500,000	$500,000
Part 2. Fixed assets	$100,000	$100,000
Long-term financing (10%)	$100,000	$100,000
Part 3. Total financing (summary of parts 1 and 2)		
Short-term (6%)	$500,000	$150,000
Long-term (10%)	100,000	450,000
	$600,000	$600,000

the firm generates $200,000 in earnings before interest and taxes, Plan A will provide aftertax earnings of $80,000, while Plan B will generate only $73,000.

Introducing varying conditions

Although Plan A, employing cheaper short-term sources of financing, appears to provide $7,000 more in return, this is not always the case. During tight money periods, short-term financing may be difficult to find or may carry exorbitant rates. Furthermore, inadequate financing may mean lost sales or financial embarrassment. For these reasons, the firm may wish to evaluate Plans A and B based on differing assumptions about the economy and the money markets.

Expected value

Past history combined with economic forecasting may indicate an 80 percent probability of normal events and a 20 percent chance of extremely tight money. Using Plan A, under normal conditions the Edwards Corporation will enjoy a $7,000 superior return over Plan B (as indicated in Table 3—7). Let us now assume that under

Table 3–7

Impact of financing plans on earnings

EDWARDS CORPORATION

Plan A

Earnings before interest and taxes	$200,000
Interest (short-term), 6% × $500,000	− 30,000
Interest (long-term), 10% × $100,000	− 10,000
Earnings before taxes	160,000
Taxes (50%)	80,000
Earnings after taxes	$ 80,000

Plan B

Earnings before interest and taxes	$200,000
Interest (short-term), 6% × $150,000	− 9,000
Interest (long-term), 10% × $450,000	− 45,000
Earnings before taxes	146,000
Taxes (50%)	73,000
Earnings after taxes	$ 73,000

disruptive tight money conditions, Plan A would provide a $15,000 lower return than Plan B because of high short-term interest rates. These conditions are summarized in Table 3—8, and an expected value of return is computed. The expected value represents the sum of the expected outcomes for the two events.

Table 3–8

Expected returns under different economic conditions

EDWARDS CORPORATION

1.	Normal events	Expected higher return under plan A		Probability of normal events		Expected outcome	
		$7,000	×	.80	=	+$5,600	
2.	Tight money	Expected lower return under Plan A		Probability of tight money			
		($15,000)	×	.20	=	(3,000)	
		Expected value of return for Plan A versus Plan B				+$2,600	

We see that even when downside risk is considered, Plan A carries a higher expected return of $2,600. For another firm in the same industry that might suffer $50,000 lower returns during tight money conditions, Plan A becomes too dangerous to undertake, as indicated in Table 3—9. Plan A's expected return is now $4,400 less than that of Plan B.

Table 3–9

Expected returns for high-risk firm

1.	Normal events	Expected higher return under Plan A $7,000	×	Probability of normal events .80	=	Expected outcome +$5,600
2.	Tight money	Expected lower return under Plan A ($50,000)	×	Probability of tight money .20	=	(10,000)

Negative expected value of return for Plan A versus Plan B   ($4,400)

Shifts in Asset Structure

Thus far, our attention has been directed to the risk associated with various financing plans. Risk-return analysis must also be carried to the asset side. A firm with heavy risk exposure due to short-term borrowing may compensate in part by carrying highly liquid assets. Conversely, a firm with established long-term debt commitments may choose to carry a heavier component of less liquid, highly profitable assets.

Either through desire or compelling circumstances, business firms have decreased the liquidity of their current asset holdings since the early 1960s. For example, in Table 3—10 we see that for U.S. nonfinancial corporations cash and cash equivalents have decreased from 19.0 percent to 10.5 percent of current assets, while inventory increased from 30.4 percent to 41.1 percent. Along these same lines, the ratio of cash and cash equivalents to current liabilities has fallen from 1 to 1 at the end of World War II to approximately 0.15 to 1 in the early 1980s.

Table 3–10

Current asset position ($ billions): U.S. nonfinancial corporations

	Cash and equivalents		Inventory		Total current assets
	Amount	Percent of current assets	Amount	Percent of current assets	Amount
1963 . . .	$ 66.7	19.0%	$107.0	30.4%	$ 351.5
1972 . . .	70.0	12.4	218.2	39.0	564.5
1978 . . .	121.3	11.8	428.3	41.7	1,028.1
1981 . . .	149.6	10.5	587.1	41.1	1,427.1

Source: *Federal Reserve Bulletin,* selected issues, and Keith V. Smith, *Management of Working Capital* (St. Paul: West, 1974), p. 9.

The reasons for diminishing liquidity can be traced in part to more sophisticated, profit-oriented financial management as well as better utilization of cash balances via the computer. Less liquidity can also be traced to the effect inflation has had on corporate balance sheets—forcing greater borrowing to carry more expensive assets and to decreasing profitability during recessions. The average current ratio for nonfinancial corporations is presented in Figure 3—11. After the recession in 1974-75, corporate liquidity increased to the highest level of the 1970s in the third quarter of 1976. Since reaching that peak, corporate liquidity has been squeezed. Generally speaking, corporations are relying more and more on short-term borrowings to carry less liquid assets—a potentially dangerous situation.

Figure 3–11

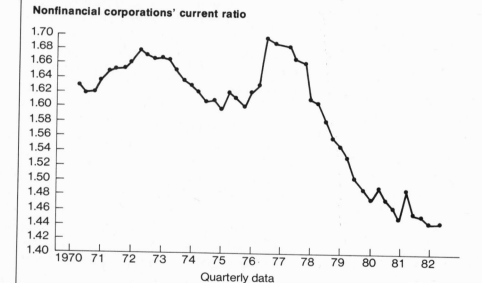

Nonfinancial corporations' current ratio

Quarterly data

Toward an Optimal Policy

As previously indicated, the firm should attempt to relate asset liquidity to financing patterns, and vice versa. In Table 3—11, a number of different working capital alternatives are presented. Along the top of the table we show asset liquidity; along the side, the type of financing arrangement. The combined impact of the two variables is shown in each of the four panels of the table.

Each firm must decide how it wishes to combine asset liquidity and financing needs. The aggressive, risk-oriented firm in panel 1

Table 3–11

Asset liquidity and financing assets

Financing plan	Low liquidity	High liquidity
Short-term	1 High profit High risk	2 Moderate profit Moderate risk
Long-term	3 Moderate profit Moderate risk	4 Low profit Low risk

of Table 3—11 will borrow stort term and carry relatively high levels of inventory and longer term receivables, hoping to increase profit. It will benefit from low-cost financing and high-return assets, but it will be vulnerable to a credit crunch. The more conservative firm, following the plan in panel 4, will utilize established long-term financing and maintain a high degree of liquidity. In panels 2 and 3, we see more moderate positions in which the firm compensates for short-term financing with highly liquid assets (2) or balances off low liquidity with precommitted, long-term financing (3).

Each financial manager must structure his or her working capital position and the associated risk-return trade-off to meet the company's needs. For firms whose cash flow patterns are predictable, typified by the public utilities sector, a low degree of liquidity can be maintained. Immediate access to capital markets, such as that enjoyed by large, prestigious firms, also allows greater risk-taking capability. In each case, the ultimate concern must be for maximizing the overall valuation of the firm through a judicious consideration of risk-return options.

In the next two chapters, we will examine the various methods for managing the individual components of working capital. In Chapter 4, we address ourselves to the techniques for managing cash, marketable securities, receivables, and inventory. In Chapter 5, we look at trade and bank credit as well as other sources of short-term funds.

Summary

Working capital management involves the financing and management of the current assets of the firm. A firm's ability to properly manage current assets and the associated liability obligations may determine how well it is able to survive in the short run. To the extent that part of the buildup in current assets is permanent, financial arrangements should carry longer maturities.

The financial manager must also give careful attention to the relationship of the production process to sales. Level production in a seasonal sales environment increases operating efficiency, but also calls for more careful financial planning. The astute financial manager must also keep an eye on the general cost of borrowing, the term structure of interest rates, and the relative volatility of short- and long-term rates.

The firm has a number of risk-return decisions to consider. Though long-term financing provides a safety margin in availability of funds, its higher cost may reduce the profit potential of the firm. On the asset side, carrying highly liquid current assets assures the bill-paying capability of the firm—but detracts from profit potential. Each firm must tailor the various risk-return trade-offs to meet its own needs. The peculiarities of a firm's industry will have a major impact on the options open to management.

4 | Current Asset Management

The financial manager must carefully allocate resources among the current assets of the firm—cash, marketable securities, accounts receivable, and inventory. In the management of cash and marketable securities, the primary concern should be for safety and liquidity—with secondary attention placed on maximizing profitability. As we move to accounts receivable and inventory, a stiffer profitability test must be met. The investment level should not be a matter of happenstance or historical determination, but must meet the same sort of return-on-investment criteria that are applied to any decision. We may need to choose between a 20 percent increase in inventory and a new plant location or a major research program. Let us examine the techniques that are applied to various forms of current assets: cash, marketable securities, accounts receivable, and inventory.

Cash Management

In the parlance of corporate financial management, the less cash you have, the better off you are. In spite of whatever lifelong teachings you might have learned about the virtues of cash, the corporate manager actively seeks to keep this nonearning asset to a minimum.

The first consideration is to ensure that inflows and outflows of cash are properly synchronized for transaction purposes. Interest-paying marketable securities, held for precautionary purposes, should only be transferred into cash when there is a scheduled need for disbursement. In determining the appropriate cash balance, the firm must carefully assess the payment pattern of customers, the speed at which suppliers and creditors process checks, and the efficiency of the banking system.

Float

Some people are shocked to realize that even the most trusted asset on a corporation's books, "cash," may not portray actual dollars at a given point in time. There are, in fact, two cash balances of importance: the corporation's recorded amount and the amount credited to the corporation by the bank. The difference between the two is labeled *float*, and it exists as a result of the lag between the time in which a check is written and the eventual clearing of the check against a corporate bank account.

Let us examine the use of float. A firm has deposited $1,000,000 in checks received from customers during the week and has written $900,000 in checks to suppliers. If the initial balance was $100,000, the corporate books would show $200,000. But what will the bank records show in the way of usable funds? Perhaps $800,000 of the checks from customers will have cleared their accounts at other banks and been credited to us, while only $400,000 of our checks may have completed a similar cycle. As indicated in Table 4—1, we have used "float" to provide us with $300,000 extra in available short-term funds.

Table 4–1

The use of float to provide funds

	Corporate books	Bank books (usable funds) (amounts actually cleared)
Initial amount	$ 100,000	$100,000
Deposits	+ 1,000,000	+ 800,000
Checks	− 900,000	− 400,000
Balance	+$ 200,000	+$500,000
		+$300,000 float

Some companies actually operate with a negative cash balance on the corporate books knowing that float will carry them through at the bank. In the above example, the firm may write $1.2 million in checks on the assumption that only $800,000 will clear by the end of the week, thus leaving it with surplus funds in its bank account. The results, shown in Table 4—2, represent the phenomenon known as "playing the float." A float of $200,000 turns a negative balance on the corporation's books into a positive temporary balance on the bank's books. Obviously, float can also work against you if checks going out are being processed more quickly than checks coming in.

Table 4–2

Playing the float

	Corporate books	Bank books (usable funds) (amounts actually cleared)
Initial amount	$ 100,000	$100,000
Deposits	+ 1,000,000*	+ 800,000*
Checks	− 1,200,000	− 800,000
Balance	−$ 100,000	+$100,000
		+$200,000 float

* Assumed to remain the same as in Table 4—1.

Improving collections

We may expedite the collection and check-clearing process through a number of strategies. A popular method is to utilize a variety of collection centers throughout our marketing area. A dress manufacturer with headquarters in Chicago may have 75 collection offices disbursed throughout the country, each performing a billing and collection-deposit function. One of the collection offices in San Francisco, using a local bank, may be able to clear a check on a San Jose bank in one day—whereas a Chicago bank would require a substantially longer time to remit and clear the check at the California bank.[1] Excess cash balances at the local banks throughout the collection system are remitted to the home office bank through a daily wire transfer.

---

[1]Checks deposited with a bank are cleared through the Federal Reserve System, through a correspondent bank, or through a locally established clearinghouse system. A check is collected when it is remitted to the payer's bank and actually paid by that bank to the payee's bank.

For those who wish to enjoy the benefits of expeditious check clearance at lower costs, a *lockbox system* may replace the network of regional collection offices. Under this plan, customers are requested to forward their checks to a post-office box in their geographic region and a local bank picks up the checks and processes them to other banks in the locality for rapid collection. Funds are then wired to the corporate home office for immediate use. The company retains many of the benefits of regional collection centers, but with reduced corporate overhead.

Extending disbursements

Perhaps you have heard of the multimillion dollar corporation with its headquarters located in the most exclusive office space in downtown Manhattan, but with its primary check disbursement center in Fargo, North Dakota. Though the firm may engage in aggressive speedup techniques in the processing of incoming checks, a slowdown pattern more aptly describes the payment procedures.

While the preceding example represents an extreme case, the slowing of disbursements is not an uncommon practice in cash management. It has even been given the title "extended disbursement float." Many full-service banks offer customers consulting services pointing out structural defects in the Federal Reserve and other collection systems that allow the firm to extend the payment period. While it is not the intent of this text to encourage or discourage such practices, their fairly widespread use is worthy of note.

Cost-benefit analysis

An efficiently maintained cash management program can be an expensive operation. The utilization of remote collection and disbursement centers involves additional costs, and banks involved in the process will require that the firm maintain adequate deposit balances or pay sufficient fees to justify their services. Though the use of a lockbox system may reduce total corporate overhead, the costs may still be substantial.

These expenses must be compared to the substantial benefits that may accrue. If a firm has an average daily remittance of $2 million and 1.5 days can be saved in the collection process by establishing a sophisticated collection network, the firm has freed up $3 million for investment elsewhere. Also, through stretching the disbursement schedule by one day, perhaps another $2 million will become available for alternate uses. An example of this process is shown in Figure 4—1. If the firm is able to earn 10 percent on the $5 million that is freed up, as much as $500,000 may be expended on the administrative costs of cash management before the new costs are equal to the generated revenue.

Electronic funds transfer

As we move into the mid-1980s, some of the techniques of delaying payment will be reduced through the techniques of *elec-*

Figure 4–1

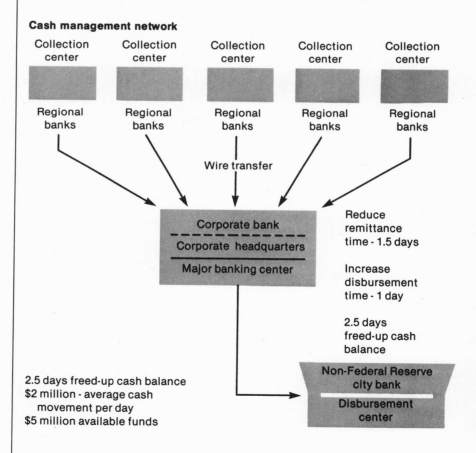

Cash management network

| Collection center | Collection center | Collection center | Collection center | Collection center |

| Regional banks | Regional banks | Regional banks | Regional banks | Regional banks |

Wire transfer

Corporate bank
- - - - - - - - - -
Corporate headquarters

Major banking center

Reduce remittance time - 1.5 days

Increase disbursement time - 1 day

2.5 days freed-up cash balance

Non-Federal Reserve city bank

Disbursement center

2.5 days freed-up cash balance
$2 million - average cash movement per day
$5 million available funds

tronic funds transfer, a system in which funds are moved between computer terminals without the use of a "check." Through the use of terminal communication between the store and the bank, your payment to the supermarket will be automatically charged against your account at the bank before you walk out the door.

Many major corporations have computerized cash management systems. For example, a firm may have 55 branch offices and 56 banks, one bank for each branch office and a lead bank in which the major corporate account is kept. At the end of each day the financial manager can check all the company's bank accounts through an online computer terminal. He or she can then transfer through the computer all excess cash balances from each branch or regional bank to the corporate lead bank for overnight investment in money market securities.

Marketable Securities

The firm may hold excess funds in anticipation of some major cash outlay, such as a dividend payment or partial retirement of debt or as a precaution against an unexpected event. When funds are being held for other than immediate transaction purposes, they should be converted from cash into interest-earning marketable securities.[2]

The financial manager has a virtual supermarket of securities from which to choose. Among the factors influencing that choice are yield, maturity, minimum investment required, safety, and marketability. Under normal conditions, the longer the maturity period of the security, the higher the yield, as indicated in Figure 4—2.

The problem in "stretching out" the maturity of your investment is not that you are legally locked in (you can generally sell your security when you need funds) but that you may have to take a loss. A $5,000 Treasury note issued initially at 9.5 percent, with three years to run, may only bring $4,500 if the going interest rate climbs to 11 percent. This risk is considerably greater as the maturity date is extended. A complete discussion of the "interest rate risk" is presented in Chapter 11, "Long-Term Debt and Lease Financing."

---

[2] The one possible exception to this principle is found in the practice of holding compensating balances at commercial banks—a topic for discussion in Chapter 5.

Figure 4–2

An examination of yield and maturity characteristics

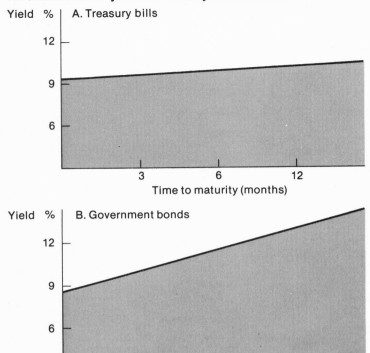

The various forms of marketable securities and investments, emphasizing the short term, are presented in Table 4—3. The key characteristics of each investment are delineated along with examples of yield as of December 1978, March 1980, and January 1983. In the first and third periods the spreads among securities are not very large, but in the second period the spreads are quite significant.

Let us examine the characteristics of each security. *Treasury bills* are short-term obligations of the federal government and are a popular place to "park funds" because of a large and active market. Although these securities are originally issued with maturities of 91 days, 182 days, and one year, the investor may buy an outstanding T bill with as little as one day remaining (perhaps two prior investors have held it for 45 days each). With the government issuing new Treasury bills weekly, a wide range of choices is always available. Treasury bills are unique in that they trade on a discount basis—meaning that the yield you recieve takes place as a result of the difference between the price you pay and the maturity value.

Treasury notes are government obligations with a maturity of three to five years, and they may be purchased with short- to intermediate-term funds. *Federal agency* securities represent the offerings of such governmental organizations as the Federal Land Bank, the Federal Home Loan Bank, and the Federal National Mortgage Association (FNMA). Though lacking the direct backing of the U.S. Treasury, they are guaranteed by the issuing agency and provide all the safety that one would normally require. There is an excellent secondary market, meaning that an investor may sell an outstanding issue in an active and liquid market prior to the maturity date. Government agency issues pay slightly higher yields than direct Treasury issues.

Table 4–3

Types of short-term investments

Investment	Maturity*	Minimum amount	Safety	Market-ability	December 1978 yield	March 24, 1980 yield	January 13, 1983 yield
Federal government securities							
Treasury bills	3 months	$ 10,000	Excellent	Excellent	8.98%	16.53%	7.67
Treasury bills	1 year	10,000	Excellent	Excellent	9.29	16.36	8.41
Treasury notes	3–5 years	5,000	Excellent	Excellent	9.01	13.86	9.77
Federal agency securities	3–5 years	5,000	Excellent	Excellent	9.21	14.40	10.34
Nongovernment securities							
Certificates of deposit	3 months	100,000	Good	Good	10.66	17.50	8.15
Commercial paper	Up to 6 months	25,000	Good	Limited	10.11	17.10	8.25
Prime banker's acceptances	90 days	None	Good	Good	10.52	17.20	8.05
Eurodollar deposits	3 months	25,000	Good	Excellent	11.66	19.06	8.81
Savings accounts	Open	None	Excellent	None†	5–5½	5–5½	5–5½
Money market funds	Open	500	Good	None†	8–8½	12½–14½	8.73
Money market account (financial institutions)	Open	2,500	Excellent	None†	—	—	8.90

*Several of the above securities can be purchased with maturities longer than those indicated. The above maturities are the most commonly quoted.

†Though not marketable, these investments are still highly liquid in that funds may be withdrawn without penalty.

Source: *Federal Reserve Bulletin* and *The Wall Street Journal.*

Another outlet for investment is the *certificates of deposit* (CD's), offered by commercial banks, savings and loans, and other financial institutions. The investor places his or her funds on deposit at a specified rate over a given time period as evidenced by the certificate received. This is a two-tier market, with small CDs ($1,000 to $10,000) carrying federally prescribed lower interest rates, while larger CDs ($100,000 and more) have higher interest provisions and a degree of marketability for those who wish to turn over their CDs prior to maturity.

Comparable in yield and quality to large certificates of deposit, *commercial paper* represents unsecured promissory notes issued to the public by large business corporations. When Ford Motor Credit Corporation is in need of short-term funds, it might choose to borrow at the bank or expand its credit resources by issuing its commercial paper to the general public in minimum units of $25,000. Commercial paper is usually held to maturity by the investor, with no active secondary market in existence. As of late 1982, $165.534 billion in commercial paper was outstanding.

Banker's acceptances are short-term securities that generally arise from foreign trade. The acceptance is a draft which is drawn on a bank for payment when presented to the bank. The difference between a <u>draft</u> and a <u>check</u> is that a company does not have to deposit funds at the bank to cover the draft until the bank has accepted the draft for payment and presented it to the company. In the case of banker's acceptances arising from foreign trade, the draft may be accepted by the bank for future payment of the required amount. This means that the exporter who now holds the banker's acceptance may have to wait 30, 60, or 90 days to collect his money. Because there is an active market for banker's acceptances (as of late 1982, $75.811 billion were outstanding), the exporter can sell his acceptance on a discount basis to any buyer and in this way receive his money before the importer receives his goods. This provides a good investment opportunity in banker's acceptances. Banker's acceptances rank close behind Treasury bills and certificates of deposits as a vehicle for viable short-term investments.

Another popular international short-term investment arising from foreign trade is the *Eurodollar certificate of deposit*. The rate on this investment is usually higher than the rates on U.S. Treasury bills and bank certificates of deposit at large U.S. money market banks. Eurodollars are U.S. dollars held on deposit by foreign banks and in turn loaned out by those banks to anyone seeking dollars. Since the U.S. dollar is the only international currency that is also used as a domestic currency abroad, any country can use it to help pay for goods. Therefore, there is a large market for Eurodollar deposits and loans, mostly centered in the London international banking market.

The lowest yielding investment may well be a passbook *savings account* at a bank or a savings and loan. The maximum rate is established by law and is generally well below that of other instruments.

Of particular interest to the smaller investor is the *money market fund*—a product of the tight money periods of the 1970s and early 1980s. For as little as $500 or $1,000, an investor may purchase shares in a money market fund, which in turn reinvests the proceeds in high-yielding $100,000 bank CDs, $25,000–$100,000 commercial paper, and other large-denomination, high-yielding securities. The investor then receives his pro rata portion of the interest proceeds daily as a credit to his shares.

The money market funds allow the small businessperson or investor to participate directly in higher yielding securities. All too often in the past, the small investor was forced to place funds in savings accounts yielding 5–5½ percent, while "smart" money was parked at higher yields in large-unit investments. Examples of money market funds are Dreyfus Liquid Assets, Inc., and Fidelity Daily Income Trust.

Beginning in December 1982, money market funds got new competition when commercial banks, savings and loans, and credit unions were permitted by the regulatory agencies and Congress to offer new money market accounts modeled after money market funds. These financial institutions are now able to pay competitive market rates on money market accounts that have a minimum balance of $2,500. These accounts may only have three deposits and three withdrawals per month, and are not meant to be transaction accounts, but a place to keep minimum and excess cash balances. They may be used by individuals or corporations, but will most likely be much more attractive to smaller firms than larger firms (which have many more investment alternatives available). These accounts are insured up to $100,000 by federal agencies, which make them slightly less risky than money market funds.

Complete deregulation of all interest-rate ceilings and minimum deposit requirements at financial institutions (by 1986) was mandated by the Monetary Control Act of 1980. The pace of deregulation has been swift and is likely to be completed before the specified time period.

Management of Accounts Receivable

An increasing portion of the investment in corporate assets has been in accounts receivable as expanding sales, fostered to some extent by inflationary pressures, have placed additional burdens on firms to carry larger balances for their customers. Frequently recessions have also stretched out the terms of payment as small customers have had to rely on suppliers for credit. Accounts receivable as a percentage of total assets has almost doubled between 1950 and the early 1980s, representing over 20 percent of total assets for the average U.S. corporation.

Accounts receivable as an investment

As is true of other current assets, accounts receivable should be thought of as an investment. The level of accounts receivable should not be adjudged too high or too low based on historical standards of industry norms, but rather the test should be whether the level of return we are able to earn from this asset equals or exceeds the potential gain from other commitments. For example, if we allow our customers five extra days to clear their accounts, our accounts receivable balance will increase—draining funds from marketable securities and perhaps drawing down the inventory level. We must ask whether we are optimizing our return, in light of appropriate risk and liquidity considerations.

An example of a buildup in accounts receivable is presented in Figure 4—3, with supportive financing provided through reducing lower yielding assets and increasing lower cost liabilities.

Credit policy administration

In considering the extension of credit, there are three primary policy variables to consider in conjunction with our profit objective.

Figure 4–3

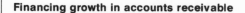

Financing growth in accounts receivable

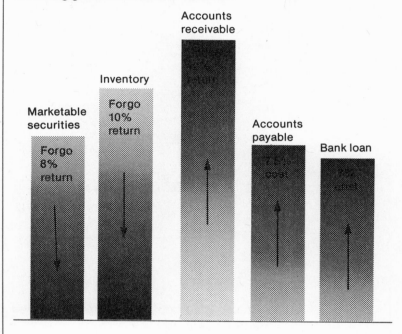

1. Credit standards.
2. Terms of credit.
3. Collection policy.

Credit standards   The firm must determine the nature of the credit risk on the basis of prior record of payment, financial stability, current net worth, and other factors. An extensive network of credit information has been developed by credit agencies throughout the country (Big Brother is watching). The most prominent source is Dun & Bradstreet, which publishes a *Reference Book* listing over 3 million business establishments. Information is given on the firm's line of business, net worth, and creditworthiness. An example of the rating system used by Dun & Bradstreet is presented in Table 4—4.

A firm with a BB2 rating has estimated financial strength, based on net worth, of $200,000–$300,000, with an overall composite credit rating of "Good." Besides the *Reference Book*, Dun & Brad-

Table 4–4

Dun & Bradstreet credit rating system

Key to ratings

	Estimated financial strength		Composite credit appraisal			
			High	Good	Fair	Limited
5A . . .	Over	$50,000,000	1	2	3	4
4A . . .	$10,000,000 to	50,000,000	1	2	3	4
3A . . .	1,000,000 to	10,000,000	1	2	3	4
2A . . .	750,000 to	1,000,000	1	2	3	4
1A . . .	500,000 to	750,000	1	2	3	4
BA . . .	300,000 to	500,000	1	2	3	4
ⒷⒷ . . .	200,000 to	300,000	1	②	3	4
CB . . .	125,000 to	200,000	1	2	3	4
CC . . .	75,000 to	125,000	1	2	3	4
DC . . .	50,000 to	75,000	1	2	3	4
DD . . .	35,000 to	50,000	1	2	3	4
EE . . .	20,000 to	35,000	1	2	3	4
FF . . .	10,000 to	20,000	1	2	3	4
GG . . .	5,000 to	10,000	1	2	3	4
HH . . .	Up to	5,000	1	2	3	4

street can also provide extensive individualized credit reports on potential customers.

Certain industries have also developed their own special credit reporting agencies, such as the Lyon Furniture Mercantile Agency and the National Credit Office (textiles). Even more important are the local credit bureaus that keep close tabs on day-to-day transactions in a given community.

Terms of trade   The stated terms of credit extension will have a strong impact on the eventual size of the accounts receivable balance. If a firm averages $5,000 in daily credit sales and allows 30-day terms, the average accounts receivable balance will be $150,000. If customers are carried for 60 days, we must maintain $300,000 in receivables and much additional financing will be required.

In establishing credit terms, the firm should also consider the use of a cash discount. Offering the terms 2/10, net 30, enables the customer to deduct 2 percent from the face amount of the bill when paying within the first 10 days, but if the discount is not taken, the customer must remit the full amount within 30 days. As later demonstrated in Chapter 5, "Sources of Short-Term Financing," the annualized cost of not taking a cash discount may be substantial.

Collection policy A third area for consideration under credit policy administration is the collection function. A number of quantitative measures may be applied to the credit department of the firm.

a. Average collection period $= \dfrac{\text{Accounts receivable}}{\text{Average daily credit sales}}$

An increase in the average collection period may be the result of a predetermined plan to extend credit terms or the consequence of poor credit administration.

b. Ratio of bad debts to credit sales.

An increasing ratio may indicate too many weak accounts or an aggressive market expansion policy.

c. Aging of accounts receivables.

We may wish to determine the amount of time that the various accounts have been on our books. If there is a buildup in receivables beyond our normal credit terms, we may wish to take remedial action. An example is presented here.

Age of receivables, May 31, 1984

Month of sales	Age of account	Amounts
May	0–30	$ 60,000
April	31–60	25,000
March	61–90	5,000
February	91–120	10,000
Total receivables		$100,000

If our normal credit terms are 30 days, we may be doing a poor job of collecting our accounts, with particular attention required on the over-90-day accounts.

An actual credit decision

We now examine a credit decision that brings together the various elements of accounts receivable management. Assume that a firm is considering selling to a group of customers that will bring $10,000 in new annual sales, of which 10 percent will be uncollectible. While this is a very high rate of nonpayment, the critical question is, What is the potential contribution to profitability?

Assume the collection cost on these accounts is 5 percent and the cost of producing and selling the product is 77 percent of the sales dollar. We are in a 40 percent tax bracket. The profit on new sales is as follows:

Additional sales	$10,000
Accounts uncollectible (10% of new sales)	1,000
Annual incremental revenue	9,000
Collection costs (5% of new sales)	500
Production and selling costs (77% of new sales)	7,700
Annual income before taxes	800
Taxes (40%)	320
Annual incremental income after taxes	$ 480

Though the return on sales is only 4.8 percent ($480/$10,000), the return on invested dollars may be considerably higher. Let us assume that the only new investment in this case is a buildup in accounts receivable. (Present working capital and fixed assets are sufficient to support the higher sales level.) Assume analysis of our accounts indicates a turnover ratio of 6 to 1 between sales and accounts receivable. Our new accounts receivable balance will average $1,667.

$$\frac{\text{Credit}}{\text{Turnover}} = \frac{\$10,000^3}{6} = \$1,667$$

Thus, we are committing an average investment of only $1,667 to provide an aftertax return of $480, so that the yield is a very attractive 28.8 percent. If the firm had a minimum required aftertax return of 10 percent, this would clearly be an acceptable investment. We might ask next if we should consider taking on 12 percent or even 15 percent in uncollectible accounts—remaining loyal to our concept of maximizing profit and forsaking any notion about risky accounts being inherently good or bad.

––––––––––

[3]We could actually argue that our out-of-pocket commitment to sales is 82 percent times $10,000, or $8,200. This would indicate an even smaller commitment to receivables.

Inventory Management

Inventory is the least liquid of current assets, and it should provide the highest yield to justify investment. While the financial manager may have direct control over the management of cash, marketable securities, and accounts receivable, control over inventory policy is generally shared with production management and marketing. Let us examine some of the key factors influencing inventory management.

Level versus seasonal production

A manufacturing firm must determine whether a plan of level or seasonal production should be followed. Level production was discussed in Chapter 3. While level (even) production throughout the year allows for maximum efficiency in the use of manpower and machinery, it may result in unnecessarily high inventory buildups prior to shipment, particularly in a seasonal business. We may have 10,000 bathing suits in stock in November.

If we produce on a seasonal basis, the inventory problem is eliminated, but we will then have unused capacity during slack periods. Furthermore, as we shift to maximum operations to meet seasonal needs, we may be forced to pay overtime wages to labor and to sustain other inefficiencies as equipment is overused.

We have a classic problem in financial analysis. Are the cost savings from level production sufficient to justify the extra expenditure in carrying inventory? Let us look at a typical case.

	Production	
	Level	Seasonal
Average inventory	$100,000	$70,000
Operating costs—after tax	50,000	60,000

Though we will have to invest $30,000 more in average inventory under level production, we will save $10,000 in operating costs. If our required rate of return is 10 percent, this would clearly be an acceptable alternative.[4]

---

[4]The problem may be further evaluated by using the capital budgeting techniques presented in Chapter 11.

Inventory policy in inflation (and deflation)

The price of copper went from $0.50 to $1.40 a pound and back again in 1973–75 and also showed sharp price volatility in the 1979–82 period. Similar price instability has taken place in wheat, sugar, lumber, and a number of other commodities. Only the most astute inventory manager can hope to prosper in this type of environment. The problem can be partially controlled by taking moderate inventory positions (do not fully commit at one price).

Another way of protecting your inventory position would be by hedging with a futures contract to sell at a stipulated price some months from now.

Rapid price movements in inventory may also have a major impact on the reported income of the firm. A firm using FIFO (first-in, first-out) accounting may experience large inventory profits when old, less expensive inventory is written off against new high prices in the marketplace. The benefits may be transitory, as the process reverses itself when prices decline.

Summary

In cash management our primary goal should be to keep our balances as low as possible consistent with the notion of maintaining adequate funds for transaction purposes. We try to speed the inflow of funds and defer their outflow. Excess short-term funds may be placed in marketable securities—with a wide selection of issues, maturities, and yields from which to choose.

The management of accounts receivable calls for the determination of credit standards and the forms of credit to be offered as well as the development of an effective collection policy. There is no such thing as bad credit—only unprofitable credit extension. Inventory is the least liquid of the current assets, so it should provide the highest yield.

5 | Sources of Short-Term Financing

In Chapter 8, we examine the cost and availability of the various outlets for short-term funds, with primary attention devoted to trade credit from suppliers, bank loans, corporate promissory notes, foreign borrowing, and loans against receivables and inventory. It is sometimes said that the only way to be sure that a loan will be approved at the bank is to convince the banker that you do not really need the money. The learning objective of this chapter will be quite the opposite—namely, to demonstrate how badly needed funds can be made available on a short-term basis from the various suppliers of credit.

Trade Credit

The largest provider of short-term credit is usually at the firm's doorstep—the manufacturer or seller of goods and services. Approximately 40 percent of short-term financing is in the form of accounts payable or trade credit. Accounts payable is a spontaneous source of funds, growing as the business expands on a seasonal or long-term basis and contracting in a like fashion.

Payment period

Trade credit is usually extended for 30 to 60 days. Many firms attempt to "stretch the payment period" in order to provide additional short-term financing. This is an acceptable form of financing as long as it is not carried to an abusive extent. Going from a 30- to a 35-day average payment period may be tolerated within the trade, while stretching payments to 65 days might alienate suppliers and cause a diminishing credit rating with Dun & Bradstreet and local credit bureaus. A major variable in determining the payment period is the possible existence of a cash discount.

Cash discount policy

A cash discount allows for a reduction in price if payment is made within a specified time period. A 2/10, net 30 cash discount means that we can deduct 2 percent if we remit our funds 10 days after billing, but failing this, we must pay the full amount by the 30th day.

On a $100 billing, we could pay $98 up to the 10th day or $100 at the end of 30 days. If we fail to take the cash discount, we will get to use $98 for 20 more days at a $2 fee. The cost is a whopping 36.72 percent. Note that we first consider the interest cost and then convert this to an annual basis. The standard formula is:

$$\text{Cost of failing to take a cash discount} = \frac{\text{Discount percent}}{100 \text{ percent} - \text{Discount percent}}$$

$$\times \frac{360}{\text{Final due date} - \text{Discount period}} \quad (5\text{—}1)$$

$$= \frac{2\%}{100\% - 2\%} \times \frac{360}{(30 - 10)}$$

$$= 2.04\% \times 18 = 36.72\%$$

Cash discount terms may vary. For example, on a 2/10, net 90 basis, it would cost us only 9.18 percent not to take the discount and to pay the full amount after 90 days.

$$\frac{2\%}{100\% - 2\%} \times \frac{360}{(90 - 10)} = 2.04\% \times 4.5 = 9.18\%$$

In each case, we must ask ourselves whether bypassing the discount and using the money for a longer period of time is the cheapest means of financing. In the first example, with a cost of 36.72 percent, it probably is not. We would be better off borrowing $98 for 20 days at some lesser rate. For example, at 10 percent interest we would pay 56 cents[1] in interest as opposed to $2 under the cash discount policy. With the 2/10, net 90 arrangement, the cost of missing the discount is only 9.18 percent and we may choose to let our suppliers carry us for an extra 80 days.

Net credit position

We defined accounts receivable as a use of funds and accounts payable as a source. The firm should closely watch the relationship between the two to determine its net credit position. If we have average daily sales of $5,000 and collect in 30 days, our accounts receivable balance will be $150,000. If this is associated with average daily purchases of $4,000 and a 25-day average payment period, our average accounts payable balance is $100,000—indicating $50,000 more in credit extended than received. Changing this situation to an average payment period of 40 days increases the accounts payable to $160,000 ($4,000 × 40). Accounts payable now exceed accounts receivable by $10,000, thus leaving funds for other needs. Larger firms tend to be net providers of trade credit (relatively high receivables), with smaller firms in the user position (relatively high payables).

Bank Credit

Banks may provide funds to finance seasonal needs, product line expansion, and long-term growth. The typical banker prefers a self-liquidating loan in which the use of funds will ensure a built-in or automatic repayment scheme. Actually, two thirds of bank loans are short term in nature. Nevertheless, through the process of renewing old loans, many of these 90- or 180-day agreements take on the characteristics of longer-term financing.

Major changes are taking place in banking today that are cen-

---

[1] $\frac{20}{360} \times 10\% \times \$100 = 56¢$

tered on the concept of "full-service banking." The modern bank-er's function is much broader than merely accepting deposits, making loans, and processing checks. At present, a banking institution may be involved in providing trust and investment services, a credit card operation, real estate lending, data processing services, and helpful advice in cash management or international trade. This wide array of services has been made possible through the development of the bank holding company—a legal entity in which one key bank owns a number of affiliate banks as well as other nonbanking subsidiaries engaged in closely related activities.

As we move into the mid-1980s, more and more banks may also engage in interstate banking activities as legislative barriers come down. The concept of a purely Texas or Illinois bank is likely to be a thing of the past. This trend is also part of the move toward greater competition among financial institutions, such as banks, savings and loans, credit unions, and brokerage houses.

We will look at a number of terms generally associated with banking (and other types of lending activity) and consider the significance of each. Attention is directed to the prime interest rate, compensating balances, the term loan arrangement, and methods of computing interest.

Prime rate

This is the rate that the bank charges its most creditworthy customers, and it is scaled up proportionally to reflect the various credit classes. At certain slack loan periods in the economy, banks may actually charge top customers less than the published prime rate; however, such activities are difficult to track. The average customer can expect to pay 1 or 2 percent above prime, while in tight money periods a builder in a speculative construction project may pay five or more percentage points over prime.

From 1954 to mid-1965, the prime rate was relatively stable, never going below 3 percent or above 5 percent, as indicated in Figure 5—1. Beginning in mid-1965 and continuing into the present, the rate became highly volatile, moving as much as 8 percentage points in a 12-month period. In the early 1980s, the prime rate went to the 20 percent range before sharply declining.

Figure 5–1

Pattern of prime interest rate movements

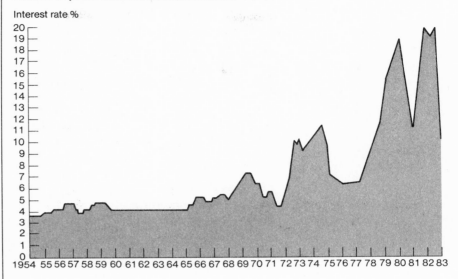

The prime rate has long been a political football, with congressmen charging that it is too high in periods of rising interest rates. In order to better justify the prime at a given point in time, Citibank of New York went to a "floating prime" in October 1971 in which the prime rate is set at ½–1½ percent above the rate on designated classes of commercial paper and other selected money market instruments. The intent was to demonstrate that bankers are not administering an artificially high rate—but moving with conditions in other markets. However, at extreme points in the economy the spread has gotten as large as 4 percent as bankers had difficulty in dealing with market conditions.

Compensating balances

In providing loans as well as other services, the bank may require that *business* customers maintain a minimum average account balance, herein referred to as a compensating balance. The required amount is usually computed as a percentage of customer loans outstanding or as a percentage of bank commitments toward future loans to a given account. A common ratio is 20 percent against outstanding loans or 10 percent against total future commitments, though market conditions tend to influence the percentages.

Some view the compensating balance requirement as an unusual arrangement. Where else would you walk into a business establishment, buy a shipment of goods, and then be told that you could not take 20 percent of the purchase home with you? If you borrow $100,000, paying 8 percent interest on the full amount with a 20 percent compensating balance requirement, you will be paying $8,000 for the use of $80,000 in funds, or an effective rate of 10 percent.

The amount that must be borrowed to end up with the desired sum of money is simply figured by taking the needed funds and dividing by $(1 - c)$, where c is the compensating balance expressed as a decimal. For example, if you need $100,000 in funds, you must borrow $125,000 to ensure that the intended amount will be available. This would be calculated as follows:

$$
\begin{aligned}
\text{Amount to be borrowed} &= \frac{\text{Amount needed}}{(1 - c)} \\
&= \frac{\$100,000}{(1 - 0.2)} \\
&= \$125,000
\end{aligned}
$$

A check on this calculation could be done to see if we actually end up with the use of $100,000

$125,000	Loan
−25,000	20% compensating balance requirement
$100,000	Available funds

The intent here is not to suggest that the compensating balance requirement represents an unfair or hidden cost. If it were not for compensating balances, quoted interest rates would be higher or gratuitous services now offered by banks would carry a price tag. Some authorities in the banking community think that this would be a move in a positive direction, forcing both banker and customer to unbundle and evaluate the full cost of services provided.

Maturity provisions

As previously indicated, bank loans have been traditionally short term in nature (though perhaps renewable). In the last decade there has been a movement to the use of the term loan, in which credit is extended for a period of one to seven years. The loan is usually repaid in monthly or quarterly installments over its life rather than in one single payment. Only superior credit applicants, as measured by working capital strength, potential profitability, and competitive position, can qualify for term loan financing. Here the banker and the business firm are said to be "climbing into bed together" because of the length of the loan.

Bankers are hesitant to fix a single interest rate to a term loan. The more common practice is to allow the interest rate to change with market conditions. Thus the interest rate on a term loan may be tied to the prime rate and will change (float) with it. Perhaps it is set at prime plus 1 percent.

Cost of commercial bank financing

The effective interest rate on a loan is based on the loan amount, the dollar interest paid, the length of the loan, and the method of repayment. It is easy enough to observe that $60 interest on a $1,000 loan for one year would carry a 6 percent interest rate, but what if the same loan were for 120 days? We use the formula:

$$\text{Effective rate} = \frac{\text{Interest}}{\text{Principal}} \times \frac{\text{Days in the year (360)}}{\text{Days loan is outstanding}} \quad (5\text{—}2)$$

$$= \frac{\$60}{\$1000} \times \frac{360}{120} = 6\% \times 3 = 18\%$$

Since we have use of the funds for only 120 days, the effective rate is 18 percent. To highlight the effect of time, if you borrowed $20 for only ten days and paid back $21, the effective interest rate would be 180 percent—a violation of almost every usury law.

$$\frac{\$1}{\$20} \times \frac{360}{10} = 5\% \times 36 = 180\%$$

Not only is the time dimension of a loan important, but also the way in which interest is charged. We have assumed that interest would be paid when the loan comes due. If the bank deducts the interest in advance (discounts the loan), the effective rate of interest increases. For example, a $1,000 one-year loan with $60 of interest deducted in advance represents the payment of interest on only $940, or an effective rate of 6.38 percent.

$$\text{Effective rate on discounted loan} = \frac{\text{Interest}}{\text{Principal} - \text{Interest}}$$

$$\times \frac{\text{Days in the year (360)}}{\text{Days loan is outstanding}} \qquad (5\text{—}3)$$

$$= \frac{\$60}{\$1,000 - \$60} \times \frac{360}{360} = \frac{\$60}{\$940} = 6.38\%$$

Interest costs with compensating balances

When a loan is made with compensating balances, the effective interest rate is the stated interest rate divided by $(1 - c)$, where c is the compensating balance expressed as a decimal. Assume that 6 percent is the stated annual rate and that a 20 percent compensating balance is required.

$$\text{Effective rate with compensating balances} = \frac{\text{Interest rate}}{(1 - c)} \qquad (5\text{—}4)$$

$$= \frac{6\%}{(1 - 0.2)}$$

$$= 7.5\%$$

If dollar amounts are used and the stated rate is unknown, Formula 5—5 can be used. The assumption is that we are paying $60 interest on a $1,000 loan, but are only able to use $800 of the funds. The loan is for a year.

$$\text{Effective rate with compensating balances} = \frac{\text{Interest}}{\text{Principal} - \text{Compensating balance in dollars}} \times \frac{\text{Days in the years (360)}}{\text{Days loan is outstanding}} \qquad (5\text{—}5)$$

$$= \frac{\$60}{\$1,000 - \$200} \times \frac{360}{360} = \frac{\$60}{\$800} = 7.5\%$$

Only in circumstances in which a firm had idle cash balances that could be used to cover compensating balance requirements would the firm not use the higher effective cost formulas in 5—4 and 5—5.

Rate on installment loans

The most confusing borrowing arrangement to the average bank customer or consumer is the installment loan. An installment loan calls for a series of equal payments over the life of the loan. Though federal legislation prohibits a misrepresentation of interest rates on loans to customers, a loan officer or an overanxious salesperson may quote a rate on an installment loan that is approximately half the true rate of interest.

Assume that you borrow $1,000 on a 12-month installment basis, with regular monthly payments to apply to interest and principal, and that the interest requirement is $60. Though it might be suggested that the rate on the loan is 6 percent, this is clearly not the case. Even though you are paying a total of $60 in interest, you do not have the use of $1,000 for one year—rather, you are paying back the $1,000 on a monthly basis, with an average outstanding loan balance for the year of approximately $500. The effective rate of interest is 11.08 percent.

$$\text{Rate on installment loan} = \frac{2 \times \text{Annual no. of payments} \times \text{Interest}}{(\text{Total no. of payments} + 1) \times \text{Principal}} \quad (5\text{—}6)$$

$$= \frac{2 \times 12 \times \$60}{13 \times \$1,000} = \frac{\$1,440}{\$13,000} = 11.08\%$$

Financing through Commercial Paper

For large, prestigious firms, commercial paper may provide an outlet for raising funds. Commercial paper represents a short-term, unsecured promissory note issued to the public in minimum units of $25,000.

The issues of commercial paper fall into two categories. First, there are the *finance companies*, such as General Motors Acceptance Corporation and CIT Financial Corporation, that issue paper to wealthy individuals, pension funds, and insurance companies. Second, we have the *industrial* or *utility* firms that use an intermediate network to distribute their paper.

Advantages of commercial paper

The growing popularity of commercial paper is attributed to a number of factors. First of all, commercial paper may be issued at 1/2-4 percent below the prime interest rate at commercial banks, as indicated in Table 5—1.

Table 5-1

Comparison of commercial paper rate to bank prime rate (annual rate) *

	Finance co. paper (directly placed) 4–6 months	Other paper (dealer-placed) 4–6 months	Average bank prime rate
1963	3.40	3.55	4.50
1964	3.83	3.97	4.50
1965	4.27	4.38	4.50
1966	5.42	5.55	5.75
1967	4.89	5.10	5.50
1968	5.69	5.90	6.50
1969	7.16	7.83	8.50
1970	7.23	7.72	8.00
1971	4.91	5.11	5.50
1972	4.52	4.69	5.25
1973	7.40	8.15	8.30
1974	8.62	9.87	11.12
1975	6.50	6.91	7.50
1976	5.22	5.35	6.84
1977	5.50	5.60	6.82
1978	7.78	7.79	9.05
1979	10.25	10.91	12.67
1980	11.28	12.29	15.27
1981	13.73	14.76	18.87
1982	11.64	12.37	13.50

*Averages for the year.
Source: *Federal Reserve Bulletins, Economic Report to the President, 1982.*

A second advantage of commercial paper is that no compensating balance requirements are associated with its issuance, though the firm is generally required to maintain commercial bank lines of approved credit equal to the amount of the paper outstanding (a procedure somewhat less costly than compensating balances). Finally, a number of firms enjoy the prestige associated with being able to float their commercial paper in what is considerd a "snobbish market" for funds.

Use of Collateral in Short-Term Financing

Almost any firm would prefer to borrow on an unsecured (no-collateral) basis; but if the borrower's credit rating is too low or its need for funds too great, the lending institution will require that certain assets be pledged. A secured credit arrangement might help the borrower to obtain funds that would otherwise be unavailable.

In any loan the lender's primary concern, however, is whether the borrower's capacity to generate cash flow is sufficient to liquidate the loan as it comes due. Few lenders would make a loan strictly on the quality of collateral. Collateral is merely a stopgap device to protect the lender when all else fails. The bank or finance company is in business to collect interest, not to repossess and re-sell assets.

Though a number of different types of assets may be pledged, our attention will be directed to accounts receivable and inventory. All states have now adopted the Uniform Commercial Code, which standardizes and simplifies the procedures for establishing the security on a loan.

Accounts Receivable Financing

Accounts receivable financing may include *pledging* accounts receivable as collateral for a loan or an outright *sale* (factoring) of receivables. Receivables financing is popular because it permits borrowing to be tied directly to the level of asset expansion at any point in time. As the level of accounts receivable goes up, we are able to borrow more.

A drawback is that this is a relatively expensive method of acquiring funds, so that it must be carefully compared to other forms of credit. Accounts receivable represent one of the firm's most valuable short-term assets, and they should be committed only where the appropriate circumstances exist. An ill-advised accounts receivable financing plan may exclude the firm from a less expensive bank term loan. Let us investigate more closely the characteristics and the costs associated with the pledging and selling of receivables.

Pledging accounts receivable

The lending institution will generally stipulate which of the accounts receivable are of sufficient quality to serve as collateral for a loan. On this basis, we may borrow 60–80 percent of the value of the acceptable collateral. The loan percentage will depend on the financial strength of the borrowing firm and on the creditworthiness of its accounts. The lender will have full recourse against the borrower in the event that any of the accounts go bad. The interest rate in a receivables borrowing arrangement is generally well in excess of the prime rate.

The interest is computed against the loan balance outstanding, a figure that may change quite frequently, as indicated in Table 5—2. In the illustration, interest is assumed to be 12 percent annually, or 1 percent per month. In month 1, we are able to borrow $8,000 against $10,000 in acceptable receivables and we must pay $80 in interest. Similar values are developed for succeeding months.

Table 5–2

Receivable loan balance

	Month 1	Month 2	Month 3	Month 4
Total accounts receivable	$11,000	$15,100	$19,400	$16,300
Acceptable accounts receivable				
(to finance company)	10,000	14,000	18,000	15,000
Loan balance (80%)	8,000	11,200	14,400	12,000
Interest 12% annual—1% per month . .	80	112	144	120

Factoring receivables

When we factor our receivables, they are sold outright to the finance company. Our customers may be instructed to remit the proceeds directly to the purchaser of the account. The factoring firm generally does not have recourse against the seller of the receivables. As a matter of practice, the finance company may do part or all of the credit analysis directly to ensure the quality of the accounts. As a potential sale is being made, the factoring firm may give immediate feedback to the seller on whether the account will be purchased.

When the factoring firm accepts an account, it may forward funds immediately to the seller, in anticipation of receiving payment 30 days later as part of the normal billing process. The factoring firm is not only absorbing risk, but is actually advancing funds to the seller a month earlier than the seller would normally receive them.

For taking the risk, the factoring firm is generally paid on a fee or commission basis equal to 1–3 percent of the invoices accepted. In addition, it is paid a lending rate for advancing the funds early. If $100,000 a month is processed at a 1 percent commission and a

12 percent annual borrowing rate, the total effective cost will be 24 percent on an *annual* basis.

1%	Commission
1%	Interest for one month (12% annual/12)
2%	Total fee monthly
2%	Monthly × 12 = 24% annual rate

If one considers that the firm selling the accounts is transferring risk as well as receiving funds early, which may allow it to take cash discounts, the rate may not be considered exorbitant. Also, the firm is able to pass on much of the credit-checking cost to the factor.

Inventory Financing

We may also borrow against inventory to acquire funds. The extent to which inventory financing may be employed is based on the marketability of the pledged goods, their associated price stability, and the perishability of the product. Another significant factor is the degree of physical control that can be exercised over the product by the lender. We can relate some of these factors to the stages of inventory production and the nature of lender control.

Stages of production

Raw materials and finished goods are likely to provide the best collateral, while goods in process may only qualify for a small percentage loan. To the extent that a firm is holding such widely traded raw materials as lumber, metals, grain, cotton, and wool, a loan of 70–80 percent or higher is possible. The lender may only have to place a few quick phone calls to dispose of the goods at market value if the borrower fails to repay the loan. For standardized finished goods, such as tires, canned goods, and building products, the same principle would apply. Goods in process, representing altered but unfinished raw materials, may qualify for a loan of only one fourth or less.

Nature of lender control

The methods for controlling pledged inventory go from the simple to the complex, providing ever greater assurances to the lender but progressively higher administrative costs.

Blanket inventory liens The simplest method is for the lender to have a general claim against the inventory of the borrower. Specific items are not identified or tagged, and there is no physical control.

Trust receipts A trust receipt is an instrument acknowledging that the borrower holds the inventory and proceeds from sales in trust for the lender. Each item is carefully marked and specified by serial number. When sold, the proceeds are transferred to the lender and the trust receipt is cancelled. Also known as floor planning, this financing device is very popular among auto and industrial equipment dealers and in the television and home appliance industries. Although it provides tighter control than does the blanket inventory lien, it still does not give the lender direct control over inventory—only a better and more legally enforceable system of tracing the goods.

Warehousing Under this arrangement, goods are physically identified, segregated, and stored under the direction of an independent warehousing company. The firm issues a warehouse receipt to the lender, and goods can be moved only with the lender's approval.

The goods may be stored on the premises of the warehousing firm, an arrangement known as *public warehousing,* or on the *borrower's premises*—under a *field warehousing* agreement. When field warehousing is utilized, it is still an independent warehousing company that exercises control over inventory.

Appraisal of inventory control devices

While the more structured methods of inventory financing appear somewhat restrictive, they are well accepted in certain industries. For example, field warehousing is popular in grain storage and food canning. Well-maintained control measures do involve substantial administrative expenses, and they raise the overall costs of borrowing. The costs of inventory financing may run 15 percent or higher. As is true of accounts receivable financing, the extension of funds is well synchronized with the need.

Summary

A firm in search of short-term financing must be aware of all the institutional arrangements that are available. The easiest access is to trade credit provided by suppliers as a natural outgrowth of the buying and reselling of goods. Larger firms tend to be net providers of trade credit, while smaller firms are net users.

Bank financing is usually in the form of short-term, self-liquidating loans. A financially strong customer will be offered the prime or lowest rate, with the rates to other accounts scaled up appropriately. The use of compensating balances tends to increase the effective yield to the bank and serves as a device to compensate the bank for the many services it provides to a commercial account.

An alternative to bank credit for the large, prestigious firm is the use of commercial paper. Though generally issued at a rate below prime, it is an impersonal means of financing that may "dry up" during difficult financing periods.

Firms are also turning to foreign sources of funds either through the Eurodollar market (foreign dollar loans) or through borrowing foreign currency directly.

By using a secured form of financing, the firm ties its borrowing requirements directly to its asset buildup. We may pledge our accounts receivable as collateral or sell them outright, as well as borrow against inventory. Though secured asset financing devices may be expensive, they may well fit the credit needs of the firm, particularly those of a small firm that cannot qualify for premium bank financing or the commercial paper market.

PART **3** | # The Capital Budgeting Process

6 | The Time Value of Money

In 1624, the Indians sold Manhattan Island at the ridiculously low figure of $24. But wait, was it really ridiculous? If the Indians had merely taken the $24 and reinvested it at 6 percent annual interest up to 1984, they would have had $31.0 billion, an amount sufficient to repurchase most of New York City. If the Indians had been slightly more astute and had invested the $24 at 7.5 percent compounded annually, they would now have close to $5,000,000,000,000 ($5 trillion)—and tribal chiefs would now rival oil sheikhs as the richest people in the world. Another popular example is that $1 received 1,984 years ago, invested at 6 percent, could now be used to purchase all the wealth in the world.

While not all examples are this dramatic, the time value of money figures in many day-to-day decisions. Understanding the effective rate on a business loan, the mortgage payment in a real estate transaction, or the true return on an investment is dependent on understanding the time value of money. As long as an investor is able to garner a positive return on idle dollars, distinctions must be made between money received today and money received in the future.

The investor/lender essentially demands that a financial "rent" be paid on his or her funds as current dollars are set aside today in anticipation of higher returns in the future.

Relationship to the Capital Outlay Decision

The decision to purchase new plant and equipment or to introduce a new product in the market requires use of capital allocating or capital budgeting techniques. Essentially, we must determine whether future benefits are sufficiently large to justify current outlays. It is important that we develop the mathematical tools of the time value of money as the first step toward making capital allocating decisions. Let us now examine the basic terminology of "time value of money."

Compound Sum— Single Amount

In determining the compound sum, we measure the future value of an amount that is allowed to grow at a given interest rate over a period of time. Assume that an investor has $1,000 and wishes to know its worth after four years if it grows at 10 percent per year. At the end of the first year, he will have $1,000 × 1.10, or $1,100. By the end of year two, the $1,100 will have grown to $1,210 ($1,100 × 1.10). The four-year pattern is indicated below.

```
1st year  $1,000 × 1.10 = $1,100
2nd year  $1,100 × 1.10 = $1,210
3rd year  $1,210 × 1.10 = $1,331
4th year  $1,331 × 1.10 = $1,464
```

After the fourth year, the investor has accumulated $1,464. Because compounding problems often cover a long period of time, a more generalized formula is necessary to describe the compounding procedure. We shall let:

S = Compound sum
P = Principal or present value
i = Interest rate
n = Number of periods

The simple formula is:

$$S = P(1 + i)^n$$

In the present case, P = \$1,000, i = 10 percent, n = 4, so we have:

$$S = \$1,000(1.10)^4, \text{ or } \$1,000 \times 1.464 = \$1,464$$

The term $(1.10)^4$ is found to equal 1.464 by multiplying 1.10 four times itself (the fourth power) or by using logarithms. An even quicker process is the use of an interest rate table, such as Table 6—1 for the compound sum of a dollar. With n = 4 and i = 10 percent, the value is also found to be 1.464.

Table 6–1

Compound sum of \$1 (IF_s)

Periods	1%	2%	3%	4%	6%	8%	10%
1	1.010	1.020	1.030	1.040	1.060	1.080	1.100
2	1.020	2.040	1.061	1.082	1.124	1.166	1.210
3	1.030	1.061	1.093	1.125	1.191	1.260	1.331
4	1.041	1.082	1.126	1.170	1.262	1.360	1.464
5	1.051	1.104	1.159	1.217	1.338	1.469	1.611
10	1.105	1.219	1.344	1.480	1.791	2.159	2.594
20	1.220	1.486	1.806	2.191	3.207	4.661	6.727

The table tells us the amount that \$1 would grow to if it were invested for any number of periods at a given interest rate. We multiply this factor times any other amount to determine the compound sum. An expanded version of Table 6—1 is presented at the back of the text in Appendix A.

In determining the compound sum, we will shorten our formula from $S = P(1 + i)^n$ to

$$S = P \times IF_s \qquad (6\text{—}1)$$

where IF_s equals the interest factor found in the table.

If \$10,000 were invested for ten years at 8 percent, the compound sum, based on Table 6—1, would be:

$$S = P \times IF_s \ (n = 10, i = 8\%)$$
$$S = \$10,000 \times 2.159 = \$21,590$$

Present Value— Single Amount

In recent years, the sports pages have been filled with stories of athletes who receive multimillion dollar contracts for signing with sports organizations. Perhaps you have wondered how the Lakers or Yankees can afford to pay such fantastic sums. The answer may lie in the concept of present value—a sum payable in the future is worth less today than the stated amount.

The present value is the exact opposite of the compound sum. For example, earlier we determined that the compound sum of $1,000 for four periods at 10 percent was $1,464. We could reverse the process to state that the present value of $1,464 received four years into the future, with a 10 percent interest or discount rate, is worth only $1,000 today. The relationship is depicted in Figure 6—1.

Figure 6–1

Relationship of present value and compound sum

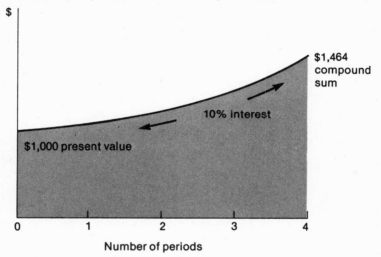

The formula for present value is derived from the original formula for the compound sum.

$$S = P(1 + i)^n \quad \text{Compound sum}$$

$$P = S\left[\frac{1}{(1 + i)^n}\right] \text{Present value}$$

The present value can be determined by solving for a mathematical solution to the above formula, or by using Table 6—2, the present value of a dollar. In the latter instance, we restate the formula for present value as:

$$P = S \times IF_{pv} \qquad\qquad (6\text{---}2)$$

Once again, IF_{pv} represents the interest factor found in appropriate Table 6—2.

Table 6–2

Present value of \$1 (IF_{pv})

Periods	1%	2%	3%	4%	6%	8%	10%
1	0.990	0.980	0.971	0.962	0.943	0.926	0.909
2	0.980	0.961	0.943	0.925	0.890	0.857	0.826
3	0.971	0.942	0.915	0.889	0.840	0.794	0.751
4	0.961	0.924	0.888	0.855	0.792	0.735	0.683
5	0.951	0.906	0.863	0.822	0.747	0.681	0.621
10	0.905	0.820	0.744	0.676	0.558	0.463	0.386
20	0.820	0.673	0.554	0.456	0.312	0.215	0.149

An expanded table is presented in Appendix B.

Let's demonstrate that the present value of \$1,464, based on our assumptions, is \$1,000 today.

$$P = S \times IF_{pv}(n = 4, i = 10\%) \text{ [Table 9--2]}$$
$$P = 1,464 \times 0.683 = \$1,000$$

Compound Sum— Annuity

Our calculations up to now have dealt with single amounts rather than annuity values, which may be defined as a series of consecutive payments or receipts of equal amount. The annuity values are generally assumed to occur at the end of each period. If we invest \$1,000 at the end of each year for four years and our funds grow at 10 percent, what is the compound sum of this annuity? We may find the compound sum for each payment and then total to find the compound sum of an annuity (Figure 6—2).

The compound sum for the annuity in Figure 6—2 is \$4,641. Although this is a four-period annuity, the first \$1,000 comes at the *end* of the first period and has but three periods to run, the second \$1,000 at the end of the second period, with two periods remaining—and so on down to the last \$1,000 at the end of the fourth period. The final payment (period 4) is not compounded at all.

Figure 6–2

Compounding process for annuity

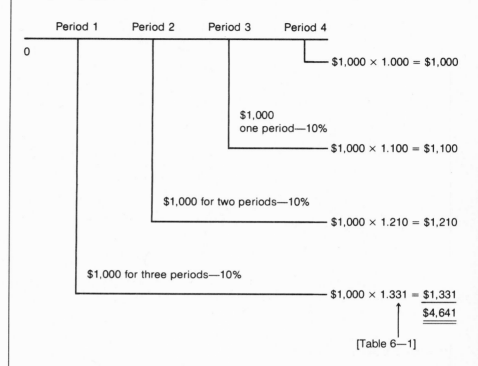

Because the process of compounding the individual values is quite tedious, special tables are also available for annuity computations. We shall refer to Table 6—3, the compound sum of an annuity of $1. Let us define R as the annuity value and use Formula 6—3 for the compound sum of an annuity.[1] Note that in the IF term the first subscript, $_s$, indicates compound sum and the second subscript, $_a$, indicates that we are dealing with an annuity.

$$S = R \times IF_{sa} \ (n = 4, i = 10\%) \tag{6—3}$$
$$S = \$1,000 \times 4.641 = \$4,641$$

---

[1] $S = R(1 + i)^{n-1} + R(1 + i)^{n-2} + \ldots R(1 + i)^1 + R(1 + i)^0$

$$= R\left[\frac{(1 + i)^n - 1}{i}\right] = R \times IF_{sa}$$

Table 6–3

Compound sum of an annuity of $1 ($IF_{sa}$)

Periods	1%	2%	3%	4%	6%	8%	10%
1	1.000	1.000	1.000	1.000	1.000	1.000	1.000
2	2.010	2.020	2.030	2.040	2.060	2.080	2.100
3	3.030	3.060	3.091	3.122	3.184	3.246	3.310
4	4.060	4.122	4.184	4.246	4.375	4.506	4.641
5	5.101	5.204	5.309	5.416	5.637	5.867	6.105
10	10.462	10.950	11.464	12.006	13.181	14.487	15.937
20	22.019	24.297	26.870	29.778	36.786	45.762	57.275

An expanded table is presented in Appendix C.

If a wealthy relative offered to set aside $2,500 a year for you for the next 20 years, how much would you have to your credit after 20 years if the funds grew at 8 percent?

$$S = R \times IF_{sa} \ (n = 20, i = 8\%)$$
$$S = \$2.500 \times 45.762 = \$114,405$$

A rather tidy sum considering that only $50,000 has been put on deposit.

Present Value— Annuity

To find the present value of an annuity, the process is reversed. In theory, each individual payment is discounted back to the present and then all of the discounted payments are added up, yielding the present value of the annuity. Table 6—4 on page 104 allows us to eliminate extensive calculations and to find our answer directly. In Formula 6—4 the term A refers to the present value of the annuity.[2] Once again, assume that R = $1,000, n = 4, and i = 10 percent—only now we want to know the present value of the annuity. Note that in the IF term the first subscript, $_{pv}$, represents present value and that the second subscript, $_a$, indicates an annuity.

$$A = R \times IF_{pva}(n = 4, i = 10\%) \qquad (6\text{—}4)$$
$$A = \$1,000 \times 3.170 = \$3,170$$

$$^2 A = R\left[\frac{1}{(1+i)}\right]^1 + R\left[\frac{1}{(1+i)}\right]^2 + \ldots R\left[\frac{1}{(1+i)}\right]^n = R\left[\frac{1 - \frac{1}{(1+i)^n}}{i}\right]$$

$$= R \times IF_{pva}$$

Table 6–4

Present value of an annuity of $1 ($IF_{pva}$)

Periods	1%	2%	3%	4%	6%	8%	10%
1	0.990	0.980	0.971	0.962	0.943	0.926	0.909
2	1.970	1.942	1.913	1.886	1.833	1.783	1.736
3	2.941	2.884	2.829	2.775	2.673	2.577	2.487
4	3.902	3.808	3.717	3.630	3.465	3.312	3.170
5	4.853	4.713	4.580	4.452	4.212	3.993	3.791
8	7.652	7.325	7.020	6.733	6.210	5.747	5.335
10	9.471	8.983	8.530	8.111	7.360	6.710	6.145
20	18.046	16.351	14.877	13.590	11.470	9.818	8.514

An expanded table is presented in Appendix D.

Determining the Annuity Value

In our prior discussion of annuities, we assumed that the unknown value was the compound sum or the present value—with specific information available on the annuity value (R), the interest rate, and the number of periods or years. In certain cases our emphasis may shift to solving for one of these other values (on the assumption that compound sum or present value is given). For now, we will concentrate on determining an unknown annuity value.

Annuity equaling a compound sum

Assuming that we wish to accumulate $4,641 after four years at a 10 percent interest rate, how much must be set aside at the end of each of the four periods? We take the previously developed statement for the compound sum of an annuity and solve for R.

$$S = R \times IF_{sa}$$

$$R = \frac{S}{IF_{sa}} \tag{6—5}$$

S is given as $4,641, and IF_{sa} (interest factor) may be determined from Table 6—3 (compound sum of an annuity). Whenever you are working with an annuity problem relating to compound sum, you employ Table 6—3, regardless of the variable that is unknown. For $n = 4$ and $i = 10$ percent, IF_{sa} is 4.641. Thus R equals $1,000.

$$R = \frac{S}{IF_{sa}} = \frac{\$4,641}{4.641} = \$1,000$$

The solution is the exact reverse of that previously presented under the discussion of compound sum of an annuity. As a second example, assume that the director of the Women's Tennis Association must set aside an equal amount for each of the next ten years in order to accumulate $100,000 in retirement funds and that the return on deposited funds is 6 percent. Solve for the annual contribution, R.

$$R = \frac{S}{IF_{sa}} \; (n = 10, i = 6\%)$$

$$R = \frac{\$100,000}{13.181} = \$7,587$$

Annuity equaling a present value

In this instance, we assume that you know the present value and that you wish to determine what size annuity can be equated to that amount. Suppose that your wealthy uncle presents you with $10,000 now to help you get through the next four years of college. If you are able to earn 6 percent on deposited funds, how much can you withdraw at the end of each year for four years? We need to know the value of an annuity equal to a given present value. We take the previously developed statement for the present value of an annuity and reverse it to solve for R.

$$A = R \times IF_{pva}$$

$$R = \frac{A}{IF_{pva}} \tag{6—6}$$

The appropriate table is Table 6—4 (present value of an annuity). We determine an answer of $2,886.

$$R = \frac{A}{IF_{pva}} \; (n = 4, i = 6\%)$$

$$R = \frac{\$10,000}{3.465} = \$2,886$$

The flow of funds would follow the pattern in Table 6—5. Annual interest is based on the beginning balance for each year.

Relationship of present value to annuity

Year	Beginning balance	Annual interest (6 percent)	Annual withdrawal	Ending balance
1	$10,000.00	$600.00	$2,886.00	$7,714.00
2	7,714.00	462.84	2,886.00	5,290.84
3	5,290.84	317.45	2,886.00	2,722.29
4	2,722.29	163.71	2,886.00	-0-

The same process can be used to indicate necessary repayments on a loan. Suppose that a homeowner signs a $40,000 mortgage to be repaid over 20 years at 8 percent interest. How much must he or she pay annually to eventually liquidate the loan? In other words, what annuity paid over 20 years is the equivalent of a $40,000 present value with an 8 percent interest rate?

$$R = \frac{A}{IF_{pva}} \, (n = 20, i = 8\%)$$

$$R = \frac{\$40,000}{9.818} = \$4,074$$

Part of the payments to the mortgage company will go toward the payment of interest, with the remainder applied to debt reduction, as indicated in Table 6—6.

Payoff table for loan (amortization table)

Period	Beginning balance	Annual payment	Annual interest (8 percent)	Repayment on principal	Ending balance
1	$40,000	$4,074	$3,200	$ 874	$39,126
2	39,126	4,074	3,130	944	38,182
3	38,182	4,074	3,055	1,019	37,163

If this same process is followed over 20 years, the balance will be reduced to zero. The student might note that the homeowner will pay over $41,000 of *interest* during the term of the loan, as indicated below.

Total payments ($4,074 for 20 years) $81,480
Repayment of principal . . . .   −40,000
Payments applied to interest $41,480

Determining the Yield on an Investment

In our discussion thus far, we have considered the following time value of money problems.

	Formula	Table	Appendix
Compound sum—single amount . . .	(9–1) $S = P \times IF_s$	9–1	A
Present value—single amount	(9–2) $P = S \times IF_{pv}$	9–2	B
Compound sum—annuity	(9–3) $S = R \times IF_{sa}$	9–3	C
Present value—annuity	(9–4) $A = R \times IF_{pva}$	9–4	D
Annuity equaling a compound sum . .	(9–5) $R = \dfrac{S}{IF_{sa}}$	9–3	C
Annuity equaling a present value . . .	(9–6) $R = \dfrac{A}{IF_{pva}}$	9–4	D

In each case, we knew three out of the four variables and solved for the fourth. We will follow the same procedure once again, but now the unknown variable will be i, the interest rate or yield on the investment.

Yield—present value of a single amount

An investment producing $1,464 after four years has a present value of $1,000. What is the interest rate or yield on the investment?

We take the basic formula for the present value of a single amount and rearrange the terms.

$$P = S \times IF_{pv}$$

$$IF_{pv} = \frac{P}{S} = \frac{\$1,000}{\$1,464} = 0.683 \qquad (6\text{—}7)$$

The determination of IF_{pv} does not give us the final answer—but, in effect, it scales down the problem so that we may ascertain the answer from Table 6—2, the present value of $1. A portion of Table 6—2 is presented below.

Periods	1%	2%	3%	4%	5%	6%	8%	10%
2	0.980	0.961	0.943	0.925	0.907	0.890	0.857	0.826
3	0.971	0.942	0.815	0.889	0.864	0.840	0.794	0.751
4	0.961	0.924	0.888	0.855	0.823	0.792	0.735	0.683

Read down the left-hand column of the table until you have located the number of periods in question (in this case $n = 4$), and read across the table for $n = 4$ until you have located the computed value of IF_{pv}. We see that for $n = 4$ and IF_{pv} equal to 0.683, the interest rate or yield is 10 percent. This is the rate that will equate $1,464 in four years to $1,000 today.

If an IF_{pv} value does not fall under a given interest rate, an approximation is possible. For example, with $n = 3$ and $IF_{pv} = 0.861$, 5 percent may be suggested as an approximate answer.

Interpolation may also be used to find a more precise answer. In the above example, we write out the two IF_{pv} values that the designated IF_{pv} (0.861) falls between and take the difference between the two.

IF_{pv} at 5% 0.864
IF_{pv} at 6% . . . . <u>0.840</u>
  0.024

We then find the difference between the IF_{pv} value at the lowest interest rate and the designated IF_{pv} value.

IF_{pv} at 5% 0.864
IF_{pv} designated . . . . . <u>0.861</u>
  0.003

We next express this value (0.003) as a fraction of the preceding value (0.024) and multiply by the difference between the two interest rates (6 percent minus 5 percent). The value is added to the lower interest rate (5 percent) to get a more exact answer of 5.125 percent rather than the estimated 5 percent.

$$5\% + \frac{0.003}{0.024}(1\%) =$$

$$5\% + 0.125\,(1\%) =$$

$$5\% + 0.125\% \quad = 5.125\%$$

Yield—present value of an annuity

We may also find the yield related to any other problem. Let's look at the present value of an annuity. Take the basic formula for the present value of an annuity, and rearrange the terms.

$$A = R \times IF_{pva}$$

$$IF_{pva} = \frac{A}{R} \tag{6—8}$$

The appropriate table is Table 6—4 (the present value of an annuity of $1). Assuming that a $10,000 investment will produce $1,490 a year for the next ten years, what is the yield on the investment?

$$IF_{pva} = \frac{A}{R} = \frac{\$10,000}{\$1,490} = 6.710$$

If the student will flip back to Table 6—4 and read across the columns for $n = 10$ periods, he will see that the yield is 8 percent.

The same type of approximated or interpolated yield that applied to a single amount can also be applied to an annuity when necessary.

Special Considerations in Time Value Analysis

We have assumed that interest was compounded or discounted on an annual basis. This assumption will now be relaxed. Contractual arrangements, such as an installment purchase agreement or a corporate bond contract, may call for semiannual, quarterly, or monthly compounding periods. The adjustment to the normal formula is quite simple. To determine n, multiply the number of years by the number of compounding periods during the year. The factor for i is then determined by dividing the quoted annual interest rate by the number of compounding periods.

Case 1. Find the compound sum of a $1,000 investment after five years at 8 percent annual interest, compounded semiannually.

$$n = 5 \times 2 = 10 \qquad i = 8 \text{ percent} \div 2 = 4 \text{ percent}$$

Since the problem calls for the compound sum of a single amount, the formula is $S = P \times IF_s$. Using Table 6—1 for $n = 10$ and $i = 4$ percent, the answer is $1,480.

$$S = P \times IF_s$$
$$S = \$1,000 \times 1.480 = \$1,480$$

Case 2. Find the present value of 20 quarterly payments of $2,000 each to be received over the next five years. The stated interest rate is 8 percent per annum. The problem calls for the present value of an annuity.

$$A = R \times IF_{pva}(n = 20, i = 2\%) \text{ [Table 6—4]}$$
$$A = \$2,000 \times 16.351 = \$32,702$$

Patterns of payment

Time value of money problems may evolve around a number of different payment or receipt patterns. Not every situation will involve a single amount or an annuity. For example, a contract may call for the payment of a different amount each year over a three-year period. To determine present value, each payment is discounted (Table 6—2) to the present and then summed.

(Assume 8% discount rate)
1. $1,000 \times 0.926 = \$\ 926$
2. $2,000 \times 0.857 = \ 1,714$
3. $3,000 \times 0.794 = \underline{\ 2,382}$
    $\$5,022$

A more involved problem might include a combination of single amounts and an annuity. If the annuity will be paid at some time in the future, it is referred to as a deferred annuity and it requires special treatment. Assume the same problem as above, but with an annuity of $1,000 that will be paid at the end of each year from the fourth through the eighth year. With a discount rate of 8 percent, what is the present value of the cash flows?

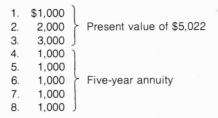

We know that the present value of the first three payments is $5,022, but what about the annuity? Let's diagram the five annuity payments.

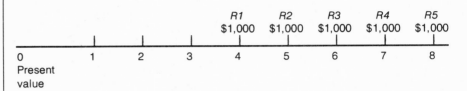

The information source is Table 6—4, the present value of an annuity of $1. For n = 5, i = 8 percent, the discount factor is 3.993— leaving a "present value" of the annuity of $3,993. However, tabular values only discount to the beginning of the first stated period of an annuity—in this case the beginning of the fourth year, as diagramed below.

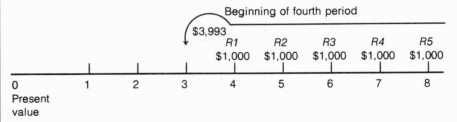

Each number represents the end of the period; that is, 4 represents the end of the fourth period.

The $3,993 must finally be discounted back to the present. Since this single amount falls at the beginning of the fourth period—in effect, the equivalent of the end of the third period—we discount back for three periods at the stated 8 percent interest rate. Using Table 6—2, we have:

$$P = S \times IF_{pv}(n = 3, i = 8\%)$$
$$P = \$3,993 \times 0.794 = \$3,170 \text{ (actual present value)}$$

The last step in the discounting process is shown below.

End of the third period—beginning of fourth period

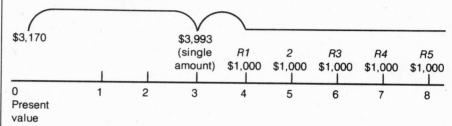

A second method for finding the present value of a deferred annuity is to:

1. Find the present value factor of an annuity for the total time period. In this case, where $n = 8, i = 8\%$, it is 5.747.
2. Find the present value factor of an annuity for the total time period (8) minus the deferred annuity period (5).

$$8 - 5 = 3$$
$$n = 3, i = 8\%$$

The value is 2.577.
3. Subtract the value in step 2 from the value in step 1, and multiply by R.

$$\begin{array}{r} 5.747 \\ -2.577 \\ \hline 3.170 \end{array}$$

$3.170 \times \$1,000 = \$3,170$ (present value of the annuity)

$3,170 is precisely the same answer for the present value of the annuity as that reached by the first method. The present value of the five-year annuity may now be added to the present value of the inflows over the first three years to arrive at the total value.

$5,022   First three period flows
+3,170   Five-year annuity
$8,192   Total present value

A special case—the bond problem

Determining the current price of a corporate bond represents a special case of present value calculations. Generally, the purchaser of a bond receives two future benefits: semiannual interest payments for the remaining life of the bond as well as a lump-sum payment at the end of the stated life of the bond. The price of the bond will reflect the present value of these two payments.

Assume that a bond has ten years to run and will provide the holder with 20 semiannual interest payments of $50 each and a $1,000 payment at the end of ten years. The annual discount rate is 8 percent, or 4 percent semiannually. What is the present value of these two forms of benefits to the bondholders?

Present value of interest payments   We are dealing with the present value of a $50 annuity for 20 periods. The discount rate is 4 percent. Using Table 6—4:

$$A = R \times IF_{pva}(n = 20, i = 4\%)$$
$$A = \$50 \times 13.590 = \$679.50$$

Present value of a lump-sum payment   This single amount will be received after 20 periods (ten years), and it should be discounted back to the present at 4 percent. Using Table 6—2:

$$P = S \times IF_{pv}(n = 20, i = 4\%)$$
$$P = \$1,000 \times 0.456 = \$456$$

The current price of the bond, reflecting both of these benefits, will be $1,135.50.

$$
\begin{array}{r}
\$\ \ 679.50 \\
456.00 \\
\hline
\$1,135.50 \\
\end{array}
$$

Some bond problems, appearing later in the text, may assume annual interest payments for ease of computation.

Special Review of the Chapter

In working a time value of money problem, the student should determine, first, whether the problem deals with compound sum or present value and, second, whether a single sum or an annuity is involved. The major calculations in Chapter 6 are summarized below.

1. *Compound sum of a single amount.*
   Formula: $S = P \times IF_s$
   Table: 6-1 or Appendix A.
   When to use: In determining the future value of a single amount.
   Sample problem statement: A invests $1,000 for four years at 10 percent interest. What is the value at the end of the fourth year?

2. *Present value of a single amount.*
   Formula: $P = S \times IF_{pv}$
   Table: 6—2 or Appendix B.
   When to use: In determining the present value of an amount to be received in the future.
   Sample problem statement: A will receive $1,000 after four years at a discount rate of 10 percent. How much is this worth today?

3. *Compound sum of an annuity.*
   Formula: $S = R \times IF_{sa}$
   Table: 6—3 or Appendix C.
   When to use: In determining the future value of a series of consecutive, equal payments (an annuity).
   Sample problem statement: A will receive $1,000 at the end of each period for four periods. What is the accumulated value (future worth) at the end of the fourth period if money grows at 10 percent?

4. *Present value of an annuity.*
   Formula: $A = R \times IF_{pva}$
   Table: 6—4 or Appendix D.
   When to use: In determining the present worth of an annuity.
   Sample problem statement: A will receive $1,000 at the end of each period for four years. At a discount rate of 10 percent, what is the current worth?

5. *Annuity equaling a compound sum.*

$$\text{Formula: } R = \frac{S}{IF_{sa}}$$

Table: 6—3 or Appendix C.

When to use: In determining the size of an annuity that will equal a future value.

Sample problem statement: A needs $1,000 after four periods. With an interest rate of 10 percent, how much must be set aside at the end of each period to accumulate this amount?

6. *Annuity equaling a present value.*

$$\text{Formula: } R = \frac{A}{IF_{pva}}$$

Table: 6—4 or Appendix D.

When to use: In determining the size of an annuity equal to a given present value.

Sample problem statements:

a. What four-year annuity is the equivalent of $1,000 today with an interet rate of 10 percent?

b. A deposits $1,000 today and wishes to withdraw funds equally over four years. How much can he withdraw at the end of each year if funds earn 10 percent?

c. A borrows $1,000 for four years at 10 percent interest. How much must be repaid at the end of each year?

7. *Determining the yield on an investment.*

Formulas	Tables	
a. $IF_{pv} = \dfrac{P}{S}$	6—2, Appendix B	Yield—present value of a single amount
b. $IF_{pva} = \dfrac{A}{R}$	6—4, Appendix D	Yield—present value of an annuity

When to use: In determining the interest rate (i) that will equate an investment with future benefits.

Sample problem statement: A invests $1,000 now, and the funds are expected to increase to $1,360 after four periods. What is the yield on the investment:

$$\text{Use } IF_{pv} = \frac{P}{S}.$$

8. *Less than annual compounding periods.*

Semiannual	Multiply $n \times 2$	Divide i by 2	$\left(\begin{array}{l}\text{then use}\\ \text{normal}\\ \text{formula}\end{array}\right)$
Quarterly	Multiply $n \times 4$	Divide i by 4	
Monthly	Multiply $n \times 12$	Divide i by 12	

When to use: If the compounding period is more (or perhaps less) frequent than once a year.

Sample problem statement: A invests $1,000 compounded semiannually at 8 percent per annum over four years. Determine the future sum.

9. *Patterns of payment—deferred annuity.*

Formulas	Tables
$A = R \times IF_{pva}$	6—4, Appendix D
$P = S \times IF_{pv}$	6—2, Appendix B

Method 1

When to use: If an annuity begins in the future.

Sample problem statement: A will receive $1,000 per period, starting at the end of the fourth period and running through the end of the eighth period. With a discount rate of 8 percent, determine the present value.

10. *Bond problem.*

Formulas	Tables
$A = R \times IF_{pva}$	6—4, Appendix D
$P = S \times IF_{pv}$	6—2, Appendix B

When to use: In determining the price of a bond based on the present value of interest payments and principal repayment.

Sample problem statement: A bond has ten years to maturity, and interest of $50 will be paid semiannually for the next ten years. Use a discount rate of 8 percent (4 percent semiannually) to determine the price of the bond.

7 | The Capital Budgeting Decision

The decision on capital outlays is among the most significant that a firm will have to make. A decision to build a new plant or expand into a foreign market may influence the performance of the firm over the next decade. The airline industry has shown a tendency to expand in excess of its needs, while other industries have insufficient capacity. The auto industry has often miscalculated its product mix and has had to shift down from one car size to another at enormous expense.

The capital budgeting decision involves the planning of expenditures for a project with a life of at least one year, and usually a considerably longer period. In the public utilities sector, a time horizon of 25 years is not unusual. The capital expenditure decision requires intensive planning to ensure that engineering and marketing information is available, product design is completed, necessary patents are acquired, and the capital markets are tapped for the necessary funds. Throughout this chapter, we will use techniques developed under the discussion of the time value of money to equate future flows to the present, while using the cost of capital as the basic discount rate.

A problem a manager faces is that, as the time horizon moves farther into the future, uncertainty becomes a greater hazard. The manager is uncertain about annual costs and inflows, product life, interest rates, economic conditions, and technological change. A good example of the vagueness of the marketplace can be observed in the hand calculator industry in the mid-1970s. A number of firms tooled up in the early 1970s in the hope of being the first to break through the $100 price range for pocket calculators, assuming that penetration of the $100 barrier would bring a larger market share and high profitability. However, technological advancement, price cutting, and the appearance of Texas Instruments in the consumer market drove prices down by 60–90 percent and made the $100 pocket calculator a museum piece. Rapid Data Systems, the first entry into the under-$100 market, went into bankruptcy. Of course, not all new developments are quite so perilous, and a number of techniques, which will be treated in the next chapter, have been devised to cope with the impact of uncertainty on decision making.

In this chapter, capital budgeting will be studied under the following major topical headings: administrative considerations, accounting flows versus cash flows, methods of ranking investment proposals, selection strategy, combining cash flow and selection strategy, and the replacement decision. In latter parts of the chapter, particular emphasis is placed on the 1981 Economic Recovery Tax Act and its impact on depreciation and capital budgeting decisions.

Administrative Considerations

A good capital budgeting program requires that a number of steps be taken in the decision-making process.

1. Search and discovery of investment opportunities.
2. Collection of data.
3. Evaluation and decision making.
4. Reevaluation and adjustment.

The search for new opportunities is the least emphasized, though perhaps the most important, of the four steps. Although it is outside the scope of this book to suggest procedures for developing an organization that is conducive to innovation and creative thinking,

Figure 7–1

Capital budgeting procedures

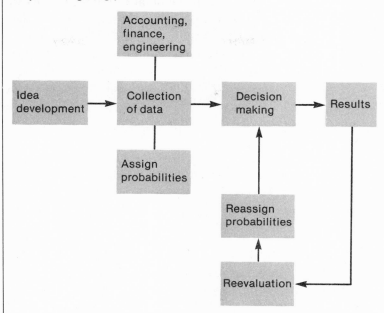

the marginal return of such an organization is likely to be high (and a high marginal return is the essence of capital budgeting).

The collection of data should go beyond engineering data and market surveys and attempt to capture the relative likelihood of the occurrence of various events. The probabilities of increases or slumps in product demand may be evaluated from statistical analysis, while other outcomes may be estimated subjectively.

After all data have been collected and evaluated, the final decision must be made. Generally, determinations involving relatively small amounts will be made at the department or division level, while major expenditures can only be approved by top management. A constant monitoring of the results of a given decision may indicate that a whole new set of probabilities must be developed, based on first-year experience, and the initial decision to choose product A over product B must be reevaluated and perhaps reversed. The preceding factors are delineated in Figure 7—1.

Accounting Flows versus Cash Flows

In most capital budgeting decisions the emphasis is on cash flow rather than reported income. Let us consider the logic of using cash flow in the capital budgeting process. Because depreciation does not represent an actual expenditure of funds in arriving at profit, it is added back to profit to determine the amount of cash flow generated. Assume that the Alston Corporation has $50,000 of new equipment to be depreciated straight-line over ten years ($5,000 per year). The firm has $20,000 in earnings before depreciation and taxes and is in a 50 percent tax bracket, as indicated in Table 7—1.

Table 7–1

Cash flow for Alston Corporation

Earnings before depreciation and taxes (cash inflow)	$20,000
Depreciation (noncash expense)	5,000
Earnings before taxes	15,000
Taxes (cash outflow)	7,500
Earnings after taxes	7,500
Depreciation	+5,000
Cash flow	$12,500

Alternative method of cash flow calculation

Cash inflow (EBDT)	$20,000
Cash outflow (taxes)	−7,500
Cash flow	$12,500

The firm shows $7,500 in earnings after taxes, but it adds back the noncash deduction of $5,000 in depreciation to arrive at a cash flow figure of $12,500. The logic of adding back depreciation becomes even greater if we consider the impact of *$20,000* in depreciation for the Alston Corp. (Table 7—2). Net earnings before and after taxes are zero, but the company has $20,000 cash in the bank.

Table 7–2

Revised cash flow for Alston Corporation

Earnings before depreciation and taxes	$20,000
Depreciation	20,000
Earnings before taxes	-0-
Taxes	-0-
Earnings after taxes	-0-
Depreciation	+20,000
Cash flow	$20,000

To the capital budgeting specialist, the use of cash flow figures is well accepted. However, top management does not always take a similar viewpoint. Assume you are the president of a firm listed on the New York Stock Exchange and must select between two alternatives. Proposal A will provide zero in aftertax earnings and $100,000 in cash flow, while Proposal B, calling for no depreciation, will provide $50,000 in aftertax earnings and cash flow. As president of a publicly traded firm, you have security analysts constantly penciling in their projections of your earnings for the next quarter and you fear your stock may drop dramatically if earnings are too low by even a small amount. Although Proposal A is superior, you may be more sensitive to aftertax earnings than to cash flow and you may therefore select Proposal B. Perhaps you are also overly concerned about the short-term impact of a decision rather than the long-term economic benefits that might accrue.

The student must be sensitive to the concessions to short-term pressures that are sometimes made by top executives. Nevertheless, in the material that follows, the emphasis is on the use of proper evaluation techniques to make the best economic choice and assure long-term wealth maximization.

Methods of Ranking Investment Proposals

Three widely used methods for evaluating capital expenditures will be considered, along with the shortcomings and advantages of each.

1. Payback method.
2. Internal rate of return.
3. Net present value.

The first method, while not conceptually sound, is often used. Approaches 2 and 3 are more acceptable, and one or the other should be applied to most situations.

Payback method

Under the payback method, we compute the time required to recoup the initial investment. Assume that we are called upon to select between Investment A and Investment B in Table 7—3.

Table 7–3

Investment alternatives ($10,000 investment)

	Cash inflows	
Year	Investment A	Investment B
1	$5,000	$2,000
2	5,000	2,000
3	2,000	2,000
4		6,000
5		6,000

The payback period for Investment A is 2 years, while Investment B requires 3⅔ years. In using the payback method to select Investment A, two important considerations are ignored. First of all, there is no consideration of inflows after the cutoff period. The $2,000 in year 3 for investment A is ignored, as is the $6,000 in year 5 for investment B. Even if the $6,000 were $60,000, it would have no impact on the decision.

Second, the method fails to consider the concept of the time value of money. If we had two $10,000 investments with the following inflow patterns, the payback method would rank them equally.

Year	Early returns	Late returns
1	$9,000	$1,000
2	1,000	9,000
3	1,000	1,000

Although both investments have a payback period of two years, the first alternative is clearly superior because the $9,000 comes in the first year rather than the second.

The payback method does have some features that help to explain its use by U.S. corporations. It is easy to understand, and it places a heavy emphasis on liquidity. An investment must recoup the initial investment quickly or it will not qualify (most corporations use a maximum time horizon of three to five years). A rapid payback may be particularly important to firms in industries characterized by rapid technological developments.

Nevertheless, the payback method, concentrating as it does on only the initial years of investment, fails to discern the optimum or most economic solution to a capital budgeting problem. The analyst is therefore required to consider the more theoretically correct methods.

Internal rate of return

The internal rate of return (IRR) calls for determining the yield on an investment, that is, calculating the interest rate that equates the cash outflows (cost) of an investment with the subsequent cash inflows. The simplest case would be an investment of $100 which provides $120 after one year, or a 20 percent internal rate of return. For more complicated situations, we use Appendix B (present value of a single amount) and Appendix D (present value of an annuity) and the techniques described in Chapter 6, "The Time Value of Money." For example, a $1,000 investment returning an annuity of $244 per year for five years provides an internal rate of return of 7 percent, as indicated by the following calculations.

1. First divide the investment (present value) by the annuity.

$$\frac{(Investment)}{(Annuity)} = \frac{\$1,000}{\$244} = 4.1 \ (IF_{pva})$$

2. Then proceed to Appendix D (present value of an annuity). The factor of 4.1 for five years indicates a yield of 7 percent.

Whenever an annuity is being evaluated, annuity interest factors (IF_{pva}) can be used to find the final IRR solution. If an uneven cash inflow is involved, we are not so lucky. We need to use a trial and error method. The first question is, Where do we start? What interest rate should we pick for our first trial? Assume that we are once again called upon to evaluate the two investment alternatives in Table 7—3, only this time using the internal rate of return to rank the two projects. Because neither proposal represents a precise annuity stream, we must use a trial and error approach to determine an answer. Let us begin with Investment A.

$10,000 investment

| Year | Cash inflows | |
	Investment A	Investment B
1	$5,000	$2,000
2	5,000	2,000
3	2,000	2,000
4		6,000
5		6,000

1. In order to find a beginning value to start our first trial, we average the inflows as if we were really getting an annuity.

$ 5,000
  5,000
  2,000
_____
$12,000 ÷ 3 = $4,000

2. Then divide the investment by the "assumed" annuity value in step 1.

$$\frac{(Investment)}{(Annuity)} = \frac{\$10,000}{\$4,000} = 2.5 \ (IF_{pva})$$

3. Proceed to Appendix D with a factor of 2.5 to arrive at a *first approximation* of the internal rate of return.

$$n \ (period) = 3$$
$$IF_{pva} \ factor = 2.5$$

The factor falls between 9 and 10 percent. This is only a first approximation—our actual answer will be closer to 10 percent or higher because our method of average cash flows theoretically moved receipts from the first two years into the last year. This averaging understates the actual internal rate of return. The same method would overstate the IRR for Investment B because it would move cash from the last two years into the first three years. Since we know that cash flows in the early years are worth more and increase our return, we can usually gauge whether our first approximation is overstated or understated.

4. We now enter into a trial and error process to arrive at an answer. Because these cash flows are uneven rather than an annuity, we need to use Appendix B. We will begin with 10 percent and then try 12 percent.

Year	10 percent		Year	12 percent
1	$5,000 × 0.909 = $ 4,545		1	$5,000 × 0.893 = $4,465
2	5,000 × 0.826 = 4,130		2	5,000 × 0.797 = 3,985
3	2,000 × 0.751 = 1,502		3	2,000 × 0.712 = 1,424
	$10,177			$9,874

At 10 percent, the present value of the inflows exceeds $10,000—we therefore use a higher discount rate. ———

At 12 percent, the present value of the inflows is less than $10,000—thus the discount rate is too high.

The answer must fall between 10 percent and 12 percent, indicating an approximate answer of 11 percent.

If we want to be more accurate, the results can be interpolated. Because the internal rate of return is achieved when the present value of the inflows (PV_I) equals the present value of the outflows (PV_O), we need to find a discount rate that equates the PV_I to the cost of $10,000 (PV_O). The total difference in present values between 10 percent and 12 percent is $303.

$10,177 . . . PV_I @ 10%	$10,177 . . . PV_I @ 10%
9,874 . . . PV_I @ 12%	10,000 . . . (cost)
$ 303	$ 177

The solution at 10 percent is $177 away from $10,000. Actually the solution is ($177/$303) percent of the way between 10 and 12 percent. Since there is a 2 percent difference between the two rates used to evaluate the cash inflows, we need to multiply the fraction by 2 percent and then add our answer to 10 percent for the final answer of:

$$10\% + (\$177/\$303)(2\%) = 11.17\% \text{ IRR}$$

In investment B, the same process will yield an answer of 18.23 percent (the student may wish to confirm this). The use of the internal rate of return calls for the prudent selection of Investment B in preference to Investment A, the exact opposite of the conclusion reached under the payback method.

	Investment A	Investment B	Selection
Payback method	2 years	3⅔ years	Investment A (quickest payback)
Internal rate of return	11.17%	18.23%	Investment B (highest yield)

The selection of any project under the internal rate-of-return method will also depend upon the yield exceeding some minimum cost standard, such as the cost of capital to the firm.

Net present value

The final method of investment selection is to determine the net present value of an investment. This is done by discounting back the inflows over the life of the investment to determine whether they equal or exceed the required investment. The basic discount rate is usually the cost of capital to the firm. Thus, inflows that arrive in later years must provide a return that at least equals the cost of financing those returns. If we once again evaluate Investments A and B—using an assumed cost of capital or a discount rate of 10 percent—we arrive at the following figures for net present value.

$10,000 investment, 10-percent discount rate

Year	Investment A		Year	Investment B	
1	5,000 × 0.909 =	$ 4,545	1	2,000 × 0.909 =	$ 1,818
2	5,000 × 0.826 =	4,130	2	2,000 × 0.826 =	1,652
3	2,000 × 0.751 =	1,502	3	2,000 × 0.751 =	1,502
		$10,177	4	6,000 × 0.683 =	4,098
			5	6,000 × 0.621 =	3,726
					$12,796
Present value of inflows . . .		$10,177	Present value of inflows . . .		$12,796
Present value of outflows . . .		10,000	Present value of outflows . . .		10,000
Net present value		$ 177	Net present value		$ 2,796

While both proposals appear to be acceptable, Investment B has a considerably higher net present value than Investment A.[2] Under most circumstances the net present value and internal rate of return methods give theoretically correct answers, and the subsequent dis-

-----

[2] A further possible refinement under the net present value method is to compute a profitability index.

$$\text{Profitability index} = \frac{\text{Present value of the inflows}}{\text{Present value of the outflows}}$$

For Investment A the profitability index is 1.0177 ($10,177/$10,000) and for Investment B it is 1.2796 ($12,796/$10,000). The profitability index can be helpful in comparing returns from different size investments by placing them on a common measuring standard. This, of course, was not necessary in this example.

cussion will be restricted to these two approaches. A summary of the various conclusions reached under the three methods follows:

	Investment A	Investment B	Selection
Payback method	2 years	3⅔ years	Investment A (quickest payout)
Internal rate of return . .	11.17%	18.23%	Investment B (highest yield)
Net present value	$177	$2,796	Investment B (highest net present value)

Selection Strategy

In both the internal rate of return and net present value methods, the profitability must equal or exceed the cost of capital for the project to be potentially acceptable. However, other distinctions are necessary—namely, whether the projects are *mutually exclusive* or not. If investments are mutually exclusive, the selection of one alternative will preclude the selection of any other alternative. Assume we are going to build a specialized assembly plant in the Midwest and four major cities are under consideration, only one of which will be picked. In this situation, we select the alternative with the highest acceptable yield or the highest net present value and disregard all others. Even if certain locations provide a marginal return in excess of the cost of capital, they will be rejected. In Table 7—4, the possible alternatives are presented.

Table 7–4

Mutually exclusive alternatives

	IRR	Net present value
Dayton	15%	$300
Columbus	12	200
St. Paul	11	100
Cost of capital	10	—
Gary	9	(100)

Among the mutually exclusive alternatives, only Dayton would be selected. Of course, if the alternatives were not mutually exclusive (much-needed multiple retail outlets), we would accept all of the alternatives that provided a return in excess of our cost of capital, and only Gary would be rejected.

Applying this logic to Investments A and B in the prior discussion and assuming a cost of capital of 10 percent, only Investment B would be accepted if the alternatives were mutually exclusive, while both would clearly qualify if they were not mutually exclusive.

	Investment A	Investment B	Accepted if mutually exclusive	Accepted if not mutually exclusive
Internal rate of return . .	11.17%	18.23%	B	A, B
Net present value	$177	$2,796	B	A, B

The discussion to this point has assumed that the internal rate of return and net present value methods will call for the same decision. Although this is generally true, there are exceptions. Two rules may be stated:

1. Both methods will accept or reject the same investments based on minimum return or cost of capital criteria. If an investment has a positive net present value, it will also have a yield in excess of the cost of capital.
2. In certain limited cases however, the two methods may give different answers in selecting the best investment from a range of acceptable alternatives.

Reinvestment assumption

It is only under this second state of events that a preference for one method over the other must be established. A prime characteristic of the internal rate of return is the assumption that all inflows can be reinvested at the yield from a given investment. For example, in the case of the aforementioned Investment A yielding 11.17 percent, the assumption is made that the dollar amounts coming in each year can, in fact, be reinvested at that rate. For Investment B, with an 18.23 percent internal rate of return, the new funds are

assumed to be reinvested at this high rate. The relationships are presented in Table 7—5.

The reinvestment assumption—internal rate of return ($10,000 investment)

Investment A (11.17% IRR)		Investment B (18.23% IRR)	
Year	Cash flow	Year	Cash flow
1	$5,000⟶	1	$2,000⟶
2	5,000⟶	2	2,000⟶
3	2,000→ reinvested at 11.17%	3	2,000⟶ reinvested at 18.23%
		4	6,000⟶
		5	6,000→

For investments with a very high IRR, it may be unrealistic to
assume that reinvestment can take place at an equally high rate.
The net present value method, depicted in Table 7—6, makes the
more conservative assumption that each inflow can be reinvested at
the cost of capital or discount rate.

The reinvestment assumption—net present value ($10,000 investment)

Investment A		Investment B	
Year	Cash flow	Year	Cash flow
1 . . .	$5,000⟶	1 . . .	$2,000⟶
2 . . .	5,000⟶	2 . . .	2,000⟶
3 . . .	2,000→ reinvested at 10% (cost of capital)	3 . . .	2,000⟶ reinvested at 10% (cost of capital)
		4 . . .	6,000⟶
		5 . . .	6,000→

The reinvestment assumption under the net present value method
allows for certain consistency. Inflows from each project are assumed to have the same (though conservative) investment opportunity. Although this may not be an accurate picture for all firms,
net present value is generally the preferred method.

Capital Rationing

At times, management may place an artificial constraint on the
amount of funds that can be invested in a given period. The executive planning committee may emerge from a lengthy capital budgeting session to announce that only $5 million may be spent on

new capital projects this year. Although $5 million may represent a large sum, it is still an artificially determined constraint and not the product of marginal analysis, in which the return for each proposal is related to the cost of capital for the firm and projects with positive net present values are accepted.

A firm may adopt a posture of capital rationing because it is fearful of growth or hesitant to use external sources of financing (perhaps debt). In a strictly economic sense, capital rationing hinders a firm from achieving maximum profitability. With capital rationing as indicated in Table 7—7, acceptable projects must be ranked and only those with the highest positive net present value are accepted.

Table 7–7

Capital rationing

	Project	Investment	Total investment	Net present value
Capital rationing solution	A	$2,000,000		$400,000
	B	2,000,000		380,000
	C	1,000,000	$5,000,000	150,000
	D	1,000,000		100,000
	E	800,000	6,800,000	40,000
Best solution	F	800,000		(30,000)

Under capital rationing, only Projects A through C, calling for $5 million in investment, will be accepted. Although Projects D and E have returns exceeding the cost of funds, as evidenced by a positive net present value, they will not be accepted with the capital rationing assumption.

Combining Cash Flow Analysis and Selection Strategy

Many of the points that we have covered will be reviewed in the context of a capital budgeting decision in which we determine the annual cash flows from an investment and compare them to the initial outlay. In order to be able to analyze a wide variety of cash flow patterns, we shall first consider the types of depreciation that are allowable under the 1981 Economic Recovery Tax Act.

Allowable depreciation is defined under the Accelerated Cost Recovery System (ACRS) standards that are part of the 1981 tax legislation. Essentially, the 1981 legislation decreased the life span over which an asset may be depreciated. Since depreciation provides tax shield benefits, the sooner the benefits can be taken, the higher the present value of the project.

According to the 1981 act, assets are to be depreciated in one of four categories as indicated in Table 7—8.

Table 7–8

Recovery periods for different types of assets

Automobiles, light-duty trucks, research and development equipment, and certain other short-lived assets	3 years
Most machinery and equipment, petroleum storage facilities, and some agricultural structures	5 years
Most public utility property, railroad tank cars, coal-fired burners, and residential mobile homes	10 years
Most real estate and longer-life public utility property that does not fall into the 10-year category	15 years

The 1981 legislation also specifies the amount of depreciation that can be taken each year. This information is presented in Table 7—9.

The depreciation schedules in Table 7—9 supersede the old methods of sum-of-the-years' digits, double declining balance, and various other techniques for tax purposes. Also salvage value is no longer set up for tax purposes. All assets are depreciated down to zero.

Actual decision

Assume a firm is evaluating a decision on whether to purchase five new trucks. The total cost is $35,000. In referring to Table 7—8, we see the trucks can be included in the three-year depreciation recovery period. We then go to Table 7—9 to determine the appropriate annual depreciation for the three-year period. The actual depreciation for the five trucks is presented in Table 7—10.

This is only one part of the analysis. We must also consider any additional profitability or cost saving benefits that will result from the purchase. In the present case, we shall assume the firm is paying transportation fees to others and can save a substantial amount by owning its own trucks. After all cash outflows (such as labor, maintenance, etc.) are considered, it is determined that the firm can

Table 7–9

Percentage depreciation that is allowable with the Accelerated Cost Recovery System (ACRS) under the 1981 Economic Recovery Tax Act

Recovery period	3-year	5-year	10-year	15-year public utility*
1	25	15	8	5
2	38	22	14	10
3	37	21	12	9
4		21	10	8
5		21	10	7
6			10	7
7			9	6
8			9	6
9			9	6
10			9	6
11				6
12				6
13				6
14				6
15				6

*Although most real estate is written off over 15 years, there is a separate real estate schedule that is more rapid than that shown for public utility property. The schedule is presented in Problem 15 at the end of the chapter.

Table 7–10

Annual dollar depreciation

Year	Depreciation base	Percentage depreciation (Table 11–9)	Depreciation
1	$35,000	25%	$ 8,750
2	35,000	38	13,300
3	35,000	37	12,950
			$35,000

save $15,500 per year for the next three years, and $8,000 per year for two more years. There is no problem with the fact that the productive life of the asset exceeds the depreciation recovery period under the Accelerated Cost Recovery System (ACRS). This is quite often the case. These cash savings are the equivalent of earnings before depreciation and taxes. They can be combined with depreciation write-off to determine cash flow. Using an analysis similar to that in the upper part of Table 7—1, we now compute annual cash flow for the trucks in Table 7—11.

Table 7–11

Cash flow related to truck purchase

	Year 1	Year 2	Year 3	Year 4	Year 5
Earnings before depreciation and taxes	$15,500	$15,500	$15,500	$8,000	$8,000
Depreciation	8,750	13,300	12,950	—	—
Earnings before taxes	6,750	2,200	2,550	8,000	8,000
Taxes (46%)	3,105	1,012	1,173	3,680	3,680
Earnings after taxes	3,645	1,188	1,377	4,320	4,320
+ Depreciation	8,750	13,300	12,950	—	—
Cash flow	$12,395	$14,488	$14,327	$4,320	$4,320

We must now discount the annual cash flows back to the present and compare them with the $35,000 initial investment. We will be using the net present value method with an assumed cost of capital of 12 percent. The analysis is presented in Table 8—12.

Table 7–12

Net present value analysis

Year	Cash flow (inflows)	Present value factor (12%)	Present value
1	$12,395	0.893	$11,069
2	14,488	0.797	11,547
3	14,327	0.712	10,201
4	4,320	0.636	2,748
5	4,320	0.567	2,449
			$38,014

Present value of inflows	$38,014
Present value of outflows (cost)	35,000
Net present value	$ 3,014

The investment shows a positive net present value and appears to be acceptable.

Investment tax credit

A potentially important variable in the capital budgeting decision is the investment tax credit (ITC). The credit represents a percentage of the purchase price that may be deducted directly from tax obligations. Under the Economic Recovery Tax Act of 1981, a three-year recovery life asset (autos, trucks etc.) is entitled to a 6 percent ITC. An asset with a life of five years or more is entitled to an ITC of 10 percent.

Normal recovery period	ITC
3 years	6%
5 years	10
10 years	10
15 years	10

Prior to the 1981 legislation, an asset had to be held for seven years or longer to get the full 10 percent investment tax credit.

In 1982 an amendment to the 1981 legislation was passed that requires half of the ITC to be subtracted from the initial depreciation base before allowing for depreciation. Let's see how the investment tax credit actually works.

In the prior example of the five trucks purchased for $35,000, which fell into the three-year recovery period, a 6 percent ITC would be available. Six percent of the $35,000 purchase price represents $2,100. This $2,100 savings in taxes effectively lowers the purchase price to $32,900.

$35,000	Purchase price
−2,100	ITC
$32,900	Net price

But now we must subtract half of the ITC from the purchase price to set up the depreciation base.

$35,000	Purchase price
1,050	Deduction of half the ITC (½ times $2,100)
$33,950	Depreciation base

With the new depreciation base, the annual depreciation is now amended to the values shown below.

Year	Depreciation base	Percentage depreciation (Table 7—9)	Depreciation
1	$33,950	25%	$ 8,488
2	33,950	38	12,901
3	33,950	37	12,561
			$33,950

The prior analysis in Table 7—11 is then changed to include the effect of the ITC on the depreciation values as shown in Table 7—13.

Table 7–13

Cash flow related to truck purchases including ITC

	Year 1	Year 2	Year 3	Year 4	Year 5
Earnings before depreciation and taxes	$15,500	$15,500	$15,500	$8,000	$8,000
Depreciation	8,488	12,901	12,561	—	—
Earnings before taxes	7,012	2,599	2,939	8,000	8,000
Taxes (46%)	3,226	1,196	1,352	3,680	3,680
Earnings after taxes	3,786	1,403	1,587	4,320	4,320
+ Depreciation	8,488	12,901	12,561	—	—
Cash flow	$12,274	$14,304	$14,148	$4,320	$4,320

We then take the present value of the amended numbers and compute the net present value as indicated in Table 7—14.

The net present value at the bottom of Table 7—14 is $1,717 higher than the net present value at the bottom of Table 7—12

Table 7–14

Net present value analysis including the ITC

Year	Cash flow (inflows)	Present value factor (12%)	Present value
1	$12,274	0.893	$10,961
2	14,304	0.797	11,400
3	14,148	0.712	10,073
4	4,320	0.636	2,748
5	4,320	0.567	2,449
			$37,631

Present value of inflows	$37,631
Present value of outflows (net price)	32,900
Net present value	$ 4,731

($4,731 vs. $3,014). In comparing the values at the bottom of both tables, we can observe that the ITC lowers the present values of the inflows slightly because of the decreased depreciation base, but more substantially decreases the outflow figure because of the tax credit. The net effect is a higher net present value.

The Replacement Decision

So far, our discussion of capital budgeting has centered on projects that are being considered as a net addition to the present plant and equipment. However, many capital budgeting decisions occur because of new technology, and these are considered replacement decisions. The financial manager often needs to determine whether a new machine with advanced technology can do the job better than the machine being used at present.

These replacement decisions include several additions to the basic capital budgeting problems presented thus far in Chapter 7. For example, we need to include the sale of the old machine in our analysis. This sale will produce a cash inflow that offsets the purchase price of the new machine. In addition, the sale of the old machine will usually have tax consequences. Some of the cash inflow from the sale can be a recovery of depreciation if the old machine is sold for less than book value. If it is sold for less than book value, this will be considered a capital loss and will provide a tax benefit.

The replacement decision can be analyzed by using a total analysis of both the old and new machine or by using an incremental analysis which emphasizes the changes in cash flows between the old and the new machine. We will emphasize the incremental approach.

Assume the Dalton Corporation purchased a computer two years ago for $100,000. The asset is being depreciated over five years under the Accelerated Cost Recovery System (ACRS). It could currently be sold in the market for $40,000. A new computer would cost $150,000 and would also be written off over five years. A 10 percent investment tax credit will be taken on the new computer. The new computer would provide cost savings and operating benefits of $38,000 per year for the next five years over the old computer. This is the equivalent of increased earnings before depreciation and taxes. The firm is in a 46 percent tax bracket and has a 10 percent cost of capital.

First of all, we need to determine the net cost of the new computer. The initial item for consideration is the price of the new computer less the investment tax credit, which gives us the net price of the new computer.

From this, we subtract the cash inflow associated with the sale of the old computer to determine at the net cost of the new computer as indicated in Table 7—15.

Table 7–15

Net cost of the new computer

Price of the new computer.	$150,000
− Investment tax credit (10%)	15,000
Net price of new computer	$135,000
− Cash inflow from sale of old computer	– – –
Net cost of new computer	– – –

The cash inflow from the sale of the old computer is based on the sale price as well as the related tax factors. In order to determine these tax factors, we first determine the book value of the old computer and compare this figure to its sales price to determine if there is a tax gain or loss. The book value of the old computer is shown in Table 7—16. You will recall, it initially cost $100,000, had a five-year depreciation life, and is now two years old.

Table 7–16

Book value of old computer

Year	Depreciation base	Percentage depreciation (Table 7—9)	Depreciation
1	$100,000	15%	$15,000
2	100,000	22	22,000
Total depreciation to date			$37,000

Purchase price	$100,000
Total depreciation to date	−37,000
Book value	$ 63,000

Since the book value of the old computer is $63,000, and the market value (previously given) is $40,000, there will be a $23,000 tax loss.

Book value	$63,000
Market value	−40,000
Tax loss on sale	$23,000

A tax loss on the sale of a depreciable asset used in business or trade may be written off against ordinary income (this is true even if it is a long-term capital loss). The Dalton Corp. is in a 46 percent tax bracket so the tax write-off is worth $10,580.

```
Tax loss on sale . . . . .    $23,000
Tax rate    . . . . . . . .        46%
Tax benefit  . . . . . . .   $10,580
```

We now add the tax benefit from the sale of the old computer to its sales value to arrive at the cash inflow from the sale of the old computer.

```
Sales price for old computer  . . . . . . . . .    $40,000
Tax benefit from sale . . . . . . . . . . . . .    +10,580
Cash inflow from sale of old computer  . . . . .   $50,580
```

The computation of the cash inflow figure now allows us to complete our analysis of the net cost of the new computer in Table 7—17. The value is $84,420.

Table 7–17

Net cost of the new computer

```
Price of the new computer. . . . . . . . . . .   $150,000
 − Investment tax credit (10%) . . . . . . . . .     15,000

Net price of new computer  . . . . . . . . . .     135,000
 − Cash inflow from sale of old computer . . . . .    50,580

Net cost of new computer . . . . . . . . . . .   $ 84,420
```

The question then becomes, are the incremental gains from the new computer compared to the old computer, large enough to justify the net cost of $84,420? We assume both will be operative over the next five years although the old computer will run out of depreciation in three more years.

We will base our cash inflow analysis on (a) the incremental gain in depreciation and the related tax shield benefits and (b) cost savings.

Incremental depreciation

The depreciation factors for the new and old computer are as follows:

	New computer	Old computer
Purchase price	$150,000	
Deduction of half of ITC	7,500	
Depreciation base	142,500	$100,000
	(over 5 years)	(3 years remaining out of original 5)

The annual depreciation on the new computer will be:

Year	Depreciation base	Percentage depreciation (Table 7—9)	Depreciation
1	$142,500	15%	$ 21,375
2	142,500	22	31,350
3	142,500	21	29,925
4	142,500	21	29,925
5	142,500	21	29,925
			$142,500

The annual depreciation on the old computer for the remaining three years would be:

Year*	Depreciation base	Percentage depreciation (Table 7—9)	Depreciation
1	$100,000	21%	$21,000
2	100,000	21	21,000
3	100,000	21	21,000

*The next three years represent the last three years for the old computer, which is already two years old.

In Table 7—18, we bring together the depreciation on the old and new computer to determine incremental depreciation and the related tax shield benefits. Since depreciation shields off other income from being taxed, it is worth the amount being depreciated times the tax rate. For example, in year one, $375 of incremental depreciation will stop an additional $375 from being taxed and with the firm in a 46 percent tax bracket, this represents a tax savings of $173. The same type of analysis applies to each subsequent year.

Table 7–18

Analysis of incremental depreciation benefits

(1) Year	(2) Depreciation on new computer	(3) Depreciation on old computer	(4) Incremental depreciation	(5) Tax rate	(6) Tax shield benefits
1	$21,375	$21,000	$ 375	0.46	$ 173
2	31,350	21,000	10,350	0.46	4,761
3	29,925	21,000	8,925	0.46	4,105
4	29,925	—	29,925	0.46	13,766
5	29,925	—	29,925	⌐46	13,766

Cost savings

The second type of benefit relates to cost savings from the new computer. As previously stated, these savings are assumed to be $38,000 per year for the next five years. The aftertax benefits are shown in Table 7—19.

Table 7–19

Analysis of incremental cost savings benefits

(1) Year	(2) Cost savings	(3) (1 − Tax rate)	(4) Aftertax savings
1	$38,000	0.54	$20,520
2	38,000	0.54	20,520
3	38,000	0.54	20,520
4	38,000	0.54	20,520
5	38,000	0.54	20.520

As indicated in Table 7—19, we take the cost savings in column (2) and multiply by one minus the tax rate. This indicates the value of the savings on an aftertax basis.

We now combine the incremental tax shield benefits from depreciation (Table 7—18) and the aftertax cost savings (Table 7—19) to arrive at total annual benefits in column (3) of Table 7—20. These benefits are discounted to the present at a 10 percent cost of capital. The present value of the inflows is $102,894 as indicated in column (5) of Table 7—20.

Table 7–20

Present value of total incremental benefits

Year	(1) Tax shield benefits from depreciation (from Table 7—18)	(2) Aftertax cost savings (from Table 7—19)	(3) Total annual benefits	(4) Present value factor (10%)	(5) Present value
1 . .	$ 173	$20,520	$20,693	0.909	$18,810
2 . .	4,761	20,520	25,281	0.826	20,882
3 . .	4,105	20,520	24,625	0.751	18,493
4 . .	13,766	20,520	34,286	0.683	23,417
5 . .	13,766	20,520	34,286	0.621	21,292

Present value of incremental benefits $102,894

We are now in a position to compare the present value of incremental benefits of $102,894 from Table 7—20 to the net cost of the new computer of $84,420 from Table 7—17.

Present value of incremental benefits $102,894
Net cost of new computer   84,420
Net present value . . . . $ 18,474

Clearly, there is a positive net present value, and the purchase of the new computer may be recommended on the basis of the financial analysis (there may be other subjective factors to consider as well). The student will be given the opportunity to examine other replacement decisions in selected end-of-chapter problems.

Summary

The capital budgeting decision involves the planning of expenditures for a project with a life of at least one year and usually a considerably longer time. Although top management is often anxious about the impact of decisions on short-term reported income, the planning of capital expenditures dictates a longer time horizon. Three primary methods are used to analyze capital investment proposals: the payback method, the internal rate of return, and the net present value. The first method is unsound, while the last two are acceptable, with net present value deserving our greatest attention.

Investment alternatives may be classified as either mutually exclusive or nonmutually exclusive. If they are mutually exclusive, the selection of one alternative will preclude the selection of all other alternatives, and projects with a positive net present value may be eliminated in favor of projects with an even higher net present value. The same is also true under capital rationing, a less than desirable method in which management arbitrarily determines the maximum amount that can be invested in any time period. The student must carefully define each situation and apply the appropriate capital budgeting technique. Tax considerations are also a major factor in capital budgeting decisions. In this chapter, the impact of the 1981 and 1982 tax legislation on depreciation and tax credits is integrated into the analysis.

8 | Valuation and the Cost of Capital

Throughout the previous chapter, a number of references were made to discounting future cash flows in solving for the present value of certain assets or financial contracts. Valuation depends on the ability to determine a discount rate or required rate of return to apply to the expected cash flow. How does an analyst determine the appropriate rate in a problem situation? Suppose that a young doctor is rendered incapable of practicing medicine due to an auto accident in the last year of his residency. The court determines that he could have made $100,000 a year for the next 30 years. What is the present value of these inflows? We must know the appropriate discount rate. If 10 percent is used, the value is $942,700; with 5 percent, the answer is $1,537,300—over half a million dollars is at stake.

In the corporate finance setting, the more likely circumstance is that an investment will be made today—promising a set of inflows in the future and we need to know the appropriate discount rate. The purpose of this chapter is to set down the methods and procedures for making such a determination.

First of all, the student should observe that if we invest money today to receive benefits in the future, we must be absolutely certain we are earning at least as much as it costs us to acquire the funds for investment—that, in essence, is the minimum acceptable return. If funds cost the firm 10 percent, then all projects must be tested to make sure they earn at least 10 percent. By using this as the discount rate, we can ascertain whether we have earned the financial cost of doing business.

The Conceptual Framework

How does the firm determine the cost of its funds or, more properly stated, the *cost of capital?* Suppose the plant superintendent wishes to borrow money at 6 percent to purchase a conveyor system, while a division manager suggests stock be sold at an effective cost of 12 percent to develop a new product. Not only would it be foolish indeed for each project to be judged against the specific means of financing used to implement it, but this would also make project selection decisions inconsistent. For example, picture financing a conveyor system having an 8 percent return with 6 percent debt and also evaluating a new product having an 11 percent return but financed with 12 percent common stock. If projects and financing are matched in this way, the project with the lowest return would be accepted and the project with the highest return would be rejected. In reality, if stock and debt are sold in equal proportions, the average cost of financing would be 9 percent (one half debt at 6 percent and one half stock at 12 percent). With a 9 percent average cost of financing, we would now reject the 8 percent conveyor system and accept the 11 percent new product. This would be a rational and consistent decision. Though an investment financed by low-cost debt might appear acceptable at first glance, the use of debt might increase the overall risk of the firm and eventually make all forms of financing more expensive. Each project must be measured against the overall cost of funds to the firm. We now consider cost of capital in a broader context.

An initial example

The determination of cost of capital can best be understood by examining the capital structure of a hypothetical firm, the Walker Corporation in Table 8—1. Note that the costs of the individual

Table 8–1

Cost of capital—Walker Corporation

		(1) Cost (aftertax)	(2) Percent of total capital	(3) Weighted cost column (1) × column (2)
Debt	K_d	6.37%	30%	1.91%
Preferred stock	K_p	10.42	10	1.04
New common stock	K_n	12.60	25	3.15
Retained earnings	K_r	9.60	35	3.36
Weighted cost of capital	K_a			9.46%

sources of financing are computed, then weights are assigned to each, and finally a weighted average cost is determined. (The costs under consideration are those related to new funds which can be used for future financing, rather than historical costs.)

Importance of Valuation

Valuation and the cost of capital are interdependent concepts. Valuation takes place in the securities markets where investors in bonds and stocks set prices based on their collective wisdom and expectations. A major part of this price setting is a function of the returns that investors require on the particular security. This market-determined rate of return depends on the market's perceived level of risk associated with the individual security and the cash flow expected to be received over the life of the investment. Also important is the idea that required rates of return are competitively determined among the many companies seeking financial capital. For example, IBM, due to its low financial risk, relatively high return, and strong market position in computers, is likely to raise debt capital at a significantly lower cost than International Harvester or Eastern Airlines, two financially troubled firms. This implies that investors are willing to accept less return for less risk.

The market-determined price then implies a required rate of return that is, in turn, the cost that the company must pay in order to raise financial capital. In this way the market allocates capital to companies based on risk, efficiency, and expected returns which are based, to a large degree, on past performance. The reward to the financial manager for efficient use of capital in the past is a lower cost of capital than that of competing companies that did not manage their financial resources as well. As we develop the methods for calculating the cost of capital for the various sources of capital, we will integrate valuation concepts with cost-of-capital concepts. Each element in the capital structure has an explicit or opportunity cost associated with it, referred to by the symbol K. Let us begin with debt.

Valuation and the cost of debt

In Chapter 6 we computed the present value of a bond having semiannual interest payments and a lump-sum principal payment at maturity. The bond price gets its value from the annuity stream of interest payments and the $1,000 principal payment at maturity. These cash flows are discounted by Y, the yield to maturity. Y is determined in the capital markets and represents the required rate of return for bonds of equal risk and maturity.

The price of a bond is equal to the present value of the interest payments discounted by the market yield to maturity added to the present value of the principal (also discounted by the market yield to maturity).

This relationship can be expressed mathematically as follows:

$$P_b = \sum_{t=1}^{n} \frac{I_t}{(1 + Y)^t} + \frac{P_n}{(1 + Y)^n} \qquad (8\text{—}1)$$

where

P_b = Price of the bond
I_t = Interest payments
P_n = Principal at maturity
t = Number corresponding to a period; running from 1 to n
n = Total number of periods
Y = Yield to maturity

Since the capital markets provide bond prices, and the interest payments and principal are known, we can always solve for Y to find the yield (refer to Chapter 6 to refresh your memory in determining the yield on an investment). More than likely, a company wishing to sell new debt would ask the company's investment banker to determine what yield would currently be competitive in the market in order to sell a new issue. The investment banker would analyze the market for bonds of equal risk and maturity, check the current tone of the market for new issues, and estimate an approximate yield to maturity. This yield would then become the interest rate payable on $1,000 principal amount. When the bond is sold, the market may adjust the actual yield up or down by bidding a price lower or higher than $1,000 par. Formula 8—1 can be used to solve the yield or an approximation formula developed in Chapter 11 can also be used. For our purposes for now, yield will simply be given.

The cost of debt is measured by the interest rate or yield paid to bondholders. The simplest case would be a $1,000 bond paying $118 annual interest—thus providing an 11.8 percent yield. Because the interest payment on debt is a tax-deductible expense, the aftertax cost to the firm is somewhat less than the actual dollars expended. For a firm in the 46 percent tax bracket, a dollar of interest will only represent a 54 cent burden to the firm. To compute the cost of the debt component in our capital structure, we multiply the yield times one minus the tax rate.[1]

$$K_d \text{ (cost of debt)} = Y \text{ (yield)} (1 - T) \qquad (8\text{—}2)$$

For the Walker Corporation, we will assume an 11.8 percent yield and a 46 percent tax rate.

$$K_d = 11.8\% \times (1 - 0.46) = 11.8\% \times 0.54 = 6.37\%$$

The 6.37 percent figure represents the cost of new debt and is not related to debt obligations already on our books.

Valuation and the cost of preferred stock

Preferred stock usually represents a perpetuity or, in other words, has no maturity date. It is valued in the stock market without any principal payment since it has no ending life. If preferred stock had a maturity date, the analysis would be similar to that of the bond

---

[1]The yield may also be thought of as representing the interest cost to the firm after consideration of all selling and distribution costs, though no explicit representation is given to these costs in relationship to debt. These costs are usually quite small, and they are often bypassed entirely in some types of loans. For those who wish to explicitly include this factor in Formula 8—1, we would have:

$$K_d = [\text{Yield} / (1 - \text{Distribution costs})] (1 - T)$$

example previously discussed. Preferred stock has a fixed dividend payment carrying a higher order of precedence than common stock dividends, but not the binding contractual obligation of interest on debt. Preferred stock, being a hybrid security, has neither the ownership privilege of common stock nor the legally enforceable provisions of debt. To value a perpetuity such as preferred stock, the calculation is simple—the fixed dividend is divided by the current required rate of return.

$$P = \frac{D_p}{K_p} \tag{8—3}$$

where

P = Price of preferred stock
D_p = Preferred stock dividend
K_p = Required rate of return

Formula 8—3 can be used to determine the price of existing preferred stock when the dividend and required rate of return are known. When we sell a new issue of preferred stock, however, the corporation's percentage cost is computed by dividing the dividend payment by the net price or proceeds received by the firm. Since a new issue of preferred has a selling cost (flotation cost), the proceeds to the firm are equal to the selling price minus the flotation cost.

$$K_p \text{ (cost of preferred stock)} = \frac{D_p}{P - F} \tag{8—4}$$

where

K_p = Cost of preferred stock
F = Flotation or selling cost

(See material above for definition for D_p and P.)

In the case of the Walker Corporation, a $10 dividend is being paid on a $100 preferred stock that carries $4 in selling costs, leaving a net price of $96. The effective cost is 10.42%.

$$K_p = \frac{\$10}{\$100 - \$4} = \frac{\$10}{\$96} = 10.42\%$$

Because a preferred stock dividend is not a tax-deductible expense, there is no downward tax adjustment.

Valuation Theory and the Cost of Common Stock

Determining the cost of common stock in the capital structure is a much more involved task. The out-of-pocket cost is the cash dividend, but is it prudent to assume that the percentage cost of common stock is simply the current year's dividend divided by the market price?

$$\frac{\text{Current dividend}}{\text{Market price}}$$

If such an approach were followed, the common stock costs for major U.S. corporations in January 1983 would be: Disney (1.9 percent), Motorola (1.9 percent), Texas Instruments (1.5 percent), and Schlumberger (2.1 percent). Ridiculous, you say! If new common stock were assumed to cost such low amounts, the firms would have no need to issue other securities and could profitably finance projects that earned only 2 or 3 percent. How, then, do we find the correct theoretical cost of common stock or equity to the firm?

Valuation approach

In determining the cost of common stock, the firm must be sensitive to the pricing and performance demands of current and future stockholders. An appropriate way to approach the problem is to develop a model for valuing common stock and to extract from this model a formula for the cost of common stock.

Dividend valuation model   The value of a share of stock may be interpreted by the shareholder as the *present value* of an expected stream of *future dividends*. Although in the short run, stockholders may be influenced by a change in earnings or other variables, the ultimate value of any holding rests with the distribution of earnings in the form of dividend payments. Though the stockholder may benefit from the retention and reinvestment of earnings by the corporation, at some point the earnings must be translated into cash flow for the stockholder. A stock valuation model based on future expected dividends can be stated as:

$$P_0 = \frac{D_1}{(1 + K_e)^1} + \frac{D_2}{(1 + K_e)^2} + \frac{D_3}{(1 + K_e)^3} + \cdots + \frac{D_\infty}{(1 + K_e)^\infty} \quad (8\text{—}5)$$

where

P_0 = Price of the stock today
D = Dividend for each year
K_e = Discount rate (required rate of return)

If a constant growth rate in dividends is assumed, Formula 8—5 can be expressed in Formula 8—6 as follows:

$$P_0 = \frac{D_0(1 + g)^1}{(1 + K_e)^1} + \frac{D_0(1 + g)^2}{(1 + K_e)^2} + \frac{D_0(1 + g)^3}{(1 + K_e)^3} + \cdots + \frac{D_0(1 + g)^\infty}{(1 + K_e)^\infty} \quad (8\text{—}6)$$

where

$D_0(1 + g)^1$ = Dividend in year 1, D_1
$D_0(1 + g)^2$ = Dividend in year 2, D_2, and so on
g = Constant growth rate in expected dividends

In other words, the current price of the stock is the present value of the future stream of dividends. If we can anticipate the growth or the pattern of future dividends and determine the discount rate, we can ascertain the price of the stock.

For example, assume the following information:

D_0 —latest 12-month dividend—assume $1.87
D_1 —first year, $2.00 (growth rate—7%)
D_2 —second year, $2.14 (growth rate—7%)
D_3 —third year, $2.29 (growth rate—7%)
etc., etc.
K_e = Discount rate—12% (required rate of return)

$$P_0 \text{ (unknown)} = \frac{\$2.00}{(1.12)^1} + \frac{\$2.14}{(1.12)^2} + \frac{\$2.29}{(1.12)^3} + \cdots$$

known
↓
Dividend
stream
Discount
rate
↓
known

In the present case, with $D_1 = \$2$ and growing at 7 percent per year, and a discount rate of 12 percent, the price of the stock would be \$40.[2] Likewise, we may know the price of the stock and the stream of dividend payments, but not know the discount rate (K_e).

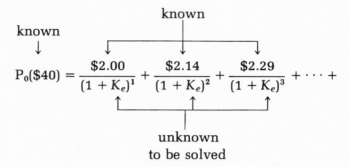

$$P_0(\$40) = \frac{\$2.00}{(1 + K_e)^1} + \frac{\$2.14}{(1 + K_e)^2} + \frac{\$2.29}{(1 + K_e)^3} + \cdots +$$

It is this latter circumstance, solving for the discount rate, or K_e, that is of particular interest to us. K_e tells us the rate of return that common stockholders will demand for receiving dividends in the future in exchange for the price of the stock today. It is the rate of return that common stockholders expect of the firm, and it represents the effective *cost of capital* assigned to common stock.

Formula for K_e Formulas have been developed that allow us to solve for K_e (the cost of common stock) with ease.

$$K_e = \frac{D_1}{P_0} + g \tag{8—7}$$

where

D_1 = First year's dividend
P_0 = Price of the stock
g = Constant dividend growth rate

Assume that the first year's dividend is expected to be \$2 per share, that the current price of the stock is \$40, and that earnings and dividends are expected to grow at 7 percent.

$$K_e = \frac{\$2}{\$40} + 7\% = 5\% + 7\% = 12\%$$

---

[2]If $K_e > g$, Formula 8—6 reduces to $P_0 = \dfrac{D_1}{K_e - g} = \dfrac{\$2}{0.12 - 0.07} = \dfrac{\$2}{0.05} = \$40.$

The stockholder demands a 12 percent return on his common stock investment. Of particular interest are the individual parts of our formula for K_e.

$$K_e = \frac{\text{First year's dividend}}{\text{Common stock price}}\left(\frac{D_1}{P_0}\right) + \text{Growth (g)}$$

The first item represents the current yield that the stockholder will receive, and the second represents anticipated growth in earnings, dividends, and, the expected increase in the yearly stock price if the price-earnings ratio stays the same from year to year or over the long run. Stockholders thus demand a current dividend yield as well as an anticipated growth rate in the future. Generally, the riskier the stock, the higher is the demanded rate of return.

Cost of common stock to the Walker Corporation

In Table 8—1, cost of capital for the Walker Corporation, which is reproduced below, we note that two common stock items are cited—the cost of new common stock (K_n) and the cost of retained earnings (K_r). Both are derived from K_e.

Reproduction of Table 8–1

		(1) Cost (aftertax)	(2) Percent of total capital	(3) Weighted cost, column (1) × column (2)
Debt	K_d	6.37%	30%	1.91%
Preferred stock	K_p	10.42	10	1.04
New common stock . .	K_n	12.60	25	3.15
Retained earnings . .	K_r	9.60	35	3.36
Weighted cost of capital	K_a			9.46%

Common stock financing becomes available either through the sale of new stock to the public or through the reinvestment of earnings belonging to current stockholders. In order to compute these two costs for the Walker Corporation, we take the basic formula for the cost of common stock (K_e) and make minor adjustments.

New common stock   If we are issuing new common stock, we must earn a slightly higher return than K_e, which represents the required rate of return of *present* stockholders—in order to cover the distribution costs of the new securities. Assume that the required return for present stockholders is 12 percent and that shares are quoted to the public at $40. A new distribution of securities must earn slightly more than 12 percent to compensate the corporation for not receiving the full $40 because of sales commissions, and other expenses. The formula for K_e is restated as K_n (the cost of new common stock) to reflect this requirement.

$$\text{Common stock} \qquad K_e = \frac{D_1}{P_0} + g$$

$$\downarrow$$

$$\text{New common stock} \qquad K_n = \frac{D_1}{P_0 - F} + g \qquad (8-9)$$

The only new term is F (flotation or selling costs).
 Assume:

$$D_1 = \$2$$
$$P_0 = \$40$$
$$F = \$4$$
$$g = 7\%$$

then

$$K_n = \frac{\$2}{\$40 - \$4} + 7\%$$
$$= \frac{\$2}{\$36} + 7\%$$
$$= 5.6\% + 7\% = 12.60\%$$

The cost of new common stock to the Walker Corporation is 12.60 percent.

Retained earnings Common stock financing may also take the form of reinvestment of retained earnings. The retained earnings, representing the past and present earnings of the firm, belong to the stockholders, and the corporation is faced with the decision to pay out the funds or reinvest them in new projects. Clearly, stockholders will only allow reinvestment in new projects that meet their return expectations. If the required rate is 12 percent, a firm with

$1 million in retained earnings should earn at least $120,000 or pay out the funds to stockholders.

We start with the basic premise that common stockholders have a required rate of return (K_e), and we make one minor adjustment. Because stockholders have to pay taxes on funds distributed to them before these funds can be reinvested, the firm may earn a little less than the required return and keep the stockholder in the same relative after tax position. The formula is:

$$\text{Cost of retained earnings } K_r = K_e(1 - tr) \qquad (8\text{—}10)$$

where

K_e = Cost of common stock
tr = Average stockholder marginal tax rate

For the Walker Corporation, K_e = 12 percent and we assume that tr = 20 percent. The cost of retained earnings is 9.60 percent.

$$K_r = K_e(1 - tr) = 12\% \, (1 - 0.2) = 9.60\%$$

Optimum Capital Structure— Weighting Costs

Having established the techniques for costing the various elements in the capital structure, we must now determine methods of assigning weights to these costs. We will attempt to weight capital components in accordance with our desire to achieve a minimum overall cost of capital.

		Cost (aftertax)	Weights
Debt	K_d	6.37%	30%
Preferred stock	K_p	10.42	10
New common stock	K_n	12.60	25
Retained earnings	K_r	9.60	35

From Table 8—1.   Weighted cost 9.46%

How does the firm decide on the appropriate weights for debt, preferred stock, and common stock financing? Though debt is the cheapest form of financing, it should be used only within reasonable limits. In the Walker Corporation example, debt carried a cost of 6.37 percent, while all other sources of financing cost at least 9.60 percent. Why not more debt? The answer is that the use of debt beyond a reasonable point may greatly increase the financial risk of the firm and thereby drive up the costs of all sources of financing. Assume you are going to start your own company and are considering three different capital structures. For ease of presentation, only debt and equity are being considered. The costs of the components in the capital structure change each time we vary the debt-equity mix (weights).

	Cost (aftertax)	Weights	Weighted cost
Financial Plan A			
Debt	5.0%	20%	1.00%
Equity	11.0	80	8.80
			9.80%
Financial Plan B			
Debt	5.5%	40%	2.20%
Equity	12.0	60	7.20
			9.40%
Financial Plan C			
Debt	7.5%	60%	4.50%
Equity	14.0	40	5.60
			10.10%

The firm is able to reduce the cost of capital with debt financing, but beyond Plan B the continued use of debt becomes unattractive and greatly increases the costs of the sources of financing. Traditional financial theory maintains that there is a U-shaped cost of capital curve relative to debt-equity mixes for the firm, as illustrated in Figure 8—1. In this example, the optimum capital structure occurs at a 40 percent debt-to-equity ratio.

Most firms are able to use 30–50 percent debt in their capital structure without exceeding norms acceptable to creditors and investors. Distinctions should be made, however, between firms that carry high or low business risks. As discussed in Chapter 2, "Operating and Financial Leverage", "a growth firm in a reasonably stable industry can afford to absorb more debt than its counterpart in cyclical industries." Examples of debt use by companies in various industries are presented in Table 8—2.

In determining the appropriate capital mix, the firm generally begins with its present capital structure and ascertains whether its current position is optimal. If not, subsequent financing should

Figure 8–1

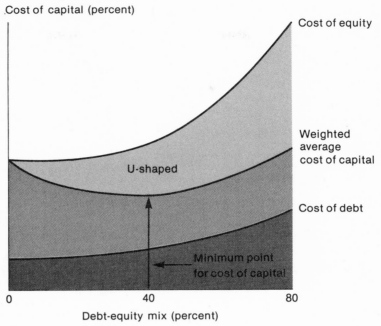

Cost of capital curve

Cost of capital (percent)

Cost of equity

Weighted average cost of capital

U-shaped

Cost of debt

Minimum point for cost of capital

0   40   80

Debt-equity mix (percent)

Table 8–2

Debt as a percentage of total assets (selected companies with industry designation)

	Percent
Getty Oil—crude petroleum and natural gas	23
American Home Products—drugs	24
Gannett—newspapers and publishing	32
General Motors—motor vehicles	36
Bethlehem Steel—blast furnaces and steelworks	40
Quaker State—petroleum refining	40
Kraft Inc.—dairy products	42
Southern Railway—railroads	44
Weyerhaeuser Co.—lumber and wood products	44
Phelps Dodge—copper	45
Revlon—perfumes and cosmetics	45
American Brands—cigarettes	49
Texas Gas Transmission—natural gas transmission	51
American Standard, Inc.—heating and plumbing equipment	52
Phillips-Van Heusen—apparel	54
Dow Chemical—chemicals	55
Gulf & Western Industries—conglomerates	60
Di Giorgio—wholesale groceries	64
Levitz Furniture—retail furniture sales	64

Source: Annual reports, Standard & Poor's Compustat tapes, and Moody's Industrial Manual.

carry the firm toward a mix that is deemed more desirable. Only the costs of new or incremental financing should be considered.

Capital Acquisition and Investment Decision Making

So far, the various costs of financial capital and the optimum capital structure have been discussed. Financial capital, as you may have figured out, consists of common stock, preferred stock, bonds, and retained earnings. These forms of financial capital appear on the corporate balance sheet under liabilities and equity. The money raised by selling these securities and retained earnings is invested in the real capital of the firm, the long-term productive assets of plant and equipment.

As discussed in Chapter 3, long-term funds are usually invested in long-term assets, with several asset-financing mixes possible over the business cycle. Obviously, a firm wants to provide all of the necessary financing at the lowest possible cost. This means selling common stock when prices are relatively high to minimize the cost of equity $K_e = (D_1/P_0) + g$. As the price increases, the dividend yield declines, and so does K_e. The financial manager also wants to sell debt at low interest rates. Since there is short-term and long-term debt, he needs to know how interest rates move over the business cycle and when to use short-term versus long-term debt, as discussed in Chapter 3.

A firm has to find a balance between debt and equity to achieve its minimum cost of capital. Although we discussed minimizing the overall cost of capital (K_a) at a single debt-to-equity ratio, in reality a firm operates within a relevant range of debt to equity before it becomes penalized with a higher overall cost because of increased risk.

Figure 8—2 shows a theoretical cost-of-capital curve at three different points in time. As we move from time period t to time period $t + 2$, falling interest rates and rising stock prices cause a downward shift in K_a. This graph illuminates two basic points: (1) the firm wants to keep its debt-to-equity ratio between x and y at all times; and (2) the firm would rather finance its long-term needs at $K_a t + 2$ than at $K_a t$. Corporations are allowed some leeway in the money and capital markets, and it is not uncommon for the debt-to-equity ratio to fluctuate between x and y over a business cycle. The firm that is at point y has lost the flexibility of increasing its debt-to-equity ratio without incurring the penalty of higher capital costs.

Figure 8–2

Cost of capital over time

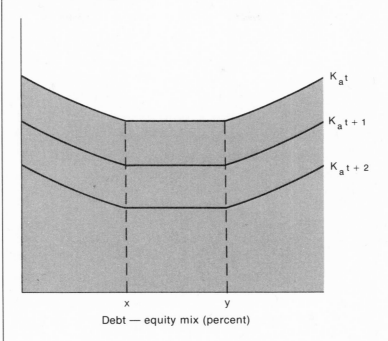

Cost of capital (K_a)

$K_a t$

$K_a t + 1$

$K_a t + 2$

x y

Debt — equity mix (percent)

Cost of capital in the capital budgeting decision

It is always the *current* cost of capital for each source of funds that is important when making a capital budgeting decision. Historical costs for past fundings may have very little to do with current costs against which present returns must be measured. When raising new financial capital, a company will tap the various sources of financing over a reasonable period of time. Regardless of the particular source of funds that the company is using for the purchase of an asset, the required rate of return or discount rate will be the weighted average cost of capital or the marginal cost of capital (the concept of marginal cost of capital is discussed in the following section). As long as the company earns its cost of capital, the common stock value of the firm will be maintained, since stockholder expectations are being met. For example, assume the Walker Corporation was considering making an investment in eight projects with the returns and costs shown in Table 8—3. These projects

Table 8–3

Investment projects available to the Walker Corporation

Projects	Expected returns	Cost ($ millions)
A	14.0%	$10
B	13.0	5
C	11.5	4
D	10.0	20
E	9.8	11
F	9.0	20
G	8.0	15
H	7.0	10
		$95 million

could be viewed graphically and merged with the weighted average cost of capital in order to make a capital budgeting decision, as indicated in Figure 8—3.

Figure 8–3

Cost of capital and investment projects for the Walker Corporation

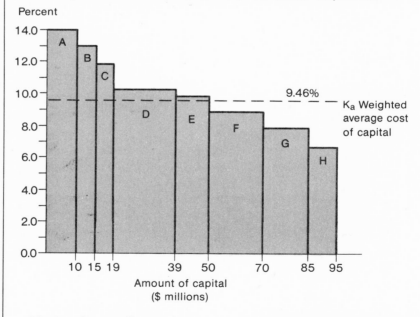

Notice that Walker is facing a total of $95 million in projects, but given the weighted average cost of capital of 9.46 percent it will choose only projects A through E, or $50 million in new assets. Selecting assets F, G, and H would probably reduce the market value of the common stock because these projects do not provide a return equal to the overall costs of raising funds. We cannot forget that the use of the weighted average cost of capital assumes that Walker Corporation is in its optimum capital structure range and the cost of each component stays constant over the range of financing.

Summary

The cost of capital for the firm is determined by computing the costs of various sources of financing and weighting them in proportion to their representation in the capital structure. The cost of each component in the capital structure is closely associated with the valuation of that source. For debt and preferred stock, the cost is directly related to the current yield, with debt adjusted downward to reflect the tax deductible nature of interest.

For common stock, the demanded return (K_e) is the current dividend yield on the security plus an anticipated rate of growth for the future. Minor adjustments are made to the formula to determine the cost of new common stock and retained earnings. A summary of the Walker Corporation's capital costs is presented in Table 8—4.

Table 8-4

Cost of components in capital structure

1. Cost of debt	$K_d = \text{Yield } (1 - T) = 6.37\%$	Yield —11.8% T —corporate tax rate—46%
2. Cost of preferred stock	$K_p = \dfrac{D_p}{P - F} = 10.42\%$	D_p —preferred dividend—$10 P —price of preferred stock—$100 F —flotation costs—$4
Cost of common stock	$K_e = \dfrac{D_1}{P_0} + g = 12\%$	D_1 —first year common dividend—$2 P_0 —price of common stock—$40 g —growth rate—7%
3. Cost of new common stock	$K_n = \dfrac{D_1}{P_0 - F} + g = 12.60\%$	Same as above, with F —flotation costs—$4
4. Cost of retained earnings	$K_r = K_e(1 - tr) = 9.60\%$	K_e —cost of common stock—12% tr —stockholder tax rate—20%

We weigh the elements in the capital structure in accordance with our desire to achieve a minimum overall cost. While debt is usually the "cheapest" form of financing, excessive debt use may increase the financial risk of the firm and drive up the costs of all sources of financing. The wise financial manager attempts to ascertain what debt component will result in the lowest overall cost of capital. Once this has been determined, the weighted average cost of capital is the discount rate we use in present-valuing future flows to ensure we are earning at least the cost of financing.

9 | Capital Markets

Security markets are generally separated into short-term and long-term markets. The short-term markets comprise securities with maturities of one year or less and are referred to as *money markets*. The securities most commonly traded in these markets, such as Treasury bills, commercial paper, and negotiable certificates of deposit, were previously discussed under working capital and cash management and will not be covered again.

The long-term markets are called *capital markets* and consist of securities having maturities greater than one year. The most common corporate securities in this category are bonds, common stock, preferred stock, and convertible securities. These securities are found on the firm's balance sheet under the designation long-term liabilities and equities. Taken together, these long-term securities comprise the firm's capital structure.

In the following chapters of this part we will be looking at how the capital markets are organized and integrated into the corporate and economic system of the United States. We will also study how corporate securities are sold by investment bankers and examine the rights, contractual obligations, and unique features of each type of security.

Competition for Funds in the Capital Markets

In order to put corporate securities into perspective, it is necessary to look at other securities that are available in the capital markets. The federal government, government agencies, state governments, and local municipalities all compete with one another for a limited supply of financial capital. The capital markets serve as a way of allocating the available capital to the most efficient user. Therefore, the ultimate investor must choose among many kinds of securities, both corporate and noncorporate. Before the investor parts with his money he desires to maximize his return for any given level of risk, and thus the expected return from the universe of securities acts as an allocating mechanism in the markets.

The size of the corporate and noncorporate capital markets is large. The total dollar amount of new security issues with maturities of more than one year rose from $40 billion in 1966 to $220 billion in 1982. This does not include the tremendous amount of funds raised in the short-term money markets. Over this time period, new issues of corporate securities averaged only 34 percent of the total, while government securities made up the other 66 percent. Figure 9—1 depicts the specific composition of long-term funds raised from 1966 through 1982.

Government securities

U.S. government securities In accordance with government fiscal policy, the U.S. Treasury manages the federal government's debt in order to balance the inflows and outflows. When deficits are incurred, the Treasury can sell short-term or long-term securities to finance the shortfall. In Figure 9—1, only long-term financing is depicted. Over the total 17 year period shown, long-term U.S. government financing averaged 31 percent of the total, second in size to corporate securities (at 34 percent). From 1966 through 1974, however, long-term financing by the Treasury averaged only 15.5 percent and was the lowest of the four groups represented in Figure 9—1. However in the 1975-78 era, the U.S. government ran up large

Figure 9–1

Composition of long-term funds raised by corporations and government

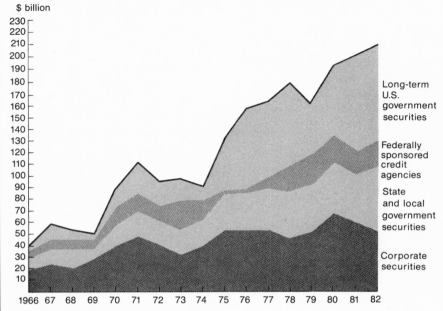

Source: *Federal Reserve Bulletin*, selected issues.

deficits. During 1979 and 1980, moderately successful attempts were made to reduce the deficit, but the recessions of the early 1980s dramatically pushed up treasury financing.

Although long-term U.S. government financing is second to corporate financing in terms of percent of long-term funds utilized over the entire 17 year time period, it has been running first in the 1980s.[1]

The average maturity on federal government debt has fallen since World War II so that the value is now close to three years. Almost one third of the debt is refunded each year and this short-term maturity creates instability in the market.

Federally sponsored credit agencies Most of the federally sponsored credit agencies are involved in making loans to the housing markets or rural farm areas. The largest of these agencies is the Federal National Mortgage Association, which is followed by the Federal Home Loan Banks. Both of these agencies are involved in

[1] When short-term U.S. government financing is added to long-term U.S. government financing, the amounts greatly increase.

the housing market. The third largest federally sponsored credit agency is the group of Farm Credit Banks. Over the period 1966–82, these agencies averaged 12 percent of the long-term financing shown in Figure 9—1. In most years their demand for funds has been at about 15-16 percent, but in 1973 it was 24.9 percent and two years later, in 1975, it had fallen to 1.5 percent.

State and local issues   These issues are sometimes referred to as municipal securities or tax exempts because the interest on them is exempt from federal income taxes and from state taxes in the state of issue. State and local municipalities were the largest sellers of long-term government securities over the 1966–74 time period. Beginning in 1975, huge federal deficit financing overshadowed state and local financing efforts, and these securities dropped to second place among government securities. They have averaged about 23 percent of the total funds raised between 1966 and 1982, and have maintained a fairly stable percentage over time.

Corporate securities

Corporate bonds   One misconception held by many investors is that corporate bond markets are dominated in size by the market for common stocks. This is far from the truth. In the new issues market, bonds averaged 75 percent of all long-term corporate securities sold from 1966 through 1982. In years of monetary tightness, when interest rates are relatively high and common stock prices are depressed, the ratio of bonds to total long-term corporate offerings has approached 87 percent.

Preferred stock   Preferred stock is the least used of all long-term securities. It has averaged only 6 percent of long-term corporate financing for the period from 1966 through 1982. The major reason for the small amount of financing by preferred stock is that the dividend is not deductible to the corporation before income taxes, as is bond interest. Given a choice between selling bonds and preferred stock, which are both fixed-income securities, most financial managers would choose bonds because they have a lower aftertax cost of capital.

Common stock   The sale of common stock during the time period 1966–82, averaged approximately 19 percent of total corporate long-term financing and a much smaller percentage of total long-term financing when government securities are included. This small percentage of new common stock financing illustrates that corporations have not been able to regularly rely on common stock for a major portion of their new long-term financing. Figure 9—2 provides comparative data on the use of various financing alternatives by U.S. corporations.[2]

Figure 9–2

Long-term corporate financing, 1966–1981

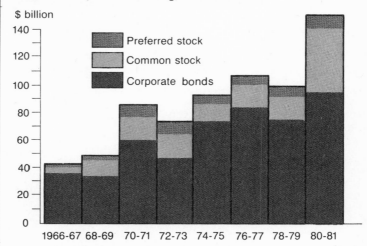

Source: *Federal Reserve Bulletin*, selected issues.

Equity financing in general   When financing by common stock and preferred stock is combined, one industry stands out. Stock financing of any significance from 1970 through the early 1980s has been done by utility companies. Utilities accounted for 33 percent of all stock financing in the early 1970s, and during the following decade the percentage rose to approximately 50 percent. It is not hard to understand this trend. Utilities in general have very high

---

[2]Because of the two-year nature of the data presentation, 1982-83 is not included in Figure 9—2.

debt-to-equity ratios relative to manufacturing firms and are therefore not very flexible in their financing strategies. They find it necessary to sell stock to keep their debt-to-equity ratios from getting too high and perhaps forcing a reduction in their credit rating.

Internal versus external sources of funds

In the 1950s and early 1960s, corporations relied primarily on internal sources of funds (cash flow from depreciation and net income) for their capital investment needs. A look at Figure 9—3 shows that the ratio of external to internal funds rose to extremely high levels in the 1970s and early 1980s. This emphasis on external markets makes the need for efficient, liquid markets more important today than ever before.

Figure 9–3

Percent of external to internal sources of funds (corporate nonfinancial sector, 1950–1982)

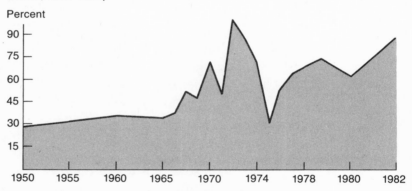

Source: *Federal Reserve Chart Book* and *Federal Reserve Bulletins*.

The rise in dependence on external funds is closely related to the inflationary spiral that started in the mid-60s. Corporations were forced to pay more and more for new equipment and capital expansion. At the same time, internally generated funds were not sufficient to replace worn-out equipment and expand capacity with new investments. Relatively low profitability during recessions of the early 1980s has also added to the dependence on externally generated funds.

A New York Stock Exchange report issued in February 1975 estimated that the external capital needs of corporations would be approximately $800 billion between 1975 and 1985. Of this amount it was estimated that $250 billion ($25 billion per year) would need to be generated from equity financing. If present savings and investment patterns continue over the 1980s, the supply of equity capital will continue to fall short of the needed amount by $7 billion per year.

The Supply of Capital Funds

Future corporate capital needs are expected to be very large partly because the high rate of inflation during the last decade has made it more expensive to replace worn-out equipment and also because the United States is a capital-intensive economy (it requires large amounts of real physical assets to generate sales dollars). What worries many corporate financial planners is the possible shortage of funds for corporate expansion in the coming years.

The flow of funds and financial intermediaries

In a three-sector economy consisting of business, government, and households, the major supplier of funds for investment is the household sector. Corporations and the federal government have traditionally been net demanders of funds. Figure 9—4 diagrams the flow of funds through our basic three-sector economy.

As households receive wages and transfer payments from the government and wages and dividends from corporations, they generally save some portion of their income. These savings are usually funneled to financial intermediaries that in turn make investments in the capital markets with the funds received from the household sector. This is known as indirect investment. The types of financial institutions that channel funds into the capital markets are specialized and diverse. Funds may flow into commercial banks, savings and loans, mutual savings banks, and credit unions. Households may also purchase mutual fund shares, invest in life insurance, or participate in some form of private pension plan or profit sharing. All these financial institutions act as intermediaries; they help make the flow of funds from one sector of the economy to another very efficient and competitive. Without intermediaries, the cost of funds

Figure 9–4   **Flow of funds through the economy**

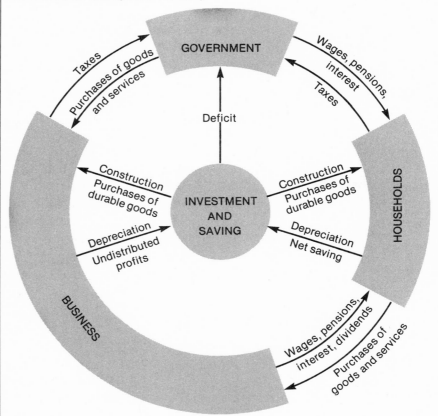

would be higher and the efficient allocation of funds to the best users at the lowest cost would not take place.

The role of the security markets

Security markets exist to aid the allocation of capital among households, corporations, and governmental units, with financial institutions acting as intermediaries. Just as financial institutions specialize in their services and investments, so are the capital markets divided into many functional subsets, with each specific market serving a certain type of security. For example, the common stocks of some of the largest corporations are traded on the New York Stock Exchange, whereas government securities are traded by government security dealers in the over-the-counter markets.

Once a security is sold for the first time as an original offering, the security trades in its appropriate market among all kinds of investors. This trading activity is known as secondary trading since funds flow among investors rather than to the corporation. The purpose of secondary trading is to provide liquidity to investors and to keep prices competitive among alternative security investments.

Security markets provide liquidity in two ways. First, they enable corporations to raise funds by selling new issues of securities rapidly and at fair, competitive prices. Second, they allow the investor who purchases securities to sell them with relative ease and speed and thereby to turn a paper asset into cash. Ask yourself the question, "Would I buy securities if there were no place to sell them?" You would probably think twice before committing funds to an illiquid investment. Without markets, corporations and governmental units would not be able to raise the large amounts of capital necessary for economic growth.

The Organization of the Security Markets

The competitive structure and organization of the security markets have changed considerably since the early 1970s. In this section we present the current organization of the markets, provide an update of significant events of the last few years, and make a small conjecture about the nature of the security markets well into the 1980s. The most common division of security markets is between organized exchanges and over-the-counter markets. Each will be examined separately.

The organized exchanges

Organized exchanges are either regional or national in scope. Each exchange has a central location where all buyers and sellers meet in an auction market to transact purchases and sales. Buyers and sellers are not actually present on the floor of the exchange but are represented by brokers who act as their agents. These brokers are registered members of the exchange. On the New York Stock Exchange, the number of members has been fixed at 1,366 since 1953, while the American Stock Exchange has a fixed limit of 650 members.

The New York Stock Exchange (NYSE) and the American Stock Exchange (AMEX) are national exchanges, and each is governed by an elected board of directors, of whom half are public directors and the other half industry representatives. Although the Midwest and Pacific Coast exchanges are the largest of the so-called regional exchanges, they trade primarily issues of large national companies. Some of the smaller exchanges, such as the Detroit, Boston, Cincinnati, and PBW, are more regional in the sense that most of the companies listed on them are headquartered or do their principal business in the region in which the exchange is located. These smaller exchanges account for a very small percentage of trading in listed securities.

Securities can only be listed and traded on an exchange with the approval of the board of governors. Until October 1976, the NYSE and AMEX were mutually exclusive and did not allow shares of stock to be listed on both exchanges. Under prodding from the Securities and Exchange Commission (SEC), both exchanges agreed to allow dual listing so that securities could be traded on both exchanges simultaneously. So far only a few companies have maintained dual listing on the NYSE and AMEX. Dual listing has long been common between the NYSE and the regional exchanges. Approximately 90 percent of the stocks traded on the Pacific and Midwest exchanges are also traded on the NYSE. This means that the shares of many large companies can be purchased on several different exchanges, which helps to make prices more competitive and less volatile.

Although dual trading has been a common practice for many years, brokers on the floor of an exchange did not have immediate price information from the other markets. In order to make prices of all competitive trades in the same stock available to all market participants at the same time, the Securities and Exchange Commission applied pressure for a consolidated tape which became reality on June 16, 1975. The consolidated tape presents the prices and volume of all shares traded on the regional exchanges and the NYSE. This information is visible to all brokers on the floor of each exchange and allows traders on each exchange to follow the activity and prices on all other exchanges as well as any over-the-counter trades in listed securities. Because of the consolidated tape, prices are more competitive and efficient.

The New York Stock Exchange

Size and liquidity The NYSE is the largest and most important of all the exchanges. In 1981 it accounted for 84.8 percent of the dollar volume of all listed stocks. Liquidity provided by the NYSE is also evident by the fact that share trading volume ranged from 40 million to 100 million shares per day. At the end of 1981, 1,565 companies were listed, having a total of 38.3 billion shares outstanding at a composite value of $1.144 trillion. We can see that the NYSE is certainly an important mechanism in the flow of funds among investors of all types.

Listing requirements Each organized exchange has some minimum requirement that a company must meet before the exchange will agree to trade its securities. Since most of the largest U.S. companies are traded on the NYSE, it is not surprising that its listing requirements are more stringent than those of the AMEX or the regionals. According to the NYSE *Fact Book*, the initial listing requirements are as follows:

1. Demonstrated earning power under competitive conditions of $2.5 million before federal income taxes for the most recent year and $2 million pretax for each of the two preceding years.
2. Net tangible assets of $16 million.
3. A total of $16 million in market value of publicly held common stock.
4. A total of 1 million common shares publicly held.
5. Two thousand holders of 100 shares or more.

Corporations choosing to be listed on exchanges have consciously decided that their stockholders and the company are best served by having a structured market available for the company's securities. In order to provide this opportunity, the company must pay annual listing fees to the exchange. In recent years, many small companies have decided to withdraw their securities from organized exchanges because the cost of continuous listing was not justified by the volume of shares traded. After withdrawal from an exchange, most companies have simply started trading on the over-the-counter market. However, IBM, a recent *annual* volume leader with over 111 million shares traded, certainly considers listing worthwhile, as do most other large, publicly-owned companies.

The over-the-counter markets

Corporations trading in the over-the-counter market (OTC) are referred to as unlisted. There is no central location for the OTC market but instead a network of dealers all over the country is linked together by computer display terminals, telephones, and teletypes. The difference between *dealers* in the OTC markets and *brokers* on exchanges is that dealers own the securities they trade while brokers act as agents for the buyers and sellers. Dealers are much like any wholesaler or retailer who stocks an inventory of goods. They price the goods to reflect their cost and to manage their inventory by seeking a balance between supply and demand.

Many dealers make markets in the same security and this creates very competitive prices. With the advent of a centralized computer to keep track of all trades and prices, dealers have up-to-the-minute price information on all competing dealers. Many people currently think that the structure of the OTC market is more competitive and cost efficient than organized exchanges.

At least 5,000 stocks are *actively* traded over-the counter, but the average price of the securities is low, so the dollar volume of the stocks traded is not as great as that of the organized exchanges. Stocks traded OTC range from large national companies, such as Coors, Tampax, and Economics Laboratory, to small regional or local companies centered in one city or state such as First Ohio Bancshares. In general, corporations trading OTC are closely held (controlled by a small group of stockholders) or have only a small regional reputation.

Although the AMEX and NYSE both trade corporate bonds and a small number of government securities, the bulk of all bond trading is done over-the-counter. Trading in government bonds, notes, and Treasury bills through government security dealers makes the OTC the largest market of all for security transactions in total dollars (though the NYSE is clearly the largest for just stocks).

The third market Stocks that are listed on organized exchanges but trade in the over-the-counter market as well are said to be trading in the third market. The third market got its start in the early 1970s because institutional investors could buy and sell large blocks of stock (10,000 shares or more) over-the-counter for a fraction of the cost of the prescribed commission on the NYSE. Since the mid-70s the organized exchanges have become more competitive. Under a mandate from the Securities and Exchange Commission, brokers on the exchanges started negotiating commissions with customers when the money involved was over $500,000. In 1972 this limit was reduced to $300,000. Finally, on May 1, 1975 (called May Day in the broker industry), commissions on all public transactions became competitive, and for the first time in 183 years fixed minimum commission rates were abolished. These competitive commissions on the organized exchanges have diminished the importance of the third market.

Security markets in the future

Security markets, and especially the stock exchanges as we know them today, may survive, but not in their present form. The U.S. Congress has mandated a national securities market which is currently being studied by the Securities and Exchange Commission advisory panel and the National Market Association, an industry group representing seven major stock markets. The latest proposal of the National Market Association would be a communications system linking the New York, American, Boston, PBW, Midwest, and Pacific Coast stock exchanges and over-the-counter trading in listed stocks. The communications system would be supervised by the National Association of Securities Dealers.

Currently these markets are tied together with a composite tape, but the proposed communications system would allow buyers and sellers of securities to make the best competitive trades at all times. The problem is that the end result would not be a national securities market but several different markets competing for business.

We think it safe to say that over the next decade securities markets will become more competitive and will be structured more like the current over-the-counter markets. Computers will do more of the paperwork and record keeping, and will eventually be used to process special orders. The transfer and registration of more stock certificates will be accomplished by a central computerized clearinghouse, and the market will be able to handle more volume in an effective fashion.

Market Efficiency

We have mentioned competitive and efficient markets all through this chapter, but so far we have not given any criteria to judge whether the U.S. securities markets are indeed competitive and efficient markets.

Criteria of efficiency

There are several concepts of market efficiency and there are many degrees of efficiency, depending on which market we are talking about. Markets in general are efficient when: (1) prices adjust rapidly to new information; (2) there is a continuous market in which each successive trade is made at a price close to the previous price (the faster the price responds to new information and the smaller the differences in price changes, the more efficient the market); and (3) the market can absorb large dollar amounts of securities without destabilizing the price.

A key variable affecting efficiency is the certainty of the income stream. The more certain the expected income, the less volatile price movements will be. Fixed income securities, with known maturities, have reasonably efficient markets. The most efficient market is that for U.S. government securities, with the short-term Treasury bill market being exemplary. Corporate bond markets are somewhat efficient, but less so than government bond markets. A question that is still widely debated and researched by academics is whether markets for common stock are truly efficient.

The efficient market hypothesis

If stock markets are efficient, it is very difficult for investors to select portfolios of common stocks that can outperform the stock market in general. The efficient market hypothesis is stated in three forms—the weak, semistrong, and strong.

The weak form simply states that past price information is unrelated to future prices, and that trends cannot be predicted and taken advantage of by investors. The semistrong form states that prices reflect all *public* information. Most of the research in this area focuses on changes in public information and on the measurement of how rapidly prices converge to a new equilibrium after new information has been released. The strong form states that all information, both *private* and *public,* is immediately reflected in stock prices. If markets are efficient, insiders and large institutions should not be able to make profits in excess of the market in general. Research on the portfolio performance of mutual funds has shown that this group of investors does no better than the market.

Our objective in bringing up this subject is to make you aware that much current research is focused on the measurement of market efficiency. As communications systems advance, information gets disseminated faster and more accurately. Furthermore, securities laws are forcing fuller disclosure of inside corporate data. It would appear that our security markets are efficient, but not perfect, in digesting information and adjusting stock prices.

Regulation of the Security Markets

Organized securities markets are regulated by the Securities and Exchange Commission (SEC) and by the self-regulation of the exchanges. The OTC market is controlled by the National Association of Securities Dealers. Three major laws govern the sale and subsequent trading of securities. The Securities Act of 1933 pertains to new issues of securities, while the Securities Exchange Act of 1934 deals with trading in the securities markets. The latest legislation is the Securities Acts amendments of 1975, whose main emphasis is on a national securities market. The primary purpose of these laws is to protect unwary investors from fraud and manipulation and to make the markets more competitive and efficient by forcing corporations to make public relevant investment information.

Securities Act of 1933

The Securities Act of 1933 was enacted after congressional investigations of the abuses present in the securities markets during the 1929 crash. Its primary purpose was to provide full disclosure of all pertinent investment information whenever a corporation sold a new issue of securities. For this reason it is sometimes referred to as the truth-in-securities act. The Securities Act has several important features which follow:

1. All offerings except government bonds and bank stocks that are to be sold in more than one state must be registered with the SEC.

2. The registration statement must be filed 20 days in advance of the date of sale and must include detailed corporate information. If the SEC finds the information misleading, incomplete, or inaccurate, it will delay the offering until the registration statement is corrected. The SEC in no way certifies that the security is fairly priced, but only that the information seems to be accurate.

3. All new issues of securities must be accompanied by a prospectus containing the same information appearing in the registration statement. Usually included in the prospectus are a list of directors and officers; their salaries, stock options, and shareholdings; financial reports certified by a CPA; a list of the underwriters; the purpose and use of the funds to be provided from the sales of securities; and any other reasonable information that investors may need before they can wisely invest their money. A preliminary prospectus may be distributed to potential buyers before the offering date, but it will not contain the offering price or the underwriting fees. It is called a "red herring" because stamped on the front in red letters are the words *preliminary prospectus.*

4. For the first time, officers of the company and other experts preparing the prospectus or the registration statement could be sued for penalties and recovery of realized losses if any information presented was fraudulent, factually wrong, or omitted.

Securities Exchange Act of 1934

This act created the Securities and Exchange Commission to enforce the securities laws. The SEC was empowered to regulate the securities markets and those companies listed on the exchanges. Specifically, the major points of the Securities Exchange Act of 1934 are as follows:

1. Guidelines for inside trading were established. Insiders must hold securities for at least six months before they can sell them. This is to prevent them from taking quick advantage of information which could result in a short-term profit. All short-term profits are payable to the corporation. Insiders were at first generally thought to be officers, directors, employees, or relatives. In the late 1960s, however, the SEC widened its interpretation to include anyone having information that was not public knowl-

edge. This could include security analysts, loan officers, large institutional holders, and many others who had business dealings with the firm.

2. The Federal Reserve's Board of Governors became responsible for setting margin requirements to determine how much credit would be available to purchasers of securities.

3. Manipulation of securities by conspiracies among investors was prohibited.

4. The SEC was given control over the proxy procedures of corporations (a proxy is an absent stockholder's vote).

5. In its regulation of companies traded on the markets, the SEC required that certain reports be filed periodically. Corporations must file quarterly financial statements and annual 10K reports with the SEC and send annual reports to stockholders. The 10K report has more financial data than the annual report and can be very useful to an investor or a loan officer. Most companies will now send 10K reports to stockholders on request.

6. The act required all security exchanges to register with the SEC. In this capacity, the SEC supervises and regulates many pertinent organizational aspects of exchanges, such as the mechanics of listing and trading.

The Securities Acts amendments of 1975

The major focus of the Securities Acts amendments of 1975 was to direct the SEC to supervise the development of a national securities market. No exact structure was put forth, but the law did assume that any national market would make extensive use of computers and electronic communication devices. In addition, the law prohibited fixed commissions on public transactions and also prohibited banks, insurance companies, and other financial institutions from buying stock exchange memberships to save commission costs for their own institutional transactions. This act is a worthwhile addition to the securities laws since it fosters greater competition and more efficient prices.

Summary

In this chapter we presented the concept of a capital market in which corporations compete for funds not only among themselves but with governmental units of all kinds. Corporations only account for about 34 percent of all funds raised in the capital market, and most of that is obtained through the sale of corporate debt. We also depicted a three-sector economy consisting of households, corporations, and governmental units and showed how funds flow through the capital markets from suppliers of funds to the ultimate users. This process is highly dependent upon the efficiency of the financial institutions that act as intermediaries in channeling the funds to the most productive users.

Security markets are divided into organized exchanges and over-the-counter markets. Brokers act as agents for stock exchange transactions, and dealers make markets over-the-counter at their own risk as owners of the securities they trade. The New York Stock Exchange is the largest of the organized exchanges. We explored some of its major characteristics, such as its relative size, the liquidity it provides corporations and investors, and its requirements for listing securities. Although the OTC market for stock is not as large as that of the organized exchanges, a majority of corporate bond trades and almost all trades in municipal and federal government securities are transacted over-the-counter.

Throughout this chapter we have tried to present the concept of efficient markets doing an important job in allocating financial capital. We find that the existing markets provide liquidity for both the corporation and the investor and that they are efficient in adjusting to new information. Because of the laws governing the markets, much information is available for investors, and this in itself creates more competitive prices. Moreover, there are very few cases of fraud and manipulation. In the future we expect even more efficient markets with a national market system patterned after that of the over-the-counter market.

10 | Investment Banking: Public and Private Placement

In Chapter 10, we will examine the role of the investment banker, the advantages and disadvantages of selling securities to the public, and the private placement of securities with insurance companies, pension funds, and other lenders. Illustrative examples are presented of H. Ross Perot and his "billion dollar" Electronic Data Systems Corporation and Nardis of Dallas—a company that "went private."

The Role of Investment Banking

The investment banker is the great link between the corporation in need of funds and the investor. As a middleman, the investment banker is responsible for designing and packaging a security offering and selling the securities to the public. The investment banking fraternity has long been thought of as an elite group—with appropriate memberships in the country club, the yacht club, and other such venerable institutions. The roller coaster performances of the security markets in the late 1960s and 70s have altered the picture somewhat. Competition has become the new way of doing business in which the fittest survive and prosper, while others drop out of the game.

Enumeration of Functions

As a middleman in the distribution of securities, the investment banker plays a number of key roles.

Underwriter   In most cases, the investment banker is a risk taker. He will contract to buy securities from the corporation and resell them to other security dealers and the public. By giving a "firm commitment" to purchase the securities from the corporation, he is said to *underwrite* any risks that might be associated with a new issue. While the risk may be fairly low in handling a bond offering for Exxon or General Electric in a stable market, such may not be the case in selling the shares of a less-known firm in a very volatile market environent.

Though most large, well-established investment bankers would not consider managing a public offering without assuming the risk of distribution, smaller investment houses may handle distributions for relatively unknown corporations on a "best-efforts" or commission basis. Only a very small percentage of new security sales are transacted in this fashion.

Market maker   During distribution and in later time periods, the investment banker may make a market in a given security—that is, engage in the buying and selling of the security to ensure a liquid market. He may also provide research on the firm to encourage active investor interest.

Adviser   The investment banker may advise clients on a continuing basis about the types of securities to be sold, the number of shares or units for distribution, and the timing of the sale. A company considering a stock issuance to the public may be persuaded, in counsel with an investment banker, to borrow the funds from an insurance company or, if stock is to be sold, to wait for two more quarters of earnings before going to the market. The investment banker also provides important advisory services in the area of mergers and acquisitions.

Agency functions   The investment banker may act as an agent for a corporation that wishes to place its securities privately with an insurance company, a pension fund, or a wealthy individual. In this instance, the investment banker will shop around among potential investors and negotiate the best possible deal for the corporation. He may also serve as an agent in merger and acquisition transactions. Because of the many critical roles that the investment banker plays, he may be requested to sit on the board of directors of the client company.

The Distribution Process

The actual distribution process requires the active participation of a number of parties. The principal or managing investment banker will call upon other investment banking houses to share the burden of risk and to aid in the distribution. To this end, they will form an underwriting syndicate comprised of as few as 2 or as many as 200 investment banking houses. In Figure 10—1, we see a typical case in which a hypothetical firm, the Maxwell Corporation, wishes to issue 250,000 additional shares of stock with Merrill Lynch as the managing underwriter and an underwriting syndicate of 15 firms.

The underwriting syndicate will purchase shares from the Max-

Figure 10–1

Distribution process in investment banking

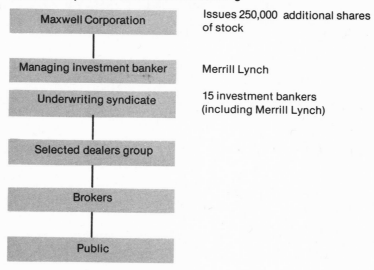

Maxwell Corporation	Issues 250,000 additional shares of stock
Managing investment banker	Merrill Lynch
Underwriting syndicate	15 investment bankers (including Merrill Lynch)
Selected dealers group	
Brokers	
Public	

well Corporation and distribute them through the channels of distribution. Syndicate members will act as wholesalers in distributing the shares to brokers and dealers who will eventually sell the shares to the public. Large investment banking houses may be vertically integrated, acting as underwriter-dealer-broker and capturing all fees and commissions.

The spread

The spread represents the total compensation for those who participate in the distribution process. If the public or retail price is $21.50 and the managing investment banker pays a price of $20.00 to the issuing company, we say there is a total spread of $1.50. The $1.50 may be divided up among the participants, as indicated in Figure 10—2.

Figure 10–2

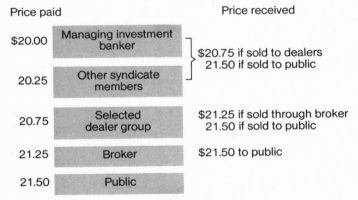

Allocation of underwriting spread

Note that the lower a party falls in the distribution process, the higher the price for shares. The managing investment banker pays $20, while dealers pay $20.75. Also, the farther down the line the securities are resold, the higher is the potential profit. If the managing investment banker resells to dealers, he makes 75 cents per share; if he resells to the public, he makes $1.50.

The total spread of $1.50 in the present case represents 7 percent of the offering price ($1.50/$21.50). Generally, the larger the dollar value of an issue, the smaller the spread is as a percentage of the offering price. Percentage figures on underwriting spreads for U.S. corporations are presented in Table 10—1. Because there is more uncertainty in the market reaction to common stock, a larger spread often exists for common stock than for other types of offerings.

Table 10–1

Underwriting compensation as a percentage of proceeds

Size of issue ($ millions)	Spread	
	Common stock	Debt
Under 0.5	11.3%	7.4%
0.5–0.9	9.7	7.2
1.0–1.9	8.6	7.0
2.0–4.9	7.4	4.2
5.0–9.9	6.7	1.5
10.0–19.9	6.2	1.0
20.0–49.9	4.9	1.0
50.0 and over	2.3	0.8

Sources: Securities and Exchange Commission, *Cost of Flotation of Registered Equity Issues, 1963–1965* (Washington, D.C.: U.S. Government Printing Office, 1970). Also Irwin Friend et al., *Investment Banking and the New Issues Market* (Cleveland: World, 1967).

Since the Maxwell Corporation stock issue is for $5.4 million (250,000 shares × $21.50), the 7 percent spread is in line with SEC figures in Table 10—1. It should be noted that the issuer bears not only the "give-up" expense of the spread in the underwriting process but also out-of-pocket costs related to legal and accounting fees, printing expenses, and so forth. On a small issue, these may represent 6-8 percent of the value of the issue. As indicated in Table 10—2, when the spread plus the out-of-pocket costs are considered, the total cost of a new issue is rather high. Of course, substantial benefits may be received in return.

Pricing the Security

Because the syndicate members purchase the stock for redistribution in the marketing channels, they must be careful about the pricing of the stock. When a stock is sold to the public for the first time (i.e., the firm is going public), the managing investment banker will do an in-depth analysis of the company to determine its value. The study will include an analysis of the firm's industry, financial characteristics, and anticipated earnings and dividend-paying ca-

Table 10–2

Total costs to issue stock (percentage of total proceeds)

Size of issue ($ millions)	Common stock		
	Spread	Out-of-pocket cost*	Total expense
Under 0.5	11.3%	7.3%	18.6%
0.5–0.9	9.7	4.9	14.6
1.0–1.9	8.6	3.0	11.6
2.0–4.9	7.4	1.7	9.1
5.0–9.9	6.7	1.0	7.7
10.0–19.9	6.2	0.6	6.8
20.0–49.9	4.9	0.8	5.7
50.0 and over	2.3	0.3	2.6

*Out-of-pocket cost of debts is approximately the same.

Source: SEC, *Flotation of Registered Equity Issues, 1963–1965* (Washington, D.C.: U.S. Government Printing Office, 1970). Also Irwin Friend et al., *Investment Banking and the New Issue Market* (Cleveland: World, 1967).

pability. Based on appropriate valuation techniques, a price will be tentatively assigned and will be compared to that enjoyed by similar firms in a given industry. If the industry's average price-earnings ratio is 10, the firm should not stray too far from this norm. Anticipated public demand will also be a major factor in pricing a new issue.

The great majority of the issues handled by investment bankers are, however, additional issues of stocks or bonds for companies already trading publicly. When additional shares are to be issued, the investment bankers will generally set the price at slightly below the current market value. This process, known as underpricing, will help ensure a receptive market for the securities.

At times an investment banker will also handle large blocks of securities for existing stockholders. Because the number of shares may be too large to trade in normal channels, the investment banker will manage the issue and underprice the stock below current prices to the public. Such a process is known as a secondary offering, in contrast to a primary offering in which corporate securities are directly sold by the corporation.

Dilution

A problem a company faces when issuing additional securities is the actual or perceived dilutive effect on shares currently outstanding. In the case of the Maxwell Corporation, the 250,000 new shares may represent a 10 percent increment to shares currently in existence. Perhaps the firm had earnings of $5 million on 2,500,000 shares prior to the offering, indicating earnings per share of $2. With 250,000 new shares to be issued, earnings per share will temporarily slip to $1.82.

Of course, the proceeds from the sale of new shares may well be expected to provide the increased earnings necessary to bring earnings back to at least $2. While financial theory dictates that a new equity issue should not be undertaken if it diminishes the overall wealth of current stockholders, there may be a perceived time lag in the recovery of earnings per share as a result of the increased shares outstanding. For this reason, there may be a temporary weakness in a stock when an issue of additional shares is proposed. In most cases, this is overcome with the passage of time.

Market stabilization

Another problem may set in when the actual public distribution begins—namely, unanticipated weakness in the stock or bond market. Since the sales group has made a firm commitment to purchase stock at a given price for redistribution, it is essential that the price of the stock remain relatively strong. Syndicate members, committed to purchasing the stock at $20 or better, could be in trouble if the sales price fell to $19 or $18. The managing investment banker is generally responsible for stabilizing the offering during the distribution period, and may accomplish this by repurchasing securities as the market price moves below the initial public offering price of $21.50.

The period of stabilization usually lasts two or three days after the initial offering, but it may extend up to 30 days for difficult-to-distribute securities. In a very poor market environment, stabilization may be virtually impossible to achieve. For example, when Federal Reserve Board Chairman Paul Volcker announced an extreme credit-tightening policy in October 1979, newly underwritten, high-quality IBM bond prices fell dramatically and Salomon Brothers and other investment bankers got trapped into approximately $10 million in losses. The bonds later recovered in value, but the investment bankers had already taken their losses.

Aftermarket

The investment banker is also interested in how well the underwritten security behaves after the distribution period—for his ultimate reputation rests on bringing strong securities to the market. This is particularly true of initial public offerings.

Research has indicated that initial public offerings often do well in the immediate aftermarket. For example, one study examined approximately 500 firms and determined that there were 10.9 percent excess returns one week after issue (excess returns refers to movement in the price of the stock above and beyond the market). There were also positive excess returns of 11.6 percent for a full month after issue, but a negative market-adjusted performance of – 3.0 percent one full year after issue. Because the managing underwriter may underprice the issue initially to ensure a successful offering, quite often there is a jump in value after the issue first goes public. However, the efficiency of the market eventually takes hold and sustained long-term performance is very much dependent on the quality of the issue and the market conditions at play.

Changes in the Investment Banking Industry

During the time period that up and down market conditions have challenged the brokerage industry, the investment banking function has been rapidly expanding. The growth in investment banking revenue has not been predominantly in the underwriting area, but rather in other functions performed. Major increases have taken place in corporate finance and merger/acquisition advisory services (currently comprising over 25 percent of investment banking revenue).

Another measure of the growth in investment banking is the number of people employed. Merrill Lynch, First Boston, Goldman Sachs, and Morgan Stanley have all at least tripled their staffs in the last 10 years. Furthermore, an earlier interest in social and family background as a prerequisite for potential employment has given way to a search for the brightest, most articulate job candidates.

The investment banking industry has remained fiercely competitive on the basis of performance. Furthermore, there has been a tremendous move toward vertical integration. Firms that were at one time primarily investment bankers, specializing in underwriting and corporate client services, have moved into more broadly based brokerage distribution services. Even more significant is the backward vertical integration that has taken place, as retail brokerage firms have acquired investment banking houses. As an example of the latter, in the late 1970s Merrill Lynch acquired White Weld & Company, a firm prominent in the investment banking industry.

Also, nonbrokerage firms are moving into the brokerage area through acquisitions. Since the acquired brokerage houses are also engaged in investment banking activities, acquiring firms are obtaining investment banking capabilities as well. Mergers during the 1980s include Prudential Insurance Company and Bache Halsey Stuart Shields; American Express and Shearson, Loeb Rhoades; and Sears Roebuck & Company and Dean Witter Reynolds (socks and stocks).

Shelf registration

In February of 1982, the Securities and Exchange Commission began allowing a process called shelf registration under SEC Rule 415. Shelf registration permits large companies, such as Exxon or Polaroid, to file one comprehensive registration statement, which outlines the firm's plans for future long-term financing. Then, when market conditions seem appropriate, the firm can issue the securities without further SEC approval. Future issues are thought to be sitting on the shelf, waiting for the appropriate time to appear.

Shelf registration is at variance with the traditional requirement that security issuers file a detailed registration statement for SEC review and approval each and every time they plan a sale. The SEC decided to allow the process of shelf registration on an experimental basis as part of an emphasis on deregulation. Whether investors are deprived of important "current" information as a result of shelf registration can only be judged with time.

One consequence of shelf registration is that there is a greater concentration of business in the investment banking industry. The strong firms such as Merrill Lynch, First Boston, Goldman Sachs, Salomon Brothers, and Morgan Stanley are acquiring more and more business, and, in some cases, are less dependent on large syndications to handle issues. Only investment banking firms with a big capital base and substantial expertise are in a position to benefit from this new registration process. Shelf registration has been most frequently used with debt issues, with relatively less utilization in the equity markets.

Size criteria for going public

Although there are no prescribed or official size criteria for approaching the public markets, the well-informed corporate financial officer of a private company should have some feel for what his or her options are. Can a company with $10 million in sales even consider a public offering?

A study indicates the following changes in various size considerations between 1969–72 and 1974–78 for 204 new public issues.

	1969–1972 ($ millions)	1974–1978 ($ millions)
Average sales volume	$8.333	$22.857
Average earnings	0.464	1.758
Average asset size	5.833	14.643

Note the substantially higher values that apply to the latter period. Actually, highly prestigious investment bankers look for larger companies to underwrite than do lesser known or regional investment banking houses. In the preceding data for 1974-78, prestigious underwriters such as First Boston and Goldman Sachs (among others) underwrote companies going public with an average sales volume of $48,486,000 and average earnings of $3,610,000. Smaller underwriters were willing to consider firms with $10-$15 million in sales and at least a million dollars in aftertax earnings.

Public versus Private Financing

Our discussion to this point has assumed that the firm was distributing stocks or bonds in the public markets (through the organized exchanges or over-the-counter, as explained in Chapter 9). However, many companies, by choice or circumstance, prefer to remain private in nature—restricting their financial activities to direct negotiations with bankers, insurance companies, and so forth. Let us evaluate the advantages and the disadvantages of public versus private financing and then explore the avenues open to a privately financed firm.

Advantages of being public

First of all, the corporation may tap the security markets for a greater amount of funds by selling securities directly to the public. With 32 million individual stockholders in the country, combined with thousands of institutional investors, the greatest pool of funds is channeled toward publicly traded securities. Furthermore, the attendant prestige of a public security may be helpful in bank negotiations, executive recruitment, and the marketing of products. Some corporations listed on the New York Stock Exchange actually allow stockholders a discount on the purchase of their product lines.

Stockholders of a heretofore private corporation may also sell part of their holdings if the corporation decides to go public. A million-share offering may contain 500,000 authorized but unissued corporate shares (a primary offering) and 500,000 existing stockholder shares (a secondary offering). The stockholder is able to achieve a higher degree of liquidity and to diversify his portfolio. A publicly traded stock with an established price may also be helpful for estate planning purposes.

Finally, going public allows the firm to play the merger game, using marketable securities for the purchase of other firms. The high visibility of a public offering may even make the firm a potential recipient of attractive offers for its own securities.

Disadvantages of being public

The company must make all information available to the public through SEC and state filings. Not only is this tedious, time consuming, and expensive, but important corporate information on profit margins and product lines must be divulged. The president must adapt himself to being a public relations representative to all interested members of the securities industry.

Another disadvantage of being public is the tremendous pressure for short-term performance placed on the firm by security analysts and large institutional investors. Quarter-to-quarter earnings reports can become more important to top management than providing a long-run stewardship for the company. A capital budgeting decision calling for the selection of Alternative A—carrying a million dollars higher net present value than Alternative B—may be discarded in favor of the latter because Alternative B adds two cents more to next quarter's earnings per share.

In a number of cases, the blessings of having a publicly quoted security may become quite the opposite. Although a security may have had an enthusiastic reception in a strong "new issues" market such as that of 1961–62, 1967–68 or 1981–82, a dramatic erosion in value may later take place, causing embarrassment and anxiety for stockholders and employers.

A final disadvantage is the high cost of going public. As indicated in Table 10—2, for issues under a million dollars the underwriting spread plus the out-of-pocket cost may run over 15 percent.

An example—EDS goes public

Perhaps no other example of the ups and downs of a public offering is more illustrative than that of H. Ross Perot and his computer service firm, Electronic Data Systems (EDS). In September 1968 Perot took his firm public, and within one month he found himself worth $300 million. This was no small accomplishment for a man who, six years earlier, had been an IBM salesman with only a few thousand dollars in the bank and a degree from the Naval Academy. Others shared in Perot's success as a handful of young systems engineers at EDS became multimillionaires overnight.

The original EDS offering—managed by P. W. Presprich, a New York investment banker—was at 118 times current earnings (the norm is 10 to 12 times earnings). After one month in the hot new issues market of 1967–68, the stock was trading at over 200 times earnings. A company with earnings of only $1.5 million had a market value well over $300 million, exceeding many of Fortune's 500 largest companies. By 1970, EDS had a quoted market value of $1.5 billion. All of this was accomplished by a firm with a few hundred employees.

It is interesting to note that Perot's main concern in the initial pricing of his stock was not to set too low a value. In the strong new issues market of the period, too many computer issues, which had been underpriced when they first crossed the tape, quickly doubled or tripled in price. Perot considered this an irrevocable loss to original shareholders who initially sold large blocks of their holdings. He was determined to avoid this by fully pricing his stock and only trading a small percentage of the total capitalization on the initial offering (only 650,000 shares out of 11.5 million). Even at a price-earnings ratio of 118 at initial trading, the stock jumped from $16.50 to $23 in one day.

In the bear markets of the 1970s, EDS suffered more than most companies and fell from a peak price of $161 in 1970 to an all-time low of $12¼ in 1974. The price-earnings ratio of 200 sank to a low of 10. Stock that was once quoted at over $1.5 billion found a new low at $150–$200 million before recovery began. Nevertheless, one need not feel sorry for centimillionaire Perot with a present net worth and corporate structure that only the most ambitious can envision. In January of 1983 the stock was selling for $50 per share, indicating a strong recovery from the low point.

Private Placement

Private placement refers to the selling of securities directly to insurance companies, pension funds, and wealthy individuals rather than through the security markets. The financing device may be employed by a growing firm that wishes to avoid or defer an initial public stock offering or by a publicly traded company that wishes to incorporate private funds into its financing package. Private placement usually takes the form of a debt instrument, though a conversion privilege to common stock is sometimes present. The relative importance of private versus public placement is indicated in Figure 10—3.

The advantages of private placement are worthy of note. First of all, there is no lengthy, expensive registration process with the SEC. Second, the firm has considerably greater flexibility in negotiating with one or a handful of insurance companies, pension funds, or bankers than is possible in a public offering. Because there is no SEC registration or underwriting, the initial costs of a private placement may be considerably lower than those of a public issue. How-

Figure 10–3

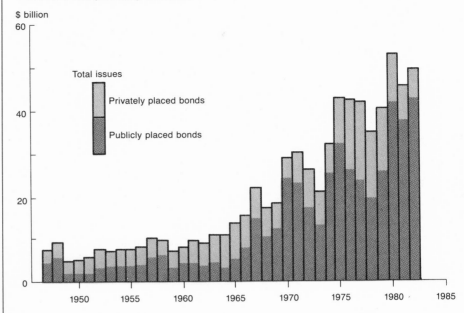

Public versus private placement

ever, the interest rate is usually higher to compensate the investor for holding a less liquid obligation.

Going private

A number of firms actually gave up their public listings to go private in the 1970s. For example, Nardis of Dallas went public in 1969 only to reverse itself and go private in 1974 by buying in all shares of stock in the public's hands. Corporate management figured that this could save $100,000 a year in annual report expenses, legal and auditing fees, and security analysts' meetings—a significant amount for a small company. A number of other companies have followed a similar pattern. The legal implications of these withdrawals are being carefully tested in the courts.

Of course, this is not to suggest that the ease of private placement could ever replace the operations of U.S. capital markets. The major thrust of corporate financing still lies in our security exchanges and our over-the-counter markets.

Summary

The role of the investment banker is critical to the distribution of securities in the U.S. economy. The investment banker serves as an underwriter or risk taker by purchasing the securities from the issuing corporation and redistributing them to the public. He also serves as an adviser to the corporation and may continue to maintain a market in the distributed securities long after they have been sold to the public.

The advantages of selling securities in the public markets must be weighed against the disadvantages. While going public may give the corporation and major stockholders greater access to funds as well as additional prestige, these advantages quickly disappear in a down market. Furthermore, the corporation must open its books to the public and orient itself to the short-term emphasis of investors.

There have been substantial increases in the average size of the corporations going public during the last decade. While during the years 1969–72 the average sales of such corporations were slightly over $8 million, by 1974–78 they had climbed to almost $23 million. The average earnings of these firms had almost quadrupled.

Shelf registration has also become an alternative to public syndications, particularly with debt issues.

Private placement—or the direct distribution of securities to large insurance companies, pension funds, and wealthy individuals—may bypass the rigors of SEC registration and allow more flexibility in terms. A number of corporations actually changed their structure from public to private during the bear market of 1973–74. Nevertheless, the vast capital needs of U.S. corporations can be met only by substantial reliance on the public markets.

11 | Long-Term Debt and Lease Financing

The Shakespearean quote of "Neither a borrower nor a lender be" hardly applies to corporate financial management. The virtues and drawbacks of debt usage were considered in Chapter 2, "Operating and financial leverage," and in Chapter 8, "The cost of capital." One can only surmise that today's financial managers, many of whom were educated in the 1950s and 1960s, remember the advantages a bit better than the disadvantages. Debt usage has been at unprecedented levels in the late 1970s and 1980s.

In Chapter 11, we will consider the importance of debt in the U.S. economy, the nature of long-term debt instruments, the mechanics of bond yields and pricing, and the decision to call back or refund an existing bond issue. Finally, lease financing will be considered as a special case of long-term debt financing. We give particular attention to accounting rule changes that affect leasing.

The Expanding Role of Debt

Corporate debt has increased more than tenfold since World War II. This growth is related to rapid business expansion, the inflationary impact on the economy, and, at times, a relatively weak stock market.

The rapid expansion of the U.S. economy has placed pressure on U.S. corporations to raise capital and will continue to do so in the future. The need for investment dollars will be two to three times greater in the 1980s than in the 1970s. In this context, a whole new set of rules has been developed for evaluating corporate bond issues. Much deterioration in borrowing qualifications has taken place. In 1967, the average U.S. manufacturing corporation had its interest covered by operating earnings at a rate of 11.7 times (operating earnings were more than 11 times as great as interest). By the early 1980s, the ratio had diminished to approximately three times. Nor has this been a short-term, cyclical phenomenon, but rather a slow, steady decline with only short-term reversals, as indicated in Figure 11—1.

Figure 11–1

Times interest earned

Interest coverage

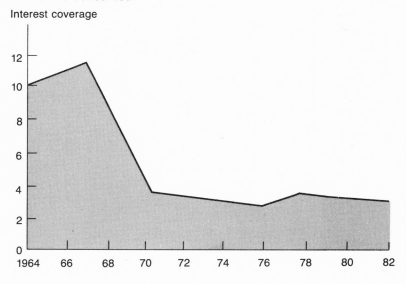

Even with a decline in the interest-paying capability of corporate borrowers, relatively few corporations actually default on their obligations and an even smaller number are liquidated. Nevertheless, a debt contract dictates the lender's potential influence over a corporation and his relative bargaining position in the event the worst comes to pass.

The Debt Contract

The corporate bond represents the basic long-term debt instrument for most large U.S. corporations. The bond agreement specifies such basic items as the par value, the coupon rate, and the maturity date.

Par value (face value).   The initial value of the bond. Most corporate bonds are traded in $1,000 units.

Coupon rate.   The actual interest rate on the bond, usually payable in semiannual installments. To the extent that interest rates in the market go above or below the coupon rate after the bond has been issued, the market price of the bond will change from the par value. A bond paying a 10 percent coupon rate on par value will not fare well in a market in which 12 percent interest is commonplace.

Maturity date.   The final date on which repayment of the bond principal is due.

The bond agreement is supplemented by a much longer document termed a bond indenture. The indenture, often containing over 100 pages of complicated legal wording, covers every minute detail surrounding the bond issue—including collateral pledged, methods of repayment, restrictions on the corporation, and procedures for initiating claims against the corporation. A financially independent trustee is appointed by the corporation to administer the provisions of the bond indenture under the guidelines of the Trust Indenture Act of 1939. Let's examine two items of interest in any bond agreement: the security provisions of the bond and the methods of repayment.

Security provisions

A secured claim is one in which specific assets are pledged to bondholders in the event of default. Only infrequently are pledged assets actually sold off and the proceeds distributed to bondholders. Typically, the defaulting corporation is reorganized and existing claims are partially satisfied by issuing new securities to the participating parties. Of course, the stronger and better secured the initial claim, the higher the quality of the new security to be received in exchange. When a defaulting corporation is reorganized for failure to meet obligations, existing management may be terminated and, in extreme cases, held legally responsible for any imprudent actions.

A number of terms are used to denote collateralized or secured debt. Under a *mortgage agreement,* real property (plant and equipment) is pledged as security for the loan. A mortgage may be *senior* or *junior* in nature, with the former requiring satisfaction of claims before payment is given to the latter. Bondholders may also attach an *after-acquired property clause,* requiring that any new property be placed under the original mortgage.

The student should realize that not all secured debt will carry every protective feature, but rather a carefully negotiated position including some safeguards and rejecting others. Generally, the greater the protection offered a given class of bondholders, the lower is the interest rate on the bond. Bondholders are willing to assume some degree of risk to receive a higher yield.

Unsecured debt

A number of corporations issue debt that is not secured by a specific claim to assets. In Wall Street jargon, the name *debenture* refers to a long-term, unsecured corporate bond. Among the major participants in debenture offerings are such prestigious firms as American Telephone and Telegraph, Exxon, International Paper, and Dow Chemical. Because of the legal problems associated with "specific" asset claims in a secured bond offering, the trend is decidedly to unsecured debt—allowing the bondholder a general claim against the corporation rather than a specific lien against an asset.

Even unsecured debt may be divided between high-ranking and subordinated debt. A *subordinated debenture* is an unsecured bond in which payment to the holder will take place only after designated senior debenture holders are satisfied. The hierarchy of creditor obligations for secured as well as unsecured debt is presented in Figure 11—2, along with consideration of the position of stockholders.

Figure 11–2   **Priority of claims**

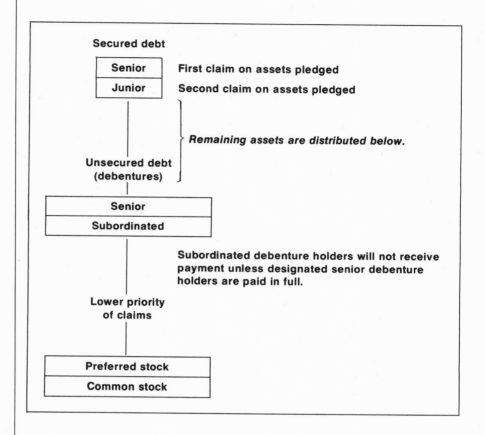

Methods of repayment

The method of repayment for bond issues may not always call for one lump-sum disbursement at the maturity date. Some Canadian and British government bonds are perpetual in nature. More interestingly, West Shore Railroad 4 percent bonds are not scheduled to mature until 2361 (almost 400 years in the future). Nevertheless, most bonds have some orderly or preplanned system of repayment. In addition to the simplest arrangement—a single-sum payment at maturity—bonds may be retired by serial payments, through sinking-fund provisions, through conversion, or by a call feature.

Serial payments   The bonds are paid off in installments over the life of the issue. Each bond has its own predetermined date of maturity and receives interest only to that point. Although the total issue may span over 20 years, 15 or 20 different maturity dates may be assigned specific dollar amounts.

Sinking-fund provision   A less structured but considerably more popular method of debt retirement is through the use of a sinking fund. Under this arrangement, semiannual or annual contributions are made by the corporation into a fund administered by a trustee for purposes of debt retirement. The trustee takes the proceeds and goes into the market to purchase bonds from willing sellers. If no willing sellers are available, a lottery system may be used among outstanding bondholders.

Conversion   A more subtle method of reducing debt outstanding is to provide for debt conversion into common stock. Although this feature is exercised at the option of the bondholder, a number of incentives or penalties may be utilized to encourage conversion.

Call feature   A call provision allows the corporation to call in or force in the debt issue prior to maturity. The corporation will pay a premium over par value of 5 to 10 percent—a bargain value to the corporation if bond prices are up. Modern call provisions usually do not take effect until the bond has been outstanding at least five to ten years. Generally the call provision declines over time, usually by ½–1 percent per year after the call period begins. A corporation may decide to call in outstanding debt issues when interest rates on new securities are considerably lower than those on previously issued debt (let's get the high cost, old debt off the books).

Bond Prices, Yields, and Ratings

The financial manager must be sensitive to interest rate changes and price movements in the bond market. The treasurer's interpretation of market conditions will influence the timing of new issues, the coupon rate offered, the maturity date, and the necessity for a call provision. Lest the student of finance think that bonds maintain stable, long-term price patterns, he or she need merely examine bond pricing during the five-year period 1967–72. When the market interest rate on outstanding 30-year, Aaa corporate bonds went from 5.10 percent to 8.10 percent, the average price of existing bonds dropped 36 percent. A conservative investor would be quite disillusioned to see a $1,000, 5.10 percent bond now quoted at $640. A similar pattern of bond price declines occurred in 1979-82. Though most bonds are virtually certain to be redeemed at their face value at maturity ($1,000 in this case), this is small consolation to the bondholder who has many decades to wait.

As indicated above, the price of a bond is intimately tied to current interest rates. A bond paying 5.10 percent ($51 a year) will fare quite poorly when the going market rate is 8.10 percent ($81 a year). In order to maintain a market in the older issue, the price is adjusted downward to reflect current market demands. The longer the life of the issue, the greater the influence of interest rate changes on the price of the bond. The same process will work in reverse if interest rates go down. A 30-year, $1,000, bond initially issued to yield 8.10 percent would go up to $1,500 if interest rates declined to 5.10 percent (assuming the bond is not callable). An illustration of interest rate effects on bond prices is presented in Table 11—1 for a bond paying 12 percent interest. Observe that not only interest rates in the market but years to maturity have a strong influence on bond prices.

Table 11–1

Interest rates and bond prices (the bond pays 12 percent interest)

Years to maturity	Rate in the market (percent)				
	8%	10%	12%	14%	16%
1	$1,037.12	$1,018.60	$1,000	$981.90	$965.44
15	1,268.20	1,124.60	1,000	894.10	806.96
25	1,449.96	1,189.30	1,000	859.60	753.24

For the last four decades, the pattern has been for long-term interest rates to move upward (Figure 11—3). Rate declines have seldom lasted more than a year, necessitating rapid action by the market participants who wished to take advantage of the situation (we will see later in the chapter how this can be done).

Figure 11–3

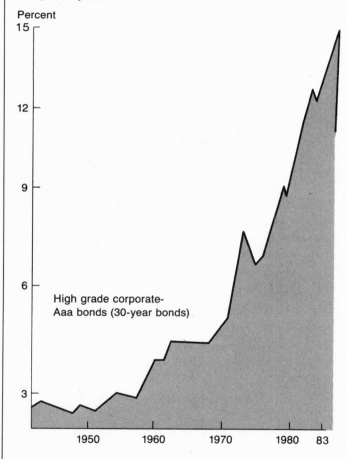

Long-term yields on debt

Percent

High grade corporate-
Aaa bonds (30-year bonds)

Bond yields

Bond yields are quoted on three different bases; coupon rate, current yield, and yield to maturity. We will apply each to a $1,000 par value bond paying $100 per year interest for ten years. The bond is currently selling in the market for $900.

Coupon rate (_nominal yield_). Stated interest payment divided by the par value.

$$\frac{\$100}{\$1,000} = 10 \text{ percent}$$

Current yield. Stated interest payment divided by the current price of the bond.

$$\frac{\$100}{\$900} = 11.11\%$$

Yield to maturity. The interest rate that will equate future interest payments and the payment at maturity to the current market price. This represents the concept of the internal rate of return, previously discussed in Chapter 8. In the present case an interest rate of approximately 11.58 percent will equate interest payments of $100 for ten years and a final payment of $1,000 to the current price of $900. A simple formula may be used to approximate yield to maturity.

$$\text{Yield to maturity} = \frac{\text{Interest}}{\text{payment}} + \dfrac{\text{Par value} - \text{Market value}}{\text{No. of periods to maturity}} \bigg/ \dfrac{}{\text{(Market price} + \text{Par value)}/2} \qquad (11\text{—}1)$$

Step 1: $\dfrac{\$100 + \dfrac{(\$1,000 - \$900)}{10}}{(\$900 + \$1,000)/2}$

Step 2: $\dfrac{\$100 + \dfrac{\$100}{10}}{\$1,900/2} = \dfrac{\$100 + \$10}{\$950} = \dfrac{\$110}{\$950} = 11.58\%$

Extensive bond tables indicating yield to maturity are also available. When financial analysts speak of bond yields, the general assumption is that they are speaking of yield to maturity. This is deemed to be the most significant measure of return.

Bond ratings

Both the issuing corporation and the investor are concerned about the rating their bond is assigned by the two major bond rating agencies—Moody's Investor Service and Standard & Poor's Corporation. The higher the rating assigned a given issue, the lower the required interest payments are to satisfy potential investors. This is because highly rated bonds carry lower risk. A major industrial corporation may be able to issue a 30-year bond at 11 percent yield to maturity because it is rated Aaa, whereas a smaller, regional firm may only qualify for a B rating and be forced to pay 13 or 13½ percent.

As an example of rating systems, Moody's Investor Service provides the following nine categories of ranking:

Aaa   Aa   A   Baa   Ba   B   Caa   Ca   C

The first two categories represent the highest quality (for example, AT&T and IBM) the next two, medium to high quality, and so on. Beginning in 1982, Moody's began applying numerical modifiers to categories Aa through B. One is the highest in a category, two is the mid-range and three is the lowest. Thus a Aa2 rating means the bond is in the mid-range of Aa. Standard & Poor's has a similar letter system with + and − modifiers.

Bonds receive ratings based on the corporation's ability to make interest payments, its consistency of performance, its size, its debt-equity ratio, its working capital position, and a number of other factors. The yield spread between higher and lower rated bonds changes with the economy. If investors are pessimistic about economic events, they will accept as much as 3 percent less return to go into securities of very high quality, whereas in more normal times the spread may be only 1.5 percent.

Combining the use of terms

Three actual bond offerings are presented in Table 11—2 to illustrate the various terms we have used. The information is taken from *Moody's Bond Record* (January 1983), a publication available at almost any library.

Table 11–2   **Outstanding bond issues**

		Rating	Price	Yield to maturity
Standard Oil of California 7's	Sinking fund debentures due 1996	Aaa	$740	11.40%
Duke Power Co. 10⅞'s	Senior mortgage bonds due 2009	A1	878	12.35%
Reynolds Metals 4½'s	Convertible debentures due 1991 (converts into 16.91 shares)	Ba3	582	13.30%

The student will recall first of all that the true return on a bond issue is measured by yield to maturity (as presented in the last column). For purposes of discussion, we will direct our attention to the Standard Oil of California bonds. We note that the oil bonds are unsecured, as indicated by the term *debenture*. Furthermore, they have a sinking-fund provision for retirement of debt. Because of the extremely high quality of the company and the sinking-fund retirement plan, the bonds are accorded an Aaa rating. Nevertheless, the bonds carry a market price of $740 because the interest rate at time of issue (7 percent) is below the demanded rate of interest of 11–11.5 percent in early 1983 for bonds of similar quality and maturity. The student may wish to make similar observations for the other two bond issues.

The Refunding Decision

Assume you are the financial vice president for a corporation that has issued bonds at 12.5 percent, only to witness a drop in interest rates to 10 percent. If you do not believe interest rates will go down further, and in fact believe that they will go back up, you may wish to redeem the expensive 12.5 percent bonds and to issue new debt at the prevailing 10 percent interest rate. This process is labeled a refunding operation. It is made feasible by the call provision which enables a corporation to buy back bonds at close to par, rather than at high market values, when interest rates are declining. Although long-term interest rates tended to move up in the 50s, 60s, 70s, and 80s, there were periods of temporary decline in interest rates that provided an excellent environment for refunding.

A capital budgeting problem

The refunding decision involves outflows in the form of financing costs related to redeeming and reissuing securities, and inflows represented by savings in annual interest costs and some tax savings. In the present case, we shall assume that the corporation issued $10 million worth of 12.5 percent debt with a 25-year maturity and that the debt has been on the books for five years. The corporation now has the opportunity to buy back the old debt at 10 percent above par (the call premium) and to issue new debt at 10 percent interest with a 20-year life. The underwriting cost for the old issue was $125,000, and the underwriting cost for the new issue is $200,000. We shall also assume that the corporation is in the 40 percent tax bracket and uses a 6 percent discount rate for refunding decisions. Since the savings from a refunding decision are certain—unlike the savings from most other capital budgeting decisions—we use the aftertax cost of new debt as the discount rate rather than the more generalized cost of capital. Actually, in this case the aftertax cost of new debt is [10 percent × (1 – Tax rate)] or 6 percent.

Restatement of facts

	Old issue	New issue
Size	$10,000,000	$10,000,000
Interest rate	12.5%	10%
Total life	25 years	20 years
Remaining life	20 years	20 years
Call premium	10%	—
Underwriting costs	$125,000	$200,000

Tax bracket—40%
Discount rate—6%

Let's go through the capital budgeting process of defining our outflows and inflows and determining the net present value.

Step A—Outflow considerations

1. Payment of call premium. The first outflow is the 10 percent call premium on $10 million, or $1 million. This prepayment penalty is necessary to call in the original issue. Being an *out-of-pocket* tax-deductible expense, the $1 million cash expenditure will cost us only $600,000 on an aftertax basis. We multiply the expense by (1 − tax rate) to get the aftertax cost.

Net cost of call premium $600,000

2. Underwriting cost on new issue. The second outflow is the $200,000 underwriting cost on the new issue. The actual cost is somewhat less because the payment is tax deductible, though the write-off must be spread over the life of the bond. While the actual $200,000 is being spent now, equal tax deductions of $10,000 a year will take place over the next 20 years (in a manner similar to depreciation).

The tax savings from a *noncash* writeoff equal the amount times the tax rate. For a company in the 40 percent tax bracket, $10,000 of annual tax deductions will provide $4,000 of tax savings each year for the next 20 years. The present value of these savings is the present value of a $4,000 annuity for 20 years at 6 percent interest:

$$\$4,000 \times 11.470 \ (n = 20, \ i = 6\%) = \$45,880$$

The net cost of underwriting the new issue is the actual expenditure now, minus the present value of future tax savings:

Actual expenditure $200,000
− PV of future tax savings 45,880
Net cost of underwriting
  expense on the new issue $154,120

Step B—Inflow considerations The major inflows in the refunding decision are related to the reduction of annual interest expense and the immediate write-off of the underwriting cost on the old issue.

3. Cost savings in lower interest rates. The corporation will enjoy a 2.5 percent drop in interest rates, from 12.5 percent to 10 percent, on $10 million of bonds.

12.5% × $10,000,000	$1,250,000
10% × $10,000,000	1,000,000
Savings	$ 250,000

Since we are in the 40 percent tax bracket, this is equivalent to $150,000 of aftertax benefits per year for 20 years. We have taken the savings and multiplied by one minus the tax rate to get the aftertax benefits. Applying a 6 percent discount rate for a 20 year annuity:

$$\$150,000 \times 11.470 \ (n = 20, i = 6\%) = \$1,720,500$$

Cost savings in lower interest rates $1,720,500

4. *Underwriting cost on old issue.* There is a further cost savings related to immediately writing off the remaining underwriting costs on the old bonds. Note that the initial amount of $125,000 was spent five years ago and was to be written off for tax purposes over 25 years at $5,000 per year. Since five years have passed, $100,000 of old underwriting costs have not been amortized.

Original amount	$125,000
Written off over five years	25,000
Unamortized old underwriting costs	$100,000

There is a tax benefit associated with the immediate write-off of old underwriting costs which we shall consider shortly.

Note, however, that this is not a total gain. We would have gotten the $100,000 additional write-off eventually if we had not called in the old bonds. By calling them in now, we simply take the write-off sooner. If we extended the write-off over the remaining life, we would have taken $5,000 a year for 20 years. Discounting this value, we show:

$$\$5,000 \times 11.470 \ (n = 20, i = 6\%) = \$57,350$$

Thus we are getting a write-off of $100,000 now rather than a present value of future write-offs of $57,350. The gain in immediate tax write-offs is $42,650. Since we are in the 40 percent tax bracket, our savings from this write-off are $17,060. The tax savings from a *noncash* tax write-off equal the amount times the tax rate.

Net gain from the underwriting cost on the old issue $17,060

Step C—Net present value We now compare our outflows and our inflows.

	Outflows				Inflows	
1.	Net cost of call premium	$600,000	3.	Cost savings in lower interest rates	$1,720,500
2.	Net cost of underwriting expense on new issue	154,120	4.	Net gain from underwriting cost on old issue	17,060
		$754,120			$1,737,560

Present value of inflows $1,737,560
Present value of outflows 754,120
Net present value . . . . . . $ 983,440

The refunding decision has a positive net present value, suggesting that interest rates have dropped to a sufficiently low level to indicate refunding is in order. The only question is, will interest rates go lower—indicating an even better time for refunding? This is a consideration that all firms must face, and there is no easy answer.

A number of other factors could be plugged into the problem. For example, there could be overlapping time periods in the refunding procedure when both issues are outstanding and the firm is paying double interest (hopefully for less than a month). The dollar amount, however, tends to be quite small and is not included in the analysis.

In working problems, the student should have minimum difficulty if he or she follows the four suggested calculations. Note, by way of review, that in each of the four calculations we had the following tax implications:

1. Payment of call premium—the cost equals the amount times (1 − Tax rate) for this *cash tax deductible expense.*
2. Underwriting costs on new issue—we pay an amount now and then amortize it over the life of the bond for tax purposes. This subsequent amortization is similar to depreciation and repre-

sents a *noncash write off* of a tax-deductible expense. The tax savings from the amortization are equal to the amount times the tax rate.

3. Cost savings in lower interest rates—cost savings are like any form of income, and we will retain the cost savings times (1 − Tax rate).

4. Underwriting cost on old issue—once again, the writing off of underwriting costs represents a *noncash write-off* of a tax-deductible expense. The tax savings from the amortization are equal to the amount times the tax rate.

Innovative Forms of Bond Financing

As interest rates continued to show increasing volatility in the late 70s and early 80s, two innovative forms of bond financing became very popular. We shall examine the zero-coupon rate bond and the floating rate bond.

The zero-coupon rate bond, as the name implies, does not pay interest. It is, however, sold at a deep discount from face value. The return to the investor is the difference between the investor's cost and the face value received at the end of the life of the bond. For example, in early 1982 BankAmerica Corporation offered $1,000 zero-coupon rate bonds with maturities of five, eight, and ten years. The five-year bonds were sold for $500, the eight-year bonds for $333.33 and the ten-year bonds for $250. All three provided an initial yield to maturity (through gain in value) of approximately 14.75 percent. The most dramatic case of a zero-coupon bond was an issue offered by PepsiCo, Inc. in 1982, in which the maturities ranged from 6 to 30 years. The 30-year $1,000 par value issue could be purchased for $26.43, providing a yield of approximately 12.75 percent. The purchase price per bond of $26.43 represents only 2.643 percent of the par value. A million dollars worth of these 30-year bonds could be initially purchased for a mere $26,430.

The advantage to the corporation is that there is immediate cash inflow to the corporation, without any outflow until the bonds mature. Furthermore, the difference between the initial bond price and the maturity value may be amortized for tax purposes by the corporation over the life of the bond. This means that the corporation will be taking annual deductions without current cash outflow.

From the investor's viewpoint, the zero-coupon bonds allow him to lock in a multiplier of the initial investment. For example, an investor may know that he will get four times his investment in 10 (or perhaps 12) years. The major drawback is that the annual increase in the value of the bonds is taxable as ordinary income as it accrues even though the bondholder does not have his or her return until maturity. For this reason most investors in zero-coupon rate bonds have tax-exempt or deferred status (pension funds, foundations, charitable organizations, Individual Retirement Accounts, etc.).

The prices of the bonds tend to be highly volatile because of changes in interest rates. Even though the bonds provide no annual interest payment, there is still an initial yield to maturity that may prove to be too high or too low with changes in the marketplace.

In August of 1982, Merrill Lynch and other brokerage houses began offering a variation of the zero-coupon rate bond through selling future interests in government securities. The securities, which are held in custody for the benefit of investors, are sold at a fraction of face value and ultimately redeemed at full value. The investor receives a multiple of the original investment and no interest, or interest which is deferred to the end of the life of the security. These securities tend to be long term (20–30 years).

A second type of innovative bond issue is the floating rate bond (already quite popular in European capital markets). In this case, instead of a change in the price of the bond, the interest rate paid on the bond changes with market conditions (usually weekly). Thus a bond that was initially issued to pay 13 percent may lower the interest payments to 10 percent during some years and raise them to 16 percent in others. The interest rate is usually tied to some overall market rate, such as the yield on Treasury bonds (perhaps 120 percent of the going yield on long-term Treasury bonds).

The advantage to the investor is that he or she has a constant (or almost constant) market value for the security even though interest rates vary. The one exception that can cause a change to this principle is that floating rate bonds often have broad limits that interest payments cannot exceed. For example, the interest rate on a 13 percent initial offering may not be allowed to go over 20 percent or below 6 percent. If long-term interest rates dictated an interest payment of 22 percent, the payment would still remain at 20 percent.

This could cause some short-term loss in market value. To date, floating rate bonds have been relatively free of this problem.

To keep matters in perspective, zero-coupon rate bonds and floating rate bonds still represent a relatively small percentage of the total market of new debt offerings. Nevertheless, they are gaining in importance and should be part of a basic understanding of long-term debt instruments.

Advantages and Disadvantages of Debt

The financial manager must consider whether debt will contribute to or detract from the firm's operations. In certain industries, such as the airlines, very heavy debt utilization is a way of life, whereas in other industries (drugs, photographic equipment) reliance is placed on other forms of capital.

Benefits of debt

The advantages of debt may be enumerated as:

1. Interest payments are tax deductible. Because the corporate tax rate approaches 50 percent, the effective aftertax cost of interest is but half the dollar amount expended.
2. The financial obligation is clearly specified and of a fixed nature (with the exception of floating rate bonds). Contrast this with selling an ownership interest in which stockholders have open-end participation in the sharing of profits.
3. In an inflationary economy, debt may be paid back with "cheaper dollars." A $1,000 bond obligation may be repaid in 10 or 20 years with dollars that have shrunk in value by 50 or 60 percent. In terms of "real dollars," or purchasing power equivalents, one might argue that the corporation should be asked to repay something in excess of $2,000. Presumably, high interest rates in inflationary periods compensate the lender for loss in purchasing power, but this is not always the case.
4. The use of debt, up to a prudent point, may lower the cost of capital to the firm. To the extent that debt does not strain the risk position of the firm, its low aftertax cost may aid in reducing the weighted overall cost of financing to the firm.

Drawbacks of debt

Finally, we must consider the disadvantages of debt:

1. Interest and principal payment obligations are set by contract and must be met regardless of the economic position of the firm.
2. Bond indenture agreements may place burdensome restrictions on the firm, such as maintenance of working capital at a given level, limits on future debt offerings, and guidelines for dividend policy. Although bondholders generally do not have the right to vote, they may take virtual control of the firm if important indenture provisions are not met.
3. Utilized beyond a given point, debt may serve as a depressant on outstanding common stock values.

Leasing as a Form of Debt

When a corporation contracts to lease an oil tanker or a computer and signs a noncancelable, long-term agreement, the transaction has all the characteristics of a debt obligation. Long-term leasing was not recognized as a debt obligation in the early post-World War II period, but since the mid-60s there has been a strong movement by the accounting profession to force companies to fully divulge all information about leasing obligations and to indicate the equivalent debt characteristics.

This position was made official for financial reporting purposes as a result of *Statement No. 13,* issued by the Financial Accounting Standards Board (FASB) in November 1976. In essence, this statement said that certain types of leases must be shown as long-term obligations on the financial statements of the firm. Prior to FASB Statement No. 13, lease obligations could merely be divulged in footnotes to financial statements and large lease obligations did not have to be included in the debt structure (except for the upcoming payment). Consider the case of firm ABC, whose balance sheet is shown in Table 11—3.

Table 11–3

Balance sheet ($ millions)

Current assets	$ 50	Current liabilities	$ 50
Fixed assets	150	Long-term liabilities	50
Total assets	$200	Total liabilities	$100
		Stockholders' equity	100
		Total liabilities and stockholders' equity	$200

Prior to the issuance of FASB *Statement No. 13*, a footnote to the financial statements might have indicated a lease obligation of $12 million a year for the next 15 years, with a present value of $100 million dollars. With the issuance of FASB *Statement No. 13*, this information has, of necessity, been moved directly to the balance sheet, as indicated in Table 11—4.

Table 11–4

Revised balance sheet ($ millions)

Current assets	$ 50	Current liabilities		$ 50
Fixed assets	150	Long-term liabilities		50
*Leased property		*Obligation under		
under capital lease	100	capital lease		100
		Total liabilities		200
		Stockholders' equity		100
Total assets	$300	Total liabilities and stockholders' equity		$300

We see that both a new asset and a new liability have been created, as indicated by the asterisks. The essence of this treatment is that a long-term, noncancelable lease is tantamount to purchasing the asset with borrowed funds, and this should be reflected on the balance sheet. Note that between the original balance sheet (Table 11—3) and the revised balance sheet (Table 11—4) the total debt to total assets ratio has gone from 50 percent to 66.7 percent.

Original

$$\frac{\text{Total debt}}{\text{Total assets}} = \frac{\$100 \text{ million}}{\$200 \text{ million}} = 50\%$$

Revised

$$\frac{\text{Total debt}}{\text{Total assets}} = \frac{\$200 \text{ million}}{\$300 \text{ million}} = 66.7\%$$

Though this represents a substantial increase in the ratio, the impact on the firm's credit rating or stock price may be minimal. To the extent that the financial markets are efficient, the information was *already* known by analysts who took the data from footnotes or other sources and made their own adjustments. Nevertheless, corporate financial officers fought long, hard, and unsuccessfully to keep the lease obligation off the balance sheet. They tend to be much less convinced about the efficiency of the marketplace.

Capital lease versus operating lease

Actually, not all leases must be capitalized (present-valued) and placed on the balance sheet. It is only under circumstances in which substantially all the benefits and risks of ownership are transferred in a lease that this treatment is necessary. Under these circumstances, we have a *capital* (or financing) lease. Identification as a capital lease and the attendant financial treatment are required whenever any *one* of the four following conditions is present:

1. The arrangement transfers ownership of the property to the lessee (the leasing party) by the end of the lease term.
2. The lease contains a bargain purchase price at the end of the lease. The option price will have to be sufficiently low so that exercise of the option appears reasonably certain.
3. The lease term is equal to 75 percent or more of the estimated life of the lease property.
4. The present value of the minimum lease payments equals 90 percent or more of the fair value of the leased property at the inception of the lease.

A lease that does not meet any of these four criteria is not regarded as a *capital* lease, but as an *operating* lease. An operating lease is usually short term and is often cancelable at the option of the lessee. Furthermore, the lessor (the owner of the asset) may provide for the maintenance and upkeep of the asset, since he is likely to get it back. An operating lease does not require the *capitalization*, or presentation, of the full obligation on the balance sheet. Operating leases are used most frequently with such assets as automobiles and office equipment, while capital leases include oil drilling equipment, airplanes and rail equipment, certain forms of real estate, and other long-term assets. The greatest volume of leasing obligations is represented by capital leases.

Income statement effect

The capital lease calls not only for present-valuing the lease obligation on the balance sheet but also for treating the arrangement for income statement purposes as if it were somewhat similar to a purchase-borrowing arrangement. Thus, under a capital lease the intangible asset account shown in Table 11—4 as "Leased property under capital lease" is amortized or written off over the life of the lease with an annual expense deduction. Also, the liability account shown in Table 11—4 as "Obligation under capital lease" is written off through regular amortization, with an implied interest expense on the remaining balance. Thus, for financial reporting purposes the annual deductions are amortization of the asset, plus implied interest expense on the remaining present value of the liability. Though the actual development of these values and accounting rules is best deferred to an accounting course, the finance student should understand the close similarity between a capital lease and borrowing to purchase an asset as far as financial reporting purposes are concerned.

An operating lease, on the other hand, usually calls for an annual expense deduction equal to the lease payment, with no specific amortization.

Advantages of leasing

Why is leasing so popular? It has emerged as a $100 billion industry, with such firms as Clark Equipment, Citicorp, and U.S. Leasing International providing an enormous amount of financing. Major reasons for the popularity of leasing include the following:

1. The lessee may lack sufficient funds or the credit capability to purchase the asset from a manufacturer, who is willing to accept a lease agreement or to arrange a lease obligation with a third party.
2. The provisions of a lease obligation may be substantially less restrictive than those of a bond indenture.

3. There may be no down payment requirement, as would generally be the case in the purchase of an asset (leasing allows for a larger indirect loan).
4. The lessor may possess particular expertise in a given industry—allowing for expert product selection, maintenance, and eventual resale. Through this process, the negative effects of obsolescence may be lessened.
5. Creditor claims on certain types of leases, such as real estate, are restricted in bankruptcy and reorganization proceedings. Leases on chattels (non-real estate items) have no such limitation.

There are also some tax factors to be considered. Where one party to a lease is in a higher tax bracket than the other party, certain tax advantages, such as an investment tax credit, may be better utilized. For example, a wealthy party may purchase an asset and take an investment tax credit, then lease the asset to another party in a lower tax bracket for actual use. Also, lease payments on the use of land are tax-deductible, whereas landownership does not allow a similar deduction for depreciation.

Finally, a firm may wish to engage in a sale-leaseback arrangement in which assets already owned by the lessee are sold to the lessor and then leased back. This process provides the lessee with an infusion of capital, while allowing the lessee to continue to use the asset. Even though the dollar costs of a leasing arrangement are often higher than the dollar costs of owning an asset, the advantages cited above may outweigh the direct cost factors.

Tax credits and deductions associated with leasing transactions became particularly popular under the 1981 Economic Recovery Tax Act. The Act contained "safe harbor" leasing provisions in which leasing transactions could be arranged for no economic purpose other than tax reduction.[1] These so called "safe harbor" leasing provisions expired in December of 1983 as mandated by the 1982 Tax Equity and Fiscal Responsibility Act.

---

[1] The typical pattern was for an unprofitable company to buy an asset and sell it to a highly profitable company and then lease it back. The profitable company generally paid the unprofitable company a minimum amount of ten percent in cash and the payments on the balance of the note were assumed to be equal to the lease payments owed by the unprofitable company. This was a *wash lease* that required no subsequent lease payments and no economic justification under the law, but because there are no longer "safe harbor" provisions, they must have economic justification.

Summary

The use of debt financing by corporations has grown very rapidly since the end of World War II, and the quality of corporate debt coverage has deteriorated.

Corporate bonds may be secured by a lien on a specific asset or may carry an unsecured designation, indicating that the bondholder possesses a general claim against the corporation.

Bond prices have been in a steady decline for the last four decades due to rising interest rates. Nevertheless, cyclical downturns in interest rates have afforded an excellent opportunity for refunding, that is replacing high-interest-rate bonds with lower-interest-rate bonds. The financial manager must consider whether the savings in interest will compensate for the additional cost of calling in the old issue and selling a new one.

Finally, the long-term, noncancelable lease should be considered as a special debt form available to the corporation. It is capitalized on the balance sheet to represent both a debt and an asset account and is amortized on a regular basis. Leasing offers a means of financing in which lessor expertise and other financial benefits can be imparted to the lessee (leasing party).

12 | Dividend Policy and Retained Earnings

A successful owner of a small business must continually decide what to do with the profits his firm has generated. One option is to reinvest in the business—purchasing new plant and equipment, expanding inventory, and perhaps hiring new employees. Another alternative, however, is to withdraw the funds from the business and invest them elsewhere. Prospective uses might include buying other stocks and bonds, purchasing a second business, or perhaps spending a "lost weekend" in Las Vegas.

A corporation and its stockholders must face exactly the same type of decision. Should funds associated with profits be retained in the business, or paid out to stockholders in the form of dividends?

The Marginal Principle of Retained Earnings

In theory, corporate directors should ask, "How can the best use of the funds be made?" The rate of return that the corporation can achieve on retained earnings for the benefit of stockholders must be compared to what stockholders could earn if the funds were paid out to them in dividends. This is known as the marginal principle of retained earnings. Each potential project to be financed by internally generated funds must provide a higher rate of return than the stockholder could achieve for himself after he has paid taxes on the distributed dividends. As discussed in Chapter 8, "Valuation and the Cost of Capital," if the stockholder can earn 10 percent on an investment of equal risk and must pay 30 percent taxes on dividends received, then the cutoff point for the corporate use of funds would be 7 percent. We speak of this as the opportunity cost of using stockholder funds.

Life cycle growth and dividends

One of the major influences on dividends is the corporate growth rate in sales and the subsequent return on assets. Figure 12—1 shows a corporate life cycle and the corresponding dividend policy that is most likely to be found at each stage. A small firm in the initial stages of development (Stage I) pays no dividends because it needs all of its profits (if there are any) for reinvestment in new productive assets. If the firm is successful in the marketplace, the demand for its products will create growth in sales, earnings, and assets and the firm will move into Stage II. At this stage, sales and returns on assets will be growing at an increasing rate and earnings will still be reinvested. In the early part of Stage II stock dividends (distribution of additional shares) may be instituted, and in the latter part of Stage II *low* cash dividends may be started to inform investors that the first is profitable, but also that it needs cash for internal acquisition.

After the growth period, the firm enters Stage III. The expansion of sales continues, but at a decreasing rate, and returns on investment may decline as more competition enters the market and tries to take away the firm's market share. During this period the firm is more and more capable of paying cash dividends, as the asset expansion rate slows and external funds become more readily available. Stock dividends and stock splits are still common in the expansion phase, and the dividend payout ratio usually increases from a low level of 5 to 15 percent of earnings to a moderate level of 25 to 40 percent of earnings. Finally at Stage IV, maturity, the firm maintains a stable growth rate in sales similar to that of the econ-

Figure 12–1

Life cycle growth and dividend policy

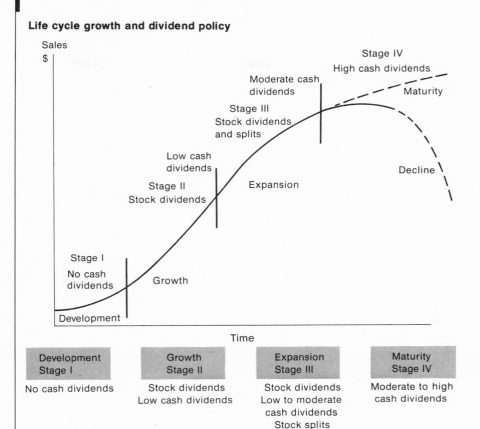

Development Stage I	Growth Stage II	Expansion Stage III	Maturity Stage IV
No cash dividends	Stock dividends Low cash dividends	Stock dividends Low to moderate cash dividends Stock splits	Moderate to high cash dividends

omy as a whole, and when risk premiums are considered, its returns on assets level out to those of the industry and the economy. In unfortunate cases, firms suffer declines in sales if product innovation and diversification have not taken place over the years. In Stage IV, assuming maturity rather than decline, dividends might range from 40 to 60 percent of earnings. These percentages will be different from industry to industry, depending on the individual characteristics of the company, such as operating and financial leverage and the volatility of sales and earnings over the business cycle.

As the chapter continues, more will be said about stock dividends, stock splits, the availability of external funds, and other variables that affect the dividend policy of the firm.

Dividends as a passive variable

In the preceding analysis, dividends were used as a "passive decision variable." They are only to be paid out if the corporation cannot make better use of the funds for the benefit of stockholders. The *active decision variable* is retained earnings. We decide how much to retain, and then the *residual is paid out in dividends*.

An incomplete theory

The only problem with the residual theory is that we have not given recognition to how stockholders feel about receiving dividends. If the stockholders' only concern is with achieving the highest return on their investment, either in the form of *corporate retained earnings remaining in the business* or as *current dividends paid out*, then there is no issue. But if stockholders have a preference for current funds, for example, over retained earnings, then our theory is incomplete. The issue is not only whether reinvestment of retained earnings or dividends provide the highest return, but also how stockholders react to the two alternatives.

While some researchers maintain that stockholders are indifferent to the division of funds between retained earnings and dividends (holding investment opportunities constant), others disagree. Though there is no conclusive proof one way or the other, the judgment of most researchers is that investors do have some preference between dividends and retained earnings.

Arguments for the relevance of dividends

A strong case can be made for the relevance of dividends because they *resolve uncertainty* in the minds of investors. Though retained earnings reinvested in the business theoretically belong to common stockholders, there is still an air of uncertainty about their eventual translation into dividends. Thus, it can be hypothesized that stockholders might apply a higher discount rate (K_e) and assign a lower valuation to funds that are retained in the business as opposed to those that are paid out.

It is also argued that dividends may be viewed more favorably than retained earnings because of the *information content* they contain. In essence, the corporation is telling the stockholder, "We are having a good year, and we wish to share the benefits with you." Though the corporation may be able to do just as well with the funds and perhaps provide even greater dividends in the future, some researchers find that "in an uncertain world in which verbal statements can be ignored or misinterpreted, dividend action does provide a clear-cut means of making a statement that speaks louder than a thousand words."[1]

The relevance of dividends in policy determination can also be argued from the viewpoint that the optimum dividend payout rate should be low. Because certain stockholders may be in high tax brackets, retention of funds in excess of investment needs might be recommended.

The primary contention in arguing for the relevance of dividend policy is that stockholders' needs and preferences go beyond the *marginal principle of retained earnings*. The issue is not only who can best utilize the funds (the corporation or the stockholder) but also what are the stockholders' preferences. In practice, it appears that most corporations adhere to the following logic. First, a determination is made of the investment opportunities of the corporation relative to a required return (marginal analysis). This is then tempered by some subjective notion of stockholders' desires. It is not surprising that corporations with unusual growth prospects and high rates of return on internal investments generally pay a relatively low dividend (the small amount may be paid out only for its informational content). For the more mature firm, an analysis of both investment opportunties and stockholder preferences may indicate that a higher rate of payout is necessary. Dividend policies of selected major U.S. corporations are presented in Table 12—1. The normal payout has been approximately 50 percent of aftertax earnings in the post-World War II period.

---

[1]Ezra Solomon, *The Theory of Financial Management* (New York:Columbia University Press, 1963), p. 142.

Table 12–1

Corporate dividend policy

	Four-year growth rate in earnings per share (1978–1982)	Dividend payout as a percentage of aftertax earnings (1982)
Category 1—Rapid growth		
Baxter Travenol Laboratories	23.3%	14.7%
Digital Equipment	33.4	0.0
Marriott	26.0	8.1
Tandy	32.0	0.0
Category 2—Slower growth		
American Telephone & Telegraph . .	9.6	59.5
GTE	1.8	66.0
Houston Industries	7.2	58.4
Toledo Edison	3.7	73.8

Dividend Stability

In considering stockholder desires in dividend policy, a primary factor is the maintenance of stability in dividend payments. Thus, corporate management must not only ask, "How many profitable investments do we have this year?" It must also ask, "What has been the pattern of dividend payments in the last three years?" Though earnings may change from year to year, the dollar amount of cash dividends tends to be much more stable, increasing in value only as new permanent levels of income are achieved. Note in Figure 12—2 the considerably greater volatility of earnings as compared to dividends for U.S. corporations in the post-World War II period.

By maintaining a record of relatively stable dividends, corporate management hopes to lower the discount rate (K_e) applied to future dividends of the firm. The operative rule appears to be that a stockholder would much prefer to receive $1 a year for three years rather than 75 cents for the first year, $1.50 for the second year, and 75 cents for the third year—for the same total of $3. Once again, we temper our policy of marginal analysis of retained earnings to include a notion of stockholder preference, with the emphasis on stability of dividends.

Figure 12-2

Corporate profits (seasonally adjusted annual rates, quarterly)

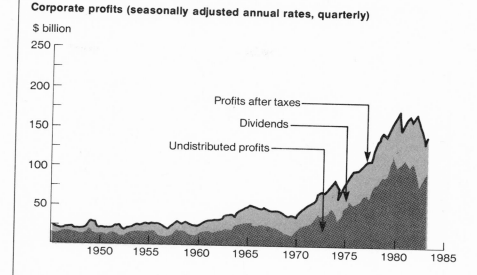

Other Factors Influencing Dividend Policy

Corporate management must also consider the legal basis of dividends, the cash flow position of the firm, and the corporation's access to capital markets. Other factors that must be considered include management's desire for control, and the tax and financial position of shareholders. Each is briefly discussed.

Legal rules

Most states forbid firms to pay dividends that would impair the initial capital contributions to the firm. For this reason, dividends may only be distributed from past and current earnings. To pay dividends in excess of this amount would mean that the corporation is returning to investors their original capital contribution (raiding the capital). If the ABC Company has the following statement of net worth, the maximum dividend payment would be $20 million.

Common stock (1 million shares at $10 par value)*	$10,000,000
Retained earnings	20,000,000
Net worth	$30,000,000

*If there is a "paid-in capital in excess of par" account, some states will allow additional dividend payments against capital, while others will not. To simplify the problem for now, paid-in capital in excess of par is not considered.

Why all the concern about impairing permanent capital? Since the firm is going to pay dividends only to those who contributed capital in the first place, what is the problem? Clearly, there is no abuse to the stockholders, but what about the creditors? They have extended credit on the assumption that a given capital base would remain intact throughout the life of the loan. While they may not object to the payment of dividends from past and current earnings, they must have the protection of keeping contributed capital in place.

Even the proscription against having dividends exceed the total of past and current earnings (retained earnings) may be inadequate to protect creditors. Because retained earnings is merely an accounting concept and in no way certifies the current liquidity of the firm, a company paying dividends equal to retained earnings may, in certain cases, jeopardize the operation of the firm. Let us examine Table 12—2.

Table 12–2

Dividend policy considerations

Cash	$ 1,000,000	Debt	$10,000,000
Accounts receivable	4,000,000	Common stock	10,000,000
Inventory	15,000,000	Retained earnings	15,000,000
Plant and equipment	15,000,000		$35,000,000
	$35,000,000		

Current earnings	$ 1,500,000
Potential dividends	15,000,000

Theoretically, management could pay up to $15,000,000 in dividends by selling off assets even though current earnings are only $1,500,000. In most cases, such frivolous action would not be taken, but the mere possibility encourages creditors to closely watch the balance sheets of corporate debtors and, at times, to impose additional limits on dividend payments as a condition for the granting of credit.

Cash position of the firm

Not only do retained earnings fail to portray the liquidity position of the firm, but there are also limitations to the use of current earnings for this purpose. As described in Chapter 1, Financial Forecasting, a growth firm producing the greatest gains in earnings may be in the poorest cash position. As sales and earnings expand rapidly, there is an accompanying buildup in receivables and inventory that may far outstrip cash flow generated through earnings. Note that the cash balance in Table 12—2 represents only two thirds of current earnings of $1,500,000. A firm must do a complete funds flow analysis before establishing a dividend policy.

Access to capital markets

The medium- to large-size firm with a good record of performance may have relatively easy access to the financial markets. A company in such a position may be willing to pay dividends now, knowing that it can sell new stocks or bonds in the future if funds are needed. Some corporations may even issue debt or stock *now* and use part of the proceeds to ensure the maintenance of current dividends. Though this policy seems at variance with the concept of a dividend as a reward, management may justify its action on the basis of maintaining stable dividends. It should be clear that in the capital shortage era of the 1970s and 80s only a relatively small percentage of firms have had sufficient ease of entry to the capital markets to modify their dividend policy in this regard. Many firms may actually defer the payment of dividends because they know that they will have difficulty in going to the capital markets for more funds.

Desire for control

Management must also consider the effect of the dividend policy on its collective ability to maintain control. The directors and officers of a small, closely held firm may be hesitant to pay any dividends at all for fear of diluting the cash position of the firm and forcing the owners to look to outside investors for financing. The funds may be available only through venture capital sources that wish to have a large say in corporate operations.

A larger firm with a broad base of shareholders may face a different type of threat in regard to dividend policy. Stockholders, spoiled by a past record of dividend payments, may demand the ouster of management if dividends are withheld.

Tax position of shareholders

While the payment of a cash dividend is generally taxable to the recipient, some feel the burden much more heavily than others. To the wealthy doctor or lawyer, dividend income can be taxed up to 50 percent. Even the average taxpayer will probably pay a 25–30 percent tax. Contrast this with the corporate receipient (such as General Motors owning Xerox stock), in which 85 percent of the dividend payment is tax exempt, and only a maximum tax of 46 percent is paid against the 15 percent balance (the overall rate is 6.9 percent). Furthermore, many large institutional investors, such as pension funds and charitable organizations, are partially or wholly tax exempt.

For the individual, dividends are taxed at an investor's ordinary tax rate. However, $100 of dividends ($200 on a joint return) may be excluded from taxation in a given year. Dividends of $1,000 for an individual investor in a 50 percent tax bracket indicate $900 of dividends should be taxed at a 50 percent rate for total taxes of $450.

Short-term capital gains (gains on securities held one year or less) are also taxed at the investor's ordinary tax rate, while long-term capital gains are taxed at 40 percent of that rate. For an investor in a 50 percent tax bracket, long-term capital gains would only be taxed at a 20 percent rate (40 percent times 50 percent). For an individual in a 45 percent tax bracket, capital gains would be taxed at 18 percent (40 percent times 45 percent). Thus, an individual in a 45 percent tax bracket would pay $180 in taxes on a $1,000 long-term capital gain.[2]

---

[2]The long-term capital gains tax rate for individuals is somewhat different than that for corporations, which is 28 percent of the gain or the ordinary (normal) tax rate, whichever is lower. The attention in this chapter will be primarily directed to individuals.

Because of differences among investors' tax rates, certain investor preferences for dividends versus capital gains have been observed in the market. This investor behavior is called the *clientele effect*. Investors in high marginal tax brackets usually prefer companies that reinvest most of their earnings, thus creating more growth in earnings and stock prices. The returns from such investments will be in the form of long-term capital gains which are taxed at lower rates than dividends. Companies following these dividend policies will most probably be found in the growth and expansion stages (see Figure 12—2). Investors in lower marginal tax brackets will have a greater preference for dividends, since the tax penalty is less at lower marginal tax rates. The clientele effect is also used to explain the advantages of a stable dividend policy that makes investors more certain about the type of return they will receive.

Dividend Payment Procedures

Now that we have examined the many factors that influence dividend policy, let us track the actual procedures for announcing and paying a dividend. Though dividends are quoted on an annual basis, the payments actually take place over four quarters during the year. For example, in 1982, IBM paid $3.44 a year in cash dividends. This meant stockholders could expect to receive 86 cents a quarter in dividends. Because the stock was selling at $96 per share in January of 1983, we say the annual dividend yield is 3.58 percent ($3.44/96).

There are actually three key dates associated with the declaration of a quarterly dividend: the ex-dividend date, the holder-of-record date, and the payment date.

We must begin with the holder-of-record date. On this date, the firm examines its books to determine who is entitled to a cash dividend. In order to have your name included on the corporate books, you must have bought or owned the stock before the ex-dividend date, which is four business days before the holder-of-record date. If you bought the stock on the ex-dividend date or later, your name will eventually be transferred to the corporate books, but you will have bought the stock without the quarterly dividend privilege. Thus we say you bought the stock ex-dividend. As an example, a stock with a holder-of-record date of March 5th will go ex-dividend on March 1st. You must buy the stock by the last day of February to get the dividend. Investors are very conscious of the date on which the stock goes ex-dividend, and the value of the stock may go down by the value of the quarterly dividend on the ex-dividend date (all other things being equal). Finally, in our example, we might assume the payment date is April 2 and checks will go out to entitled stockholders on or about this time.

Stock Dividend

A stock dividend represents of distribution of additional shares to common stockholders. The typical size of such dividends is in the 10 percent range, so that a stockholder with ten shares might receive one new share in the form of a stock dividend. Larger distributions of 20–25 percent or more are usually considered to have the characteristics of a stock split, a topic to be discussed later in the chapter.

Accounting considerations for a stock dividend

Assume that prior to the declaration of a stock dividend the XYZ Corporation has the net worth position indicated in Table 12—3.

Table 12–3

XYZ Corporation's financial position before stock dividend

Capital accounts	Common stock (1,000,000 shares at $10 par)	$10,000,000
	Capital in excess of par	5,000,000
	Retained earnings	15,000,000
	Net worth	$30,000,000

If a 10 percent stock dividend is declared, shares outstanding will increase by 100,000 (10 percent times 1,000,000 shares). An accounting transfer will take place between retained earnings and the two capital stock accounts based on the market value of the stock dividend. If the stock is selling at $15 a share, we will assign $1,000,000 to common stock (100,000 shares times $10 par) and $500,000 to capital in excess of par. The net worth position of XYZ after the transfer is shown in Table 12—4.

Table 12–4

XYZ Corporation's financial position after stock dividend

Common stock (1,100,000 shares at $10) . . .	$11,000,000
Capital in excess of par	5,500,000
Retained earnings	13,500,000
Net worth	$30,000,000

Value to investor

An appropriate question might be, is a stock dividend of real value to the investor? Suppose that your finance class collectively purchased $1,000 worth of assets and issued ten shares of stock to each class member. Three days later it is announced that each stockholder will receive an extra share. Has anyone benefited from the stock dividend? Of course not! The asset base remains the same ($1,000), and your proportionate ownership in the business is unchanged (everyone got the same new share). You merely have more paper to tell you what you already knew.

The same logic is essentially true in the corporate setting. In the case of the XYZ Corporation, shown in Tables 12—3 and 12—4, we assumed that 1 million shares were outstanding before the stock dividend and 1.1 million shares afterward. Now let us assume that the corporation had aftertax earnings of $6.6 million. Without the stock dividend, earnings per share would be $6.60, and with the dividend $6.00.

$$\text{Earnings per share} = \frac{\text{Earnings after taxes}}{\text{Shares outstanding}}$$

Without stock dividend:

$$= \frac{\$6.6 \text{ million}}{1 \text{ million shares}} = \$6.60$$

With stock dividend:

$$= \frac{\$6.6 \text{ million}}{1.1 \text{ million shares}} = \$6.00$$
$$(10\% \text{ decline})$$

Earnings per share have gone down by exactly the same percentage that shares outstanding increased. For further illustration, assuming that Stockholder A had 10 shares before the stock dividend and 11 afterward, what are his total claims to earnings? As expected, they remain the same at $66.

$$\text{Claims to earnings} = \text{Shares} \times \text{Earnings per share}$$

Without stock dividend:

$$10 \times \$6.60 = \$66$$

With stock dividend:

$$11 \times \$6.00 = \$66$$

Taking the analogy one step farther, assuming the stock sold at 20 times earnings before and after the stock dividend, what is the total market value of the portfolio in each case?

$$\text{Total market value} = \text{Shares} \times \left(\frac{\text{Price/earnings}}{\text{ratio}} \times \frac{\text{Earnings}}{\text{per share}} \right)$$

Without stock dividend:

$$10 \times (20 \times \$6.60)$$
$$10 \times \$132 = \$1,320$$

With stock dividend:

$$11 \times (20 \times \$6.00)$$
$$11 \times \$120 = \$1,320$$

The total market value is unchanged. Note that if the stockholder sells off the 11th share to acquire cash, his stock portfolio will be worth $120 less than it was worth before the stock dividend.

Possible value of stock dividends

There are limited circumstances under which a stock dividend may be more than a financial sleight of hand. If at the time a stock dividend is declared, the cash dividend per share remains constant, the stockholder will receive greater total cash dividends. Assume that the annual cash dividend for the XYZ Corporation will remain $1 per share even though earnings per share decline from $6.60 to $6.00. In this instance a stockholder moving from 10 to 11 shares as the result of a stock dividend has a $1 increase in total dividends. The overall value of his portfolio may then increase in response to larger dividends.

Use of stock dividends

Stock dividends are most frequently used by growth companies as a form of "informational content" in explaining the retention of funds for reinvestment purposes. This was indicated in the discussion of the life cycle of the firm earlier in the chapter. A corporation president may state that "instead of doing more in the way of cash dividends, we are providing a stock dividend. The funds remaining in the corporation will be used for highly profitable investment opportunities." The market reaction to such an approach may be neutral or slightly positive.

A second use of stock dividends may be to camouflage the inability of the corporation to pay cash dividends and to cover up the ineffectiveness of management in generating cash flow. The president may proclaim, "Though we are unable to pay cash dividends, we wish to reward you with a 15 percent stock dividend." Well-informed investors are likely to react very negatively.

Stock Splits

A stock split is similar to a stock dividend, only more shares are distributed. For example, a two-for-one stock split would double the number of shares outstanding. In general, the rules of the New York Stock Exchange and the Financial Accounting Standards Board encourage distributions in excess of 20–25 percent to be handled as stock splits.

The accounting treatment for a stock split is somewhat different from that for a stock dividend in that there is no transfer of funds from retained earnings to the capital accounts, but merely a reduction in par value and a proportionate increase in the number of shares outstanding. For example, a two-for-one stock split for the XYZ Corporation would necessitate the accounting adjustments shown in Table 12—5.

In this case, all adjustments are in the common stock account. Because the number of shares are doubled and the par value halved, the market price of the stock should drop proportionately. There has been much discussion in the financial literature about the im-

Table 12–5

XYZ Corporation before and after stock split

Before

Common stock (1 million shares at $10 par)	$10,000,000
Capital in excess of par	5,000,000
Retained earnings	15,000,000
	$30,000,000

After

Common stock (2 million shares at $5 par)	$10,000,000
Capital in excess of par	5,000,000
Retained earnings	15,000,000
	$30,000,000

pact of a split on overall stock value. While there might be some positive benefit, that benefit is virtually impossible to capture after the announcement of a split has taken place. Perhaps a $66 dollar stock will drop only to $36 after a two-for-one split, but one must act very early in the process to benefit.

The primary purpose of a stock split is to lower the price of a security into a more popular trading range. A stock selling for over $50 per share may be excluded from consideration by many small investors. Splits are popular because only the stronger companies that have witnessed substantial growth in market price are in a position to participate in them.

Repurchase of Stock as an Alternative to Dividends

A firm with excess cash and inadequate investment opportunities may choose to repurchase its own shares in the market rather than pay a cash dividend. For this reason the stock repurchase decision may be thought of as an alternative to the payment of cash dividends.

We will show that the benefits of the stockholder are equal under either alternative, at least in theory. For purposes of study, assume that the Morgan Corporation's financial position may be described by the data in Table 12—6.

The firm has $2 million in excess cash, and it wishes to compare the value to stockholders of a $2 cash dividend (on the million shares outstanding) as opposed to spending the funds to repurchase shares in the market. If the cash dividend is paid, the shareholder will have $30 in stock and the $2 cash dividend. On the other hand, the $2 million may be used to repurchase shares at slightly over market value (to induce sale). The overall benefit to

Table 12–6

Financial data of Morgan Corporation

Earnings after taxes	$3,000,000
Shares	1,000,000
Earnings per share	$3
Price-earnings ratio	10
Market price per share	$30
Excess cash	$2,000,000

stockholders is that earnings per share will go up as the number of shares outstanding is decreased. If the price-earnings ratio of the stock remains constant, then the price of the stock should also go up. If a purchase price of $32 is used to induce sale, then 62,500 shares will be purchased.

$$\frac{\text{Excess funds}}{\text{Purchase price per share}} = \frac{\$2,000,000}{\$32} = 62,500 \text{ shares}$$

Total shares outstanding are reduced to 937,500 (1,000,000 − 62,500). Revised earnings per share for the Morgan Corporation become:

$$\frac{\text{Earnings after taxes}}{\text{Shares}} = \frac{\$3,000,000}{937,500} = \$3.20$$

Since the price-earnings ratio for the stock is 10, the market value of the stock should go to $32. Thus, we see that the consequences of the two alternatives are presumed to be the same.

(1) *Funds used for cash dividend*	(2) *Funds used to repurchase stock*
Market value per share . . . $30	Market value per share . . . $32
Cash dividend per share . . . <u>2</u>	
$32	

In either instance, the total value is presumed to be $32. Theoretically, the stockholder would be indifferent with respect to the two alternatives. This changes somewhat, however, when taxes and transaction costs are brought into the decision-making process. Let us look at taxes first. While the cash dividend is immediately taxed as ordinary income in alternative (1), the gain in alternative (2) is likely to be taxed at approximately 40 percent of that rate as a form of capital gains. Furthermore, the tax will be incurred only when the stock is sold. From a tax viewpoint, the repurchase of shares may provide maximum benefits. On the other hand, one can argue that dividends put cash in the stockholder's hands without any transaction costs, while the cash flow from alternative (2) can be realized only by selling stock at the higher price.

Other reasons for repurchase

In addition to using the repurchase decision as an alternative to cash dividends, corporate management may acquire its own shares in the market because it believes they are selling at a low price. A corporation president who sees his firm's stock decline by 50–75 percent over a six-month period may determine that the stock is the best investment available to the corporation. Heavy repurchases of this nature took place in the 1973–74 bear market and again in 1981–82.

By repurchasing shares, the corporation is able to maintain a constant demand for its own securities and perhaps to stave off further decline, at least temporarily. Reacquired shares may also be used for employee stock options or as part of a tender offer in a merger or an acquisition.

Dividend Reinvestment Plans

During the 1970s, many companies started dividend reinvestment plans for their shareholders. These plans take various forms, but basically they provide the investor with an opportunity to buy additional shares of stock with the cash dividend paid by the company. Some plans, such as that of American Telephone and Telegraph, will sell treasury stock or authorized but unissued shares to the stockholders. With this type of plan the company is the beneficiary of increased cash flow, since dividends paid are returned to the company for reinvestment in common stock. These types of plans have been very popular with cash-short utilities, and very often utilities will allow shareholders a 5 percent discount from market value at the time of purchase. This is justified because no investment banking or underwriting fees need be paid.

Under the 1981 Economic Recovery Tax Act, individuals are able to treat otherwise taxable dividends paid by a qualified *public utility* as tax free if the dividends are reinvested with the company in its stock. This privilege can be applied up to $750 annually for an individual ($1,500 on a joint return). It is available only through 1985.

The reader should note that a public utility must be specifically qualified for this program (a stockbroker can easily supply information on this point). Stock received as a qualified dividend will have a zero tax basis. When it is sold, all the proceeds will be taxable. However, if the stock is held for over one year, it will qualify for long-term capital gains as would normally be the case.

Under a second popular dividend reinvestment plan, the company's transfer agent, usually a bank, buys shares of stock in the market for the stockholder. This plan provides no cash flow for the company, but it is a service to the shareholder, who benefits from much lower transaction costs, the right to own fractional shares, and more flexibility in choosing between cash and common stock. Usually a shareholder can also add cash payments of up to $1,000 per month to his or her dividend payments and receive the same lower transaction costs. Shareholder accounts are kept at the bank, and quarterly statements are provided. Shares will be sent out to stockholders on request or will be sold on request for a commission that is usually lower than that charged by a broker.

Summary

The first consideration in the establishment of a dividend policy is the firm's ability to reinvest the funds versus that of the stockholder. To the extent that the firm is able to earn a higher return (after consideration of taxes), reinvestment of retained earnings may be justified. However, we must temper this "highest return theory" with a consideration of stockholder preferences and the firm's need for earnings retention and growth as presented in the life cycle growth curve.

Stockholders may be given a greater payout than the optimum determined by rational analysis in order to resolve their uncertainty about the future and for informational content purposes. Conversely, stockholders may prefer a greater than normal retention in order to defer the income tax obligation associated with cash dividends. Another important consideration in establishing a dividend policy may be the stockholders' desire for steady dividend payments.

Lesser factors influencing dividend policy are legal rules relating to maximum payment, the cash position of the firm, and the firm's access to capital markets. One must also consider the desire for control by corporate management and stockholders.

An alternative (or a supplement) to cash dividends may be the use of stock dividends and stock splits. While neither of these financing devices directly changes the intrinsic value of the stockholder position, they may provide communication to stockholders and bring the stock price into a more acceptable trading range. A stock dividend may take on some actual value when total cash dividends are allowed to increase. Nevertheless, the alert investor will watch for abuses of stock dividends—situations in which the corporation indicates that something of great value is taking place when, in fact, the new shares that are created merely represent the same proportionate interest for each shareholder.

The decision to repurchase shares may be thought of as an alternative to the payment of a cash dividend. Decreasing shares outstanding will cause earnings per share, and hopefully the market price, to go up. The increase in the market price may be equated to the size of the cash dividend forgone.

Many firms are now offering stockholders the option of reinvesting cash dividends in the company's common stock. Cash-short companies have been using dividend reinvestment plans in order to raise external funds. Other companies simply provide a service to stockholders by allowing them to purchase shares in the market for low transaction costs.

Appendixes

Appendix A   Compound sum of $1, IF_s $S = P(1+i)^n$

Percent

Period	1%	2%	3%	4%	5%	6%	7%	8%	9%	10%	11%
1	1.010	1.020	1.030	1.040	1.050	1.060	1.070	1.080	1.090	1.100	1.110
2	1.020	1.040	1.061	1.082	1.103	1.124	1.145	1.166	1.188	1.210	1.232
3	1.030	1.061	1.093	1.125	1.158	1.191	1.225	1.260	1.295	1.331	1.368
4	1.041	1.082	1.126	1.170	1.216	1.262	1.311	1.360	1.412	1.464	1.518
5	1.051	1.104	1.159	1.217	1.276	1.338	1.403	1.469	1.539	1.611	1.685
6	1.062	1.126	1.194	1.265	1.340	1.419	1.501	1.587	1.677	1.772	1.870
7	1.072	1.149	1.230	1.316	1.407	1.504	1.606	1.714	1.828	1.949	2.076
8	1.083	1.172	1.267	1.369	1.477	1.594	1.718	1.851	1.993	2.144	2.305
9	1.094	1.195	1.305	1.423	1.551	1.689	1.838	1.999	2.172	2.358	2.558
10	1.105	1.219	1.344	1.480	1.629	1.791	1.967	2.159	2.367	2.594	2.839
11	1.116	1.243	1.384	1.539	1.710	1.898	2.105	2.332	2.580	2.853	3.152
12	1.127	1.268	1.426	1.601	1.796	2.012	2.252	2.518	2.813	3.138	3.498
13	1.138	1.294	1.469	1.665	1.886	2.133	2.410	2.720	3.066	3.452	3.883
14	1.149	1.319	1.513	1.732	1.980	2.261	2.579	2.937	3.342	3.797	4.310
15	1.161	1.346	1.558	1.801	2.079	2.397	2.759	3.172	3.642	4.177	4.785
16	1.173	1.373	1.605	1.873	2.183	2.540	2.952	3.426	3.970	4.595	5.311
17	1.184	1.400	1.653	1.948	2.292	2.693	3.159	3.700	4.328	5.054	5.895
18	1.196	1.428	1.702	2.206	2.407	2.854	3.380	3.996	4.717	5.560	6.544
19	1.208	1.457	1.754	2.107	2.527	3.026	3.617	4.316	5.142	6.116	7.263
20	1.220	1.486	1.806	2.191	2.653	3.207	3.870	4.661	5.604	6.727	8.062
25	1.282	1.641	2.094	2.666	3.386	4.292	5.427	6.848	8.623	10.835	13.585
30	1.348	1.811	2.427	3.243	4.322	5.743	7.612	10.063	13.268	17.449	22.892
40	1.489	2.208	3.262	4.801	7.040	10.286	14.974	21.725	31.409	45.259	65.001
50	1.645	2.692	4.384	7.107	11.467	18.420	29.457	46.902	74.358	117.39	184.57

Appendix A (concluded)   Compound sum of $1

Percent

Period	12%	13%	14%	15%	16%	17%	18%	19%	20%	25%	30%
1	1.120	1.130	1.140	1.150	1.160	1.170	1.180	1.190	1.200	1.250	1.300
2	1.254	1.277	1.300	1.323	1.346	1.369	1.392	1.416	1.440	1.563	1.690
3	1.405	1.443	1.482	1.521	1.561	1.602	1.643	1.685	1.728	1.953	2.197
4	1.574	1.630	1.689	1.749	1.811	1.874	1.939	2.005	2.074	2.441	2.856
5	1.762	1.842	1.925	2.011	2.100	2.192	2.288	2.386	2.488	3.052	3.713
6	1.974	2.082	2.195	2.313	2.436	2.565	2.700	2.840	2.986	3.815	4.827
7	2.211	2.353	2.502	2.660	2.826	3.001	3.185	3.379	3.583	4.768	6.276
8	2.476	2.658	2.853	3.059	3.278	3.511	3.759	4.021	4.300	5.960	8.157
9	2.773	3.004	3.252	3.518	3.803	4.108	4.435	4.785	5.160	7.451	10.604
10	3.106	3.395	3.707	4.046	4.411	4.807	5.234	5.696	6.192	9.313	13.786
11	3.479	3.836	4.226	4.652	5.117	5.624	6.176	6.777	7.430	11.642	17.922
12	3.896	4.335	4.818	5.350	5.936	6.580	7.288	8.064	8.916	14.552	23.298
13	4.363	4.898	5.492	6.153	6.886	7.699	8.599	9.596	10.699	18.190	30.288
14	4.887	5.535	6.261	7.076	7.988	9.007	10.147	11.420	12.839	22.737	39.374
15	5.474	6.254	7.138	8.137	9.266	10.539	11.974	13.590	15.407	28.422	51.186
16	6.130	7.067	8.137	9.358	10.748	12.330	14.129	16.172	18.488	35.527	66.542
17	6.866	7.986	9.276	10.761	12.468	14.426	16.672	19.244	22.186	44.409	86.504
18	7.690	9.024	10.575	12.375	14.463	16.879	19.673	22.091	26.623	55.511	112.46
19	8.613	10.197	12.056	14.232	16.777	19.748	23.214	27.252	31.948	69.389	146.19
20	9.646	11.523	13.743	16.367	19.461	23.106	27.393	32.429	38.338	86.736	190.05
25	17.000	21.231	26.462	32.919	40.874	50.658	62.669	77.388	95.396	264.70	705.64
30	29.960	39.116	50.950	66.212	85.850	111.07	143.37	184.68	237.38	807.79	2,620.0
40	93.051	132.78	188.88	267.86	378.72	533.87	750.38	1,051.7	1,469.8	7,523.2	36,119.
50	289.00	450.74	700.23	1,083.7	1,670.7	2,566.2	3,927.4	5,988.9	9,100.4	70,065.	497,929.

Source: Maurice Joy, *Introduction to Financial Management* (Homewood, Ill.: Richard D. Irwin, Inc., 1977).

Appendix B Present value of $1, IF_{pv} $P = S\left[\dfrac{1}{(1+i)^n}\right]$

Percent

Period	1%	2%	3%	4%	5%	6%	7%	8%	9%	10%	11%	12%
1	0.990	0.980	0.971	0.962	0.952	0.943	0.935	0.926	0.917	0.909	0.901	0.893
2	0.980	0.961	0.943	0.925	0.907	0.890	0.873	0.857	0.842	0.826	0.812	0.797
3	0.971	0.942	0.915	0.889	0.864	0.840	0.816	0.794	0.772	0.751	0.731	0.712
4	0.961	0.924	0.885	0.855	0.823	0.792	0.763	0.735	0.708	0.683	0.659	0.636
5	0.951	0.906	0.863	0.822	0.784	0.747	0.713	0.681	0.650	0.621	0.593	0.567
6	0.942	0.888	0.837	0.790	0.746	0.705	0.666	0.630	0.596	0.564	0.535	0.507
7	0.933	0.871	0.813	0.760	0.711	0.665	0.623	0.583	0.547	0.513	0.482	0.452
8	0.923	0.853	0.789	0.731	0.677	0.627	0.582	0.540	0.502	0.467	0.434	0.404
9	0.914	0.837	0.766	0.703	0.645	0.592	0.544	0.500	0.460	0.424	0.391	0.361
10	0.905	0.820	0.744	0.676	0.614	0.558	0.508	0.463	0.422	0.386	0.352	0.322
11	0.896	0.804	0.722	0.650	0.585	0.527	0.475	0.429	0.388	0.350	0.317	0.287
12	0.887	0.788	0.701	0.625	0.557	0.497	0.444	0.397	0.356	0.319	0.286	0.257
13	0.879	0.773	0.681	0.601	0.530	0.469	0.415	0.368	0.326	0.290	0.258	0.229
14	0.870	0.758	0.661	0.577	0.505	0.442	0.388	0.340	0.299	0.263	0.232	0.205
15	0.861	0.743	0.642	0.555	0.481	0.417	0.362	0.315	0.275	0.239	0.209	0.183
16	0.853	0.728	0.623	0.534	0.458	0.394	0.339	0.292	0.252	0.218	0.188	0.163
17	0.844	0.714	0.605	0.513	0.436	0.371	0.317	0.270	0.231	0.198	0.170	0.146
18	0.836	0.700	0.587	0.494	0.416	0.350	0.296	0.250	0.212	0.180	0.153	0.130
19	0.828	0.686	0.570	0.475	0.396	0.331	0.277	0.232	0.194	0.164	0.138	0.116
20	0.820	0.673	0.554	0.456	0.377	0.312	0.258	0.215	0.178	0.149	0.124	0.104
25	0.780	0.610	0.478	0.375	0.295	0.233	0.184	0.146	0.116	0.092	0.074	0.059
30	0.742	0.552	0.412	0.308	0.231	0.174	0.131	0.099	0.075	0.057	0.044	0.033
40	0.672	0.453	0.307	0.208	0.142	0.097	0.067	0.046	0.032	0.022	0.015	0.011
50	0.608	0.372	0.228	0.141	0.087	0.054	0.034	0.021	0.013	0.009	0.005	0.003

Appendix B (concluded)   **Present value of $1**

Percent

Period	13%	14%	15%	16%	17%	18%	19%	20%	25%	30%	35%	40%	50%
1	0.885	0.877	0.870	0.862	0.855	0.847	0.840	0.833	0.800	0.769	0.741	0.714	0.667
2	0.783	0.769	0.756	0.743	0.731	0.718	0.706	0.694	0.640	0.592	0.549	0.510	0.444
3	0.693	0.675	0.658	0.641	0.624	0.609	0.593	0.579	0.512	0.455	0.406	0.364	0.296
4	0.613	0.592	0.572	0.552	0.534	0.515	0.499	0.482	0.410	0.350	0.301	0.260	0.198
5	0.543	0.519	0.497	0.476	0.456	0.437	0.419	0.402	0.320	0.269	0.223	0.186	0.132
6	0.480	0.456	0.432	0.410	0.390	0.370	0.352	0.335	0.262	0.207	0.165	0.133	0.088
7	0.425	0.400	0.376	0.354	0.333	0.314	0.296	0.279	0.210	0.159	0.122	0.095	0.059
8	0.376	0.351	0.327	0.305	0.285	0.266	0.249	0.233	0.168	0.123	0.091	0.068	0.039
9	0.333	0.300	0.284	0.263	0.243	0.225	0.209	0.194	0.134	0.094	0.067	0.048	0.026
10	0.295	0.270	0.247	0.227	0.208	0.191	0.176	0.162	0.107	0.073	0.050	0.035	0.017
11	0.261	0.237	0.215	0.195	0.178	0.162	0.148	0.135	0.086	0.056	0.037	0.025	0.012
12	0.231	0.208	0.187	0.168	0.152	0.137	0.124	0.112	0.069	0.043	0.027	0.018	0.008
13	0.204	0.182	0.163	0.145	0.130	0.116	0.104	0.093	0.055	0.033	0.020	0.013	0.005
14	0.181	0.160	0.141	0.125	0.111	0.099	0.088	0.078	0.044	0.025	0.015	0.009	0.003
15	0.160	0.140	0.123	0.108	0.095	0.084	0.074	0.065	0.035	0.020	0.011	0.006	0.002
16	0.141	0.123	0.107	0.093	0.081	0.071	0.062	0.054	0.028	0.015	0.008	0.005	0.002
17	0.125	0.108	0.093	0.080	0.069	0.060	0.052	0.045	0.023	0.012	0.006	0.003	0.001
18	0.111	0.095	0.081	0.069	0.059	0.051	0.044	0.038	0.018	0.009	0.005	0.002	0.001
19	0.098	0.083	0.070	0.060	0.051	0.043	0.037	0.031	0.014	0.007	0.003	0.002	0
20	0.087	0.073	0.061	0.051	0.043	0.037	0.031	0.026	0.012	0.005	0.002	0.001	0
25	0.047	0.038	0.030	0.024	0.020	0.016	0.013	0.010	0.004	0.001	0.001	0	0
30	0.026	0.020	0.015	0.012	0.009	0.007	0.005	0.004	0.001	0	0	0	0
40	0.008	0.005	0.004	0.003	0.002	0.001	0.001	0.001	0	0	0	0	0
50	0.002	0.001	0.001	0.001	0	0	0	0	0	0	0	0	0

Source: Maurice Joy, *Introduction to Financial Management* (Homewood, Ill.: Richard D. Irwin, Inc. 1977).

Appendix C   Compound sum of an annuity of $1, IF_{sa} $S = R\left[\dfrac{(1+I)^n - 1}{i}\right]$

Percent

Period	1%	2%	3%	4%	5%	6%	7%	8%	9%	10%	11%
1	1.000	1.000	1.000	1.000	1.000	1.000	1.000	1.000	1.000	1.000	1.000
2	2.010	2.020	2.030	2.040	2.050	2.060	2.070	2.080	2.090	2.100	2.110
3	3.030	3.060	3.091	3.122	3.153	3.184	3.215	3.246	3.278	3.310	3.342
4	4.060	4.122	4.184	4.246	4.310	4.375	4.440	4.506	4.573	4.641	4.710
5	5.101	5.204	5.309	5.416	5.526	5.637	5.751	5.867	5.985	6.105	6.228
6	6.152	6.308	6.468	6.633	6.802	6.975	7.153	7.336	7.523	7.716	7.913
7	7.214	7.434	7.662	7.898	8.142	8.394	8.654	8.923	9.200	9.487	9.783
8	8.286	8.583	8.892	9.214	9.549	9.897	10.260	10.637	11.028	11.436	11.859
9	9.369	9.755	10.159	10.583	11.027	11.491	11.978	12.488	13.021	13.579	14.164
10	10.462	10.950	11.464	12.006	12.578	13.181	13.816	14.487	15.193	15.937	16.722
11	11.567	12.169	12.808	13.486	14.207	14.972	15.784	16.645	17.560	18.531	19.561
12	12.683	13.412	14.192	15.026	15.917	16.870	17.888	18.977	20.141	21.384	22.713
13	13.809	14.680	15.618	16.627	17.713	18.882	20.141	21.495	22.953	24.523	26.212
14	14.947	15.974	17.086	18.292	19.599	21.015	22.550	24.215	26.019	27.975	30.095
15	16.097	17.293	18.599	20.024	21.579	23.276	25.129	27.152	29.361	31.772	34.405
16	17.258	18.639	20.157	21.825	23.657	25.673	27.888	30.324	33.003	35.950	39.190
17	18.430	20.012	21.762	23.698	25.840	28.213	30.840	33.750	36.974	40.545	44.501
18	19.615	21.412	23.414	25.645	28.132	30.906	33.999	37.450	41.301	45.599	50.396
19	20.811	22.841	25.117	27.671	30.539	33.760	37.379	41.446	46.018	51.159	56.939
20	22.019	24.297	26.870	29.778	33.066	36.786	40.995	45.762	51.160	57.275	64.203
25	28.243	32.030	36.459	41.646	47.727	54.865	63.249	73.106	84.701	98.347	114.41
30	34.785	40.588	47.575	56.085	66.439	79.058	94.461	113.28	136.31	164.49	199.02
40	48.886	60.402	75.401	95.026	120.80	154.76	199.64	259.06	337.89	442.59	581.83
50	64.463	84.579	112.80	152.67	209.35	290.34	406.53	573.77	815.08	1,163.9	1,668.8

Appendix C (concluded)   **Compound sum of an annuity of $1**

Percent

Period	12%	13%	14%	15%	16%	17%	18%	19%	20%	25%	30%
1	1.000	1.000	1.000	1.000	1.000	1.000	1.000	1.000	1.000	1.000	1.000
2	2.120	2.130	2.140	2.150	2.160	2.170	2.180	2.190	2.200	2.250	2.300
3	3.374	3.407	3.440	3.473	3.506	3.539	3.572	3.606	3.640	3.813	3.990
4	4.779	4.850	4.921	4.993	5.066	5.141	5.215	5.291	5.368	5.766	6.187
5	6.353	6.480	6.610	6.742	6.877	7.014	7.154	7.297	7.442	8.207	9.043
6	8.115	8.323	8.536	9.754	8.977	9.207	9.442	0.683	9.930	11.259	12.756
7	10.089	10.405	10.730	11.067	11.414	11.772	12.142	12.523	12.916	15.073	17.583
8	12.300	12.757	13.233	13.727	14.240	14.773	15.327	15.902	16.499	19.842	23.858
9	14.776	15.416	16.085	16.786	17.519	18.285	19.086	19.923	20.799	25.802	32.015
10	17.549	18.420	19.337	20.304	21.321	22.393	23.521	24.701	25.959	33.253	42.619
11	20.655	21.814	23.045	24.349	25.733	27.200	28.755	30.404	32.150	42.566	56.405
12	24.133	25.650	27.271	29.002	30.850	32.824	34.931	37.180	39.581	54.208	74.327
13	28.029	29.985	32.089	34.352	36.786	39.404	42.219	45.244	48.497	68.760	97.625
14	32.393	34.883	37.581	40.505	43.672	47.103	50.818	54.841	59.196	86.949	127.91
15	37.280	40.417	43.842	47.580	51.660	56.110	60.965	66.261	72.035	109.69	167.29
16	42.753	46.672	50.980	55.717	60.925	66.649	72.939	79.850	87.442	138.11	218.47
17	48.884	53.739	59.118	65.075	71.673	78.979	87.068	96.022	105.93	173.64	285.01
18	55.750	61.725	68.394	75.836	84.141	93.406	103.74	115.27	128.12	218.05	371.52
19	63.440	70.749	78.969	88.212	98.603	110.29	123.41	138.17	154.74	273.56	483.97
20	72.052	80.947	91.025	102.44	115.38	130.03	146.63	165.42	186.69	342.95	630.17
25	133.33	155.62	181.87	212.79	249.21	292.11	342.60	402.04	471.98	1,054.8	2,348.80
30	241.33	293.20	356.79	434.75	530.31	647.44	790.95	966.7	1,181.9	3,227.2	8,730.0
40	767.09	1,013.7	1,342.0	1,779.1	2,360.8	3,134.5	4,163.21	5,529.8	7,343.9	30,089.	120,393.
50	2,400.0	3,459.5	4,994.5	7,217.7	10,436.	15,090.	21,813.	31,515.	45,497.	280,256.	165,976.

Source: Maurice Joy, *Introduction to Financial Management* (Homewood, Ill.: Richard D. Irwin, Inc. 1977).

Appendix D   Present value of an annuity of $1, IF_{pva} $A = R \left[\dfrac{1 - \dfrac{1}{(1+i)^n}}{i} \right]$

Percent

Period	1%	2%	3%	4%	5%	6%	7%	8%	9%	10%	11%	12%
1	0.990	0.980	0.971	0.962	0.952	0.943	0.935	0.926	0.917	0.909	0.901	0.893
2	1.970	1.942	1.913	1.886	1.859	1.833	1.808	1.783	1.759	1.736	1.713	1.690
3	2.941	2.884	2.829	2.775	2.723	2.673	2.624	2.577	2.531	2.487	2.444	2.402
4	3.902	3.808	3.717	3.630	3.546	3.465	3.387	3.312	3.240	3.170	3.102	3.037
5	4.853	4.713	4.580	4.452	4.329	4.212	4.100	3.993	3.890	3.791	3.696	3.605
6	5.795	5.601	5.417	5.242	5.076	4.917	4.767	4.623	4.486	4.355	4.231	4.111
7	6.728	6.472	6.230	6.002	5.786	5.582	5.389	5.206	5.033	4.868	4.712	4.564
8	7.652	7.325	7.020	6.733	6.463	6.210	5.971	5.747	5.535	5.335	5.146	4.968
9	8.566	8.162	7.786	7.435	7.108	6.802	6.515	6.247	5.995	5.759	5.537	5.328
10	9.471	8.983	8.530	8.111	7.722	7.360	7.024	6.710	6.418	6.145	5.889	5.650
11	10.368	9.787	9.253	8.760	8.306	7.887	7.499	7.139	6.805	6.495	6.207	5.938
12	11.255	10.575	9.954	9.385	8.863	8.384	7.943	7.536	7.161	6.814	6.492	6.194
13	12.134	11.348	10.635	9.986	9.394	8.853	8.358	7.904	7.487	7.103	6.750	6.424
14	13.004	12.106	11.296	10.563	9.899	9.295	8.745	8.244	7.786	7.367	6.982	6.628
15	13.865	12.849	11.939	11.118	10.380	9.712	9.108	8.559	8.061	7.606	7.191	6.811
16	14.718	13.578	12.561	11.652	10.838	10.106	9.447	8.851	8.313	7.824	7.379	6.974
17	15.562	14.292	13.166	12.166	11.274	10.477	9.763	9.122	8.544	8.022	7.549	7.102
18	16.398	14.992	13.754	12.659	11.690	10.828	10.059	9.372	8.756	8.201	7.702	7.250
19	17.226	15.678	14.324	13.134	12.085	11.158	10.336	9.604	8.950	8.365	7.839	7.366
20	18.046	16.351	14.877	13.590	12.462	11.470	10.594	9.818	9.129	8.514	7.963	7.469
25	22.023	19.523	17.413	15.622	14.094	12.783	11.654	10.675	9.823	9.077	8.422	7.843
30	25.808	22.396	19.600	17.292	15.372	13.765	12.409	11.258	10.274	9.427	8.694	8.055
40	32.835	27.355	23.115	19.793	17.159	15.046	13.332	11.925	10.757	9.779	8.951	8.244
50	39.196	31.424	25.730	21.482	18.256	15.762	13.801	12.233	10.962	9.915	9.042	8.304

Appendix D (concluded)   **Present value of an annuity of $1**

Percent

Period	13%	14%	15%	16%	17%	18%	19%	20%	25%	30%	35%	40%	50%
1	0.885	0.877	0.870	0.862	0.855	0.847	0.840	0.833	0.800	0.769	0.741	0.714	0.667
2	1.668	1.647	1.626	1.605	1.585	1.566	1.547	1.528	1.440	1.361	1.289	1.224	1.111
3	2.361	2.322	2.283	2.246	2.210	2.174	2.140	2.106	1.952	1.816	1.696	1.589	1.407
4	2.974	2.914	2.855	2.798	2.743	2.690	2.639	2.589	2.362	2.166	1.997	1.849	1.605
5	3.517	3.433	3.352	3.274	3.199	3.127	3.058	2.991	2.689	2.436	2.220	2.035	1.737
6	3.998	3.889	3.784	3.685	3.589	3.498	3.410	3.326	2.951	2.643	2.385	2.168	1.824
7	4.423	4.288	4.160	4.039	3.922	3.812	3.706	3.605	3.161	2.802	2.508	2.263	1.883
8	4.799	4.639	4.487	4.344	4.207	4.078	3.954	3.837	3.329	2.925	2.598	2.331	1.922
9	5.132	4.946	4.772	4.607	4.451	4.303	4.163	4.031	3.463	3.019	2.665	2.379	1.948
10	5.426	5.216	5.019	4.833	4.659	4.494	4.339	4.192	3.571	3.092	2.715	2.414	1.965
11	5.687	5.453	5.234	5.029	4.836	4.656	4.486	4.327	3.656	3.147	2.752	2.438	1.977
12	5.918	5.660	5.421	5.197	4.988	4.793	4.611	4.439	3.725	3.190	2.779	2.456	1.985
13	6.122	5.842	5.583	5.342	5.118	4.910	4.715	4.533	3.780	3.223	2.799	2.469	1.990
14	6.302	6.002	5.724	5.468	5.229	5.008	4.802	4.611	3.824	3.249	2.814	2.478	1.993
15	6.462	6.142	5.847	5.575	5.324	5.092	4.876	4.675	3.859	3.268	2.825	2.484	1.995
16	6.604	6.265	5.954	5.668	5.405	5.162	4.938	4.730	3.887	3.283	2.834	2.489	1.997
17	6.729	6.373	6.047	5.749	5.475	5.222	4.988	4.775	3.910	3.295	2.840	2.492	1.998
18	6.840	6.467	6.128	5.818	5.534	5.273	5.033	4.812	3.928	3.304	2.844	2.494	1.999
19	6.938	6.550	6.198	5.877	5.584	5.316	5.070	4.843	3.942	3.311	2.848	2.496	1.999
20	7.025	6.623	6.259	5.929	5.628	5.353	5.101	4.870	3.954	3.316	2.850	2.497	1.999
25	7.330	6.873	6.464	6.097	5.766	5.467	5.195	4.948	3.985	3.329	2.856	2.499	2.000
30	7.496	7.003	6.566	6.177	5.829	5.517	5.235	4.979	3.995	3.332	2.857	2.500	2.000
40	7.634	7.105	6.642	6.233	5.871	5.548	5.258	4.997	3.999	3.333	2.857	2.500	2.000
50	7.675	7.133	6.661	6.246	5.880	5.554	5.262	4.999	4.000	3.333	2.857	2.500	2.000

Source: Maurice Joy, *Introduction to Financial Management* (homewood, Ill.: Richard D. Irwin, Inc., 1977).

Appendix E Tables of squares and square roots

N	N^2	$\sqrt{N}$	$\sqrt{10N}$	N	N^2	$\sqrt{N}$	$\sqrt{10N}$
				50	2 500	7.071 068	22.36068
1	1	1.000 000	3.162 278	51	2 601	7.141 428	22.58318
2	4	1.414 214	4.472 136	52	2 704	7.211 103	22.80351
3	9	1.732 051	5.477 226	53	2 809	7.280 110	23.02173
4	16	2.000 000	6.324 555	54	2 916	7.348 469	23.23790
5	25	2.236 068	7.071 068	55	3 025	7.416 198	23.45208
6	36	2.449 490	7.745 967	56	3 136	7.483 315	23.66432
7	49	2.645 751	8.366 600	57	3 249	7.549 834	23.87467
8	64	2.828 427	8.944 272	58	3 364	7.615 773	24.08319
9	81	3.000 000	9.486 833	59	3 481	7.681 146	24.28992
10	100	3.162 278	10.00000	60	3 600	7.745 967	24.49490
11	121	3.316 625	10.48809	61	3 721	7.810 250	24.69818
12	144	3.464 102	10.95445	62	3 844	7.874 008	24.89980
13	169	3.605 551	11.40175	63	3 969	7.937 254	25.09980
14	196	3.741 657	11.83216	64	4 096	8.000 000	25.29822
15	225	3.872 983	12.24745	65	4 225	8.062 258	25.49510
16	256	4.000 000	12.64911	66	4 356	8.124 038	25.69047
17	289	4.123 106	13.03840	67	4 489	8.185 353	25.88436
18	324	4.242 641	13.41641	68	4 624	8.246 211	26.07681
19	361	4.358 899	13.78405	69	4 761	8.306 824	26.26785
20	400	4.472 136	14.14214	70	4 900	8.366 600	26.45751
21	441	4.582 576	14.49138	71	5 041	8.426 150	26.64583
22	484	4.690 416	14.83240	72	5 184	8.485 281	26.83282
23	529	4.795 832	15.16575	73	5 329	8.544 004	27.01851
24	576	4.898 979	15.49193	74	5 476	8.602 325	27.20294
25	625	5.000 000	15.81139	75	5 625	8.660 254	27.38613
26	676	5.099 020	16.12452	76	5 776	8.717 798	27.56810
27	729	5.196 152	16.43168	77	5 929	8.774 964	27.74887
28	784	5.291 503	16.73320	78	6 084	8.831 761	27.92848
29	841	5.385 165	17.02939	79	6 241	8.888 194	28.10694
30	900	5.477 226	17.32051	80	6 400	8.944 272	28.28427
31	961	5.567 764	17.60682	81	6 561	9.000 000	28.46050
32	1 024	5.656 854	17.88854	82	6 724	9.055 385	28.63564
33	1 089	5.744 563	18.16590	83	6 889	9.110 434	28.80972
34	1 156	5.830 952	18.43909	84	7 056	9.165 151	28.98275
35	1 225	5.916 080	18.70829	85	7 225	9.219 544	29.15476
36	1 296	6.000 000	18.97367	86	7 396	9.273 618	29.32576
37	1 369	6.082 763	19.23538	87	7 569	9.327 379	29.49576
38	1 444	6.164 414	19.49359	88	7 744	9.380 832	29.66479
39	1 521	6.244 998	19.74842	89	7 921	9.433 981	29.83287
40	1 600	6.324 555	20.00000	90	8 100	9.486 833	30.00000
41	1 681	6.403 124	20.24846	91	8 281	9.539 392	30.16621
42	1 764	6.480 741	20.49390	92	8 464	9.591 663	30.33150
43	1 849	6.557 439	20.73644	93	8 649	9.643 651	30.49590
44	1 936	6.633 250	20.97618	94	8 836	9.695 360	30.65942
45	2 025	6.708 204	21.21320	95	9 025	9.746 794	30.82207
46	2 116	6.782 330	21.44761	96	9 216	9.797 959	30.98387
47	2 209	6.855 655	21.67948	97	9 409	9.848 858	31.14482
48	2 304	6.928 203	21.90890	98	9 604	9.899 495	31.30495
49	2 401	7.000 000	22.13594	99	9 801	9.949 874	31.46427
50	2 500	7.071 068	22.36068	100	10 000	10.00000	31.62278

N	N^2	$\sqrt{N}$	$\sqrt{10N}$	N	N^2	$\sqrt{N}$	$\sqrt{10N}$
100	10 000	10.00000	31.62278	150	22 500	12.24745	38.72983
101	10 201	10.04988	31.78050	151	22 801	12.28821	38.85872
102	10 404	10.09950	31.93744	152	23 104	12.32883	39.98718
103	10 609	10.14889	32.09361	153	23 409	12.36932	39.11521
104	10 816	10.19804	32.24903	154	23 716	12.40967	39.24283
105	11 025	10.24695	32.40370	155	24 025	12.44990	39.37004
106	11 236	10.29563	32.55764	156	24 336	12.45000	39.49684
107	11 449	10.34408	32.71085	157	24 649	12.52996	39.62323
108	11 664	10.39230	32.86335	158	24 964	12.56981	39.74921
109	11 881	10.44031	33.01515	159	25 281	12.60952	39.87480
110	12 100	10.48809	33.16625	160	25 600	12.64911	40.00000
111	12 321	10.53565	33.31666	161	25 921	12.68858	40.12481
112	12 544	10.58301	33.46640	162	26 244	12.72792	40.24922
113	12 769	10.63015	33.61547	163	26 569	12.76715	40.37326
114	12 996	10.67708	33.76389	164	26 896	12.80625	40.49691
115	13 225	10.72381	33.91165	165	27 225	12.84523	40.62019
116	13 456	10.77033	34.05877	166	27 556	12.88410	40.74310
117	13 689	10.81665	34.20526	167	27 889	12.92285	40.86563
118	13 924	10.86278	34.35113	168	28 224	12.96148	40.98780
119	14 161	10.90871	34.49638	169	28 561	13.00000	41.10961
120	14 400	10.95445	34.64102	170	28 900	13.03840	41.23106
121	14 641	11.00000	34.78505	171	29 241	13.07670	41.35215
122	14 884	11.04536	34.92850	172	29 584	13.11488	41.47288
123	15 129	11.09054	35.07136	173	29 929	13.15295	41.59327
124	15 376	11.13553	35.21363	174	30 276	13.19091	41.71331
125	15 625	11.18034	35.35534	175	30 625	13.22876	41.83300
126	15 876	11.22497	35.49648	176	30 976	13.26650	41.95235
127	16 129	11.26943	35.63706	177	31 329	13.30413	42.07137
128	16 384	11.31371	35.77709	178	31 684	13.34166	42.19005
129	16 641	11.35782	35.91657	179	32 041	13.37909	42.30839
130	16 900	11.40175	36.05551	180	32 400	13.41641	42.42641
131	17 161	11.44552	36.19392	181	32 761	13.45362	42.54409
132	17 424	11.48913	36.33180	182	33 124	13.49074	42.66146
133	17 689	11.53256	36.46917	183	33 489	13.52775	42.77850
134	17 956	11.57584	36.60601	184	33 856	13.56466	42.89522
135	18 225	11.61895	36.74235	185	34 225	13.60147	43.01163
136	18 496	11.66190	36.87818	186	34 596	13.63818	43.12772
137	18 769	11.70470	37.01351	187	34 969	13.67479	43.24350
138	19 044	11.74734	37.14835	188	35 344	13.71131	43.35897
139	19 321	11.78983	37.28270	189	35 721	13.74773	43.47413
140	19 600	11.83216	37.41657	190	36 100	13.78405	43.58899
141	19 881	11.87434	37.54997	191	36 481	13.82027	43.70355
142	20 164	11.91638	37.68289	192	36 864	13.85641	43.81780
143	20 449	11.95826	37.81534	193	37 249	13.89244	43.93177
144	20 736	12.00000	37.94733	194	37 636	13.92839	44.04543
145	21 025	12.04159	38.07887	195	38 025	13.96424	44.15880
146	21 316	12.08305	38.20995	196	38 416	14.00000	44.27189
147	21 609	12.12436	38.34058	197	38 809	14.03567	44.38468
148	21 904	12.16553	38.47077	198	39 204	14.07125	44.49719
149	22 201	12.20656	38.60052	199	39 601	14.10674	44.60942
150	22 500	12.24745	38.72983	200	40 000	14.14214	44.72136

Appendix E (*continued*)   Tables of squares and square roots

N	N²	√N	√10N	N	N²	√N	√10N
200	40 000	14.14214	44.72136	250	62 500	15.81139	50.00000
201	40 401	14.17745	44.83302	251	63 001	15.84298	50.09990
202	40 804	14.21267	44.94441	252	63 504	15.87451	50.19960
203	41 209	14.24781	45.05552	253	64 009	15.90597	50.29911
204	41 616	14.28296	45.16636	254	64 516	15.93738	50.39841
205	42 025	14.31782	45.27693	255	65 025	15.96872	50.49752
206	42 436	14.35270	45.38722	256	65 536	16.00000	50.59644
207	42 849	14.38749	45.49725	257	66 049	16.03122	50.69517
208	43 264	14.42221	45.60702	258	66 564	16.06238	50.79370
209	43 681	14.45683	45.71652	259	67 081	16.09348	50.89204
210	44 100	14.49138	45.82576	260	67 600	16.12452	50.99020
211	44 521	14.52584	45.93474	261	68 121	16.15549	51.08816
212	44 944	14.56022	46.04346	262	68 644	16.18641	51.18594
213	45 369	14.59452	46.15192	263	69 169	16.21727	51.28353
214	45 796	14.62874	46.26013	264	69 696	16.24808	51.38093
215	46 225	14.66288	46.36809	265	70 225	16.27882	51.47815
216	46 656	14.69694	46.47580	266	70 756	16.30951	51.57519
217	47 089	14.73092	46.58326	267	71 289	16.34013	51.67204
218	47 524	14.76482	46.69047	268	71 824	16.37071	51.76872
219	47 961	14.79865	46.79744	269	72 361	16.40122	51.86521
220	48 400	14.83240	46.90415	270	72 900	16.43168	51.96152
221	48 841	14.86607	47.01064	271	73 441	16.46208	52.05766
222	49 284	14.89966	47.11688	272	73 984	16.49242	52.15362
223	49 729	14.93318	47.22288	273	74 529	16.52271	52.24940
224	50 176	14.96663	47.32864	274	75 076	16.55295	52.34501
225	50 625	15.00000	47.43416	275	75 625	16.58312	52.44044
226	51 076	15.03330	47.53946	276	76 176	16.61325	52.53570
227	51 529	15.06652	47.64452	277	76 729	16.64332	52.63079
228	51 984	15.09967	47.74935	278	77 284	16.67333	52.72571
229	52 441	15.13275	47.85394	279	77 841	16.70329	52.82045
230	52 900	15.16575	47.95832	280	78 400	16.73320	52.91503
231	53 361	15.19868	48.06246	281	78 961	16.76305	53.00943
232	53 824	15.23155	48.16638	282	79 524	16.79286	53.10367
233	54 289	15.26434	48.27007	283	80 089	16.82260	53.19774
234	54 756	15.29706	48.37355	284	80 656	16.85230	53.29165
235	55 225	15.32971	48.47680	285	81 225	16.88194	53.38539
236	55 696	15.36229	48.57983	286	81 796	16.91153	53.47897
237	56 169	15.39480	48.68265	287	82 369	16.94107	53.57238
238	56 644	15.42725	48.78524	288	82 944	16.97056	53.66563
239	57 121	15.45962	48.88763	289	83 521	17.00000	53.75872
240	57 600	15.49193	48.98979	290	84 100	17.02939	53.85165
241	58 081	15.52417	49.09175	291	84 681	17.05872	53.94442
242	58 564	15.55635	49.19350	292	85 264	17.08801	54.03702
243	59 049	15.58846	49.29503	293	85 849	17.11724	54.12947
244	59 536	15.62050	49.39636	294	86 436	17.14643	54.22177
245	60 025	15.65248	49.49747	295	87 025	17.17556	54.31390
246	60 516	15.68439	49.59839	296	87 616	17.20465	54.40588
247	61 009	15.71623	49.69909	297	88 209	17.23369	54.49771
248	61 504	15.74802	49.79960	298	88 804	17.26268	54.58938
249	62 001	15.77973	49.89990	299	89 401	17.29162	54.68089
250	62 500	15.81139	50.00000	300	90 000	17.32051	54.77226

N	N²	√N	√10N	N	N²	√N	√10N
300	90 000	17.32051	54.77226	350	122 500	18.70829	59.16080
301	90 601	17.34935	54.86347	351	123 201	18.73499	59.24525
302	91 204	17.37815	54.95453	352	123 904	18.76166	59.32959
303	91 809	17.40690	55.04544	353	124 609	18.78829	59.41380
304	92 416	17.43560	55.13620	354	125 316	18.81489	59.49790
305	93 025	17.46425	55.22681	355	126 025	18.84144	59.58188
306	93 636	17.49288	55.31727	356	126 736	18.86796	59.66574
307	94 249	17.52142	55.40758	357	127 449	18.89444	59.74948
308	94 864	17.54993	55.49775	358	128 164	18.92089	59.83310
309	95 481	17.57840	55.58777	359	128 881	18.94730	59.91661
310	96 100	17.60682	55.67764	360	129 600	18.97367	60.00000
311	96 721	17.63519	55.76737	361	130 321	19.00000	60.08328
312	97 344	17.66352	55.85696	362	131 044	19.02630	60.16644
313	97 969	17.69181	55.94640	363	131 769	19.05256	60.24948
314	98 596	17.72005	56.03670	364	132 496	19.07878	60.33241
315	99 225	17.74824	56.12486	365	133 225	19.10497	60.41523
316	99 856	17.77639	56.21388	366	133 956	19.13113	60.49793
317	100 489	17.80449	56.30275	367	134 689	19.15724	60.58052
318	101 124	17.83255	56.39149	368	135 424	19.18333	60.66300
319	101 761	17.86057	56.48008	369	136 161	19.20937	60.74537
320	102 400	17.88854	56.56854	370	136 900	19.23538	60.82763
321	103 041	17.91647	56.65686	371	137 641	19.26136	60.90977
322	103 684	17.94436	56.74504	372	138 384	19.28730	60.99180
323	104 329	17.97220	56.83309	373	139 129	19.31321	61.07373
324	104 976	18.00000	56.92100	374	139 876	19.33908	61.15554
325	105 625	18.02776	57.00877	375	140 625	19.36492	61.23724
326	106 276	18.05547	57.09641	376	141 376	19.39072	61.31884
327	106 929	18.08314	57.18391	377	142 129	19.41649	61.40033
328	107 584	18.11077	57.27128	378	142 884	19.44222	61.48170
329	108 241	18.13836	57.35852	379	143 641	19.46792	61.56298
330	108 900	18.16590	57.44563	380	144 000	19.49359	61.64414
331	109 561	18.19341	57.53260	381	145 161	19.51922	61.72520
332	110 224	18.22087	57.61944	382	145 924	19.54483	61.80615
333	110 889	18.24829	57.70615	383	146 689	19.57039	61.88699
334	111 556	18.27567	57.79273	384	147 456	19.59592	61.96773
335	112 225	18.30301	57. 87918	385	148 225	19.62142	62.04837
336	112 896	18.33030	57.96551	386	148 996	19.64688	62.12890
337	113 569	18.35756	58.05170	387	149 769	19.67232	62.20932
338	114 224	18.38478	57.13777	388	150 544	19.69772	62.28965
339	114 921	18.41195	58.22371	389	151 321	19.72308	62.36986
340	115 600	18.43909	58.30952	390	152 100	19.74842	62.44998
341	116 281	18.46619	58.39521	391	152 881	19.77372	62.52999
342	116 694	18.49324	58.48077	392	153 664	19.79899	62.60990
343	117 649	18.52026	58.56620	393	154 449	19.82423	62.68971
344	118 336	18.54724	58.65151	394	155 236	19.84943	62.76942
345	119 025	18.57418	58.73670	395	156 025	19.87461	62.84903
346	119 716	18.60108	58.82176	396	156 816	19.89975	62.92853
347	120 409	18.62794	58.90671	397	157 609	19.92486	63.00794
348	121 104	18.65476	58.99152	398	158 404	19.94994	63.08724
349	121 801	18.68154	59.07622	399	159 201	19.97498	63.16645
350	122 500	18.70829	59.16080	400	160 000	20.00000	63.24555

Appendix E (*continued*)   Tables of squares and square roots

N	N²	√N	√10N	N	N²	√N	√10N
400	160 000	20.00000	63.24555	450	202 500	21.21320	67.08204
401	160 801	20.02498	63.32456	451	203 401	21.23676	67.15653
402	161 604	20.04994	63.40347	452	204 304	21.26029	67.23095
403	162 409	20.07486	63.48228	453	205 209	21.28380	67.30527
404	163 216	20.09975	63.56099	454	206 116	21.30728	67.37952
405	164 025	20.12461	63.63961	455	207 025	21.33073	67.45369
406	164 836	20.14944	63.71813	456	207 936	21.35416	67.52777
407	165 649	20.17424	63.79655	457	208 849	21.37756	67.60178
408	166 464	20.19901	63.87488	458	209 764	21.40093	67.67570
409	167 281	20.22375	63.95311	459	210 681	21.42429	67.74954
410	168 100	20.24846	64.03124	460	211 600	21.44761	67.82330
411	168 921	20.27313	64.10928	461	212 521	21.47091	67.89698
412	169 744	20.29778	64.18723	462	213 444	21.49419	67.97058
413	170 569	20.32240	64.26508	463	214 369	21.51743	68.04410
414	171 396	20.34699	64.34283	464	215 296	21.54066	68.11755
415	172 225	20.37155	64.42049	465	216 225	21.56386	68.19091
416	173 056	20.39608	64.49806	466	217 156	21.58703	68.26419
417	173 889	20.42058	64.57554	467	218 089	21.61018	68.33740
418	174 724	20.44505	64.65292	468	219 024	21.63331	68.41053
419	175 561	20.46949	64.73021	469	219 961	21.65641	68.48357
420	176 400	20.49390	64.80741	470	220 900	21.67948	68.55655
421	177 241	20.51828	64.88451	471	221 841	21.70253	68.62944
422	178 084	20.54264	64.96153	472	222 784	21.72556	68.70226
423	178 929	20.56696	65.03845	473	223 729	21.74856	68.77500
424	179 776	20.59126	65.11528	474	224 676	21.77154	68.84706
425	180 625	20.61553	65.19202	475	225 625	21.79449	68.92024
426	181 476	20.63977	65.26808	476	226 576	21.81742	68.99275
427	182 329	20.66398	65.34524	477	227 529	21.84033	69.06519
428	183 184	20.68816	65.42171	478	228 484	21.86321	69.13754
429	184 041	20.71232	65.49809	479	229 441	21.88607	69.20983
430	184 900	20.73644	65.57439	480	230 400	21.90800	69.28203
431	185 761	20.76054	65.65059	481	231 361	21.93171	69.35416
432	186 624	20.78461	65.72671	482	232 324	21.95450	69.42622
433	187 489	20.80865	65.80274	483	233 280	21.97726	69.50820
434	188 356	20.83267	65.87868	484	234 256	22.00000	69.57011
435	189 225	20.85665	65.95453	485	235 225	22.02272	69.64194
436	190 096	20.88061	66.03030	486	236 196	22.04541	69.71370
437	190 969	20.90454	66.10598	487	237 169	22.06808	69.78530
438	191 844	20.92845	66.18157	488	238 144	22.09072	69.85700
439	192 721	20.95233	66.25708	489	239 121	22.11334	69.92853
440	193 600	20.97618	66.33250	490	240 100	22.13594	70.00000
441	194 481	21.00000	66.40783	491	241 081	22.15852	70.07139
442	195 364	21.02380	66.48308	492	242 064	22.18107	70.14271
443	196 249	21.04757	66.55825	493	243 049	22.20360	70.21396
444	197 136	21.07131	66.63332	494	244 036	22.22611	70.28513
445	198 025	21.09502	66.70832	495	245 025	22.24860	70.35624
446	198 916	21.11871	66.78323	496	246 016	22.27106	70.42727
447	199 809	21.14237	66.85806	497	247 009	22.29350	70.49823
448	200 704	21.16601	66.93280	498	248 004	22.31519	70.56912
449	201 601	21.18962	67.00746	499	249 001	22.33831	70.63993
450	202 500	21.21320	67.08204	500	250 000	22.36068	70.71068

N	N²	√N	√10N	N	N²	√N	√10N
500	250 000	22.36068	70.71068	550	302 500	23.45208	74.16198
501	251 001	22.38303	70.78135	551	303 601	23.47339	74.22937
502	252 004	22.40536	70.85196	552	304 704	23.49468	74.29670
503	253 009	22.42766	70.92249	553	305 809	23.51595	74.36397
504	254 016	22.44994	70.99296	554	306 916	23.53720	74.43118
505	255 025	22.47221	71.06335	555	308 025	23.55844	74.49832
506	256 036	22.49444	71.13368	556	309 136	23.57965	74.56541
507	257 049	22.51666	71.20393	557	310 249	23.60085	74.63243
508	258 064	22.53886	71.27412	558	311 364	23.62202	74.69940
509	259 081	22.56103	71.34424	559	312 481	23.64318	74.76630
510	260 100	22.58318	71.41428	560	313 600	23.66432	74.83315
511	261 121	22.60531	71.48426	561	314 721	23.68544	74.89993
512	262 144	22.62742	71.55418	562	315 844	23.70654	74.96666
513	263 169	22.64950	71.62402	563	316 969	23.72762	75.03333
514	264 196	22.67157	71.69379	564	318 096	23.74686	75.09993
515	265 225	22.69361	71.76350	565	319 225	23.76973	75.16648
516	266 256	22.71563	71.83314	566	320 356	23.79075	75.23297
517	267 289	22.73763	71.90271	567	321 489	23.81176	75.29940
518	268 324	22.75961	71.97222	568	322 624	23.83275	75.36577
519	269 361	22.78157	72.04165	569	323 761	23.85372	75.43209
520	270 400	22.80351	72.11103	570	324 900	23.87467	75.49834
521	271 441	22.82542	72.18033	571	326 041	23.89561	75.56454
522	272 484	22.84732	72.24957	572	327 184	23.91652	75.63068
523	273 529	22.86919	72.31874	573	328 329	23.93742	75.69676
524	274 576	22.89105	72.38784	574	329 476	23.95830	75.76279
525	275 625	22.91288	72.45688	575	330 625	23.97916	75.82875
526	276 676	22.93469	72.52586	576	331 776	24.00000	75.89466
527	277 729	22.95648	72.59477	577	332 929	24.02082	75.96052
528	278 784	22.97825	72.66361	578	334 084	24.04163	76.02631
529	279 841	23.00000	72.73239	579	335 241	24.06242	76.09205
530	280 900	23.02173	72.80110	580	336 400	24.08319	76.15773
531	281 961	23.04344	72.86975	581	337 561	24.10394	76.22336
532	283 024	23.06513	72.93833	582	338 724	24.12468	76.28892
533	284 089	23.08679	73.00685	583	339 889	24.14539	76.35444
534	285 156	23.10844	73.07530	584	341 056	24.16609	76.41989
535	286 225	23.13007	73.14369	585	342 225	24.18677	76.48529
536	287 296	23.15167	73.21202	586	343 396	24.20744	76.55064
537	288 369	23.17326	73.28028	587	344 569	24.22808	76.61593
538	289 444	23.19483	73.34848	588	345 744	24.24871	76.68116
539	290 521	23.21637	73.41662	589	346 921	24.26932	76.74634
540	291 600	23.23790	73.48469	590	348 100	24.28992	76.81146
541	292 681	23.25941	73.55270	591	349 281	24.31049	76.87652
542	293 764	23.28089	73.62056	592	350 464	24.33105	76.94154
543	294 849	23.30236	73.68853	593	351 649	24.35159	77.00649
544	295 936	23.32381	73.75636	594	352 836	24.37212	77.07140
545	297 025	23.34524	73.82412	595	354 025	24.39262	77.13624
546	298 116	23.36664	73.89181	596	355 216	24.41311	77.20104
547	299 209	23.38803	73.95945	597	356 409	24.43358	77.26578
548	300 304	23.40940	74.02702	598	357 604	24.45404	77.33046
549	301 401	23.43075	74.09453	599	358 801	24.47448	77.39509
550	302 500	23.45208	74.16198	600	360 000	24.49490	77.45967

Appendix E (*continued*)   Tables of squares and square roots

N	N²	√N	√10N	N	N²	√N	√10N
600	360 000	24.49490	77.45967	650	422 500	25.49510	80.62258
601	361 201	24.51530	77.52419	651	423 801	25.51470	80.68457
602	362 404	24.53569	77.58868	652	425 409	25.53240	80.80130
603	363 609	24.55606	77.65307	653	426 409	25.55386	80.80842
604	364 816	24.57641	77.71744	654	427 716	25.57342	80.87027
605	366 025	24.59675	77.78175	655	429 025	25.59297	80.93207
606	367 736	24.61707	77.84600	656	430 336	25.61250	80.99383
607	368 449	24.63737	77.91020	657	431 649	25.63201	81.05554
608	369 664	24.65766	77.97435	658	432 964	25.65151	81.11720
609	370 881	24.67793	78.03845	659	434 281	25.67100	81.17881
610	372 100	24.69818	78.10250	660	435 600	25.69047	81.24038
611	373 321	24.71841	78.16649	661	436 921	25.70992	81.30191
612	374 544	24.73863	78.23043	662	438 244	25.72936	81.36338
613	375 769	24.75884	78.29432	663	439 569	25.74879	81.42481
614	376 996	24.77902	78.35815	664	440 896	25.76820	81.48620
615	378 225	24.79919	78.42194	665	442 225	25.78759	81.54753
616	379 456	24.81935	78.48567	666	443 556	25.80698	81.60882
617	380 689	24.83948	78.54935	667	444 889	25.82634	81.67007
618	381 924	24.85961	78.61298	668	446 224	25.84570	81.73127
619	383 161	24.87971	78.67655	669	447 561	25.86503	81.79242
620	384 400	24.89980	78.74008	670	448 900	25.88436	81.85353
621	385 641	24.91987	78.80355	671	450 241	25.90367	81.91459
622	386 884	24.93993	78.86698	672	451 584	25.92296	81.97561
623	388 129	24.95997	78.93035	673	452 929	25.94224	82.03658
624	389 376	24.97999	78.99367	674	454 276	25.96151	82.09750
625	390 625	25.00000	79.05694	675	455 625	25.98076	82.15838
626	391 876	25.01999	79.12016	676	456 976	26.00000	82.21922
627	393 129	25.03997	79.18333	677	458 329	26.01922	82.28001
628	394 384	25.05993	79.24645	678	459 684	26.03843	82.34076
629	395 641	25.07987	79.30952	679	461 041	26.05763	82.40146
630	396 900	25.09980	79.37254	680	462 400	26.07681	82.46211
631	398 161	25.11971	79.43551	681	463 761	26.09598	82.52272
632	399 424	25.13961	79.49843	682	465 124	26.11513	82.58329
633	400 689	25.15949	79.56130	683	466 489	26.13427	82.64381
634	401 956	25.17936	79.62412	684	467 856	26.15339	82.70429
635	403 225	25.19921	79.68689	685	469 225	26.17250	82.76473
636	404 496	25.21904	79.74961	686	470 596	26.19160	82.82512
637	405 769	25.23886	79.81228	687	471 969	26.21068	82.88546
638	407 044	25.25866	79.87490	688	473 344	26.22975	82.94577
639	408 321	25.27845	79.93748	689	474 721	26.24881	83.00602
640	409 600	25.29822	80.00000	690	476 100	26.26785	83.06624
641	410 881	25.31798	80.06248	691	477 481	26.28688	83.12641
642	412 164	25.33772	80.12490	692	478 864	26.30589	83.18654
643	413 449	25.35744	80.18728	693	480 249	26.32489	83.24662
644	414 736	25.37716	80.24961	694	481 636	26.34388	83.30666
645	416 025	25.39685	80.31189	695	483 025	26.36285	83.36666
646	417 316	25.41653	80.37413	696	484 416	26.38181	83.42661
647	418 609	25.43619	80.43631	697	485 809	26.40076	83.48653
648	419 904	25.45584	80.49845	698	487 204	26.41969	83.54639
649	421 201	25.47548	80.56054	699	488 601	26.43861	83.60622
650	422 500	25.49510	80.62258	700	490 000	26.45751	83.66600

N	N²	√N	√10N	N	N²	√N	√10N
700	490 000	26.45751	83.66600	750	562 500	27.38613	86.60254
701	491 401	26.47640	83.72574	751	564 001	27.40438	86.66026
702	492 804	26.49528	83.78544	752	565 504	27.42262	86.71793
703	494 209	26.51415	83.84510	753	567 009	27.44085	86.77557
704	495 616	26.53300	83.90471	754	568 516	27.45906	86.83317
705	497 025	26.55184	83.96428	755	570 025	27.47726	86.89074
706	498 436	26.57066	84.02381	756	571 536	27.49545	86.94826
707	499 849	26.58947	84.08329	757	573 049	27.51363	87.00575
708	501 264	26.60827	84.14274	758	574 564	27.53180	87.06320
709	502 681	26.62705	84.20214	759	576 081	27.54995	87.12061
710	504 100	26.64583	84.26150	760	577 600	27.56810	87.17798
711	505 521	26.66458	84.32082	761	579 121	27.58623	87.23531
712	506 944	26.68333	84.38009	762	580 644	27.60435	87.29261
713	508 369	26.70206	84.43933	763	582 169	27.62245	87.34987
714	509 796	26.72078	84.49852	764	583 696	27.64055	87.40709
715	511 225	26.73948	84.55767	765	585 225	27.65863	87.46428
716	512 656	26.75818	84.61578	766	586 756	27.67671	87.52143
717	514 089	26.77686	84.67585	767	588 289	27.69476	87.57854
718	515 524	26.79552	84.73488	768	589 824	27.71281	87.63561
719	516 961	26.81418	84.79387	769	591 361	27.73085	87.69265
720	518 400	26.83282	84.85281	770	592 900	27.74887	87.74964
721	519 841	26.85144	84.91172	771	594 441	27.76689	87.80661
722	521 284	26.87006	84.97058	772	595 984	27.78489	87.86353
723	522 729	26.88866	85.02941	773	597 529	27.80288	87.92042
724	524 176	26.90725	85.08819	774	599 076	27.82086	87.97727
725	525 625	26.92582	85.14693	775	600 625	27.83882	88.03408
726	527 076	26.94439	85.20563	776	602 176	27.85678	88.09086
727	528 529	26.96294	85.26429	777	603 729	27.87472	88.14760
728	529 984	26.98148	85.32294	778	605 284	27.89265	88.20431
729	531 411	27.00000	85.38150	779	606 841	27.91057	88.26098
730	532 900	27.01851	85.44004	780	608 400	27.92848	88.31761
731	534 361	27.03701	85.49854	781	609 961	27.94638	88.37420
732	535 824	27.05550	85.55700	782	611 524	27.96426	88.43076
733	537 289	27.07397	85.61542	783	613 089	27.98214	88.48729
734	538 756	27.09243	85.67380	784	614 656	28.00000	88.54377
735	540 225	27.11088	85.73214	785	616 225	28.01785	88.60023
736	541 696	27.12932	85.79044	786	617 796	28.03569	88.65664
737	543 169	27.14774	85.84870	787	619 369	28.05352	88.71302
738	544 644	27.16616	85.90693	788	620 944	28.07134	88.76936
739	546 121	27.18455	85.96511	789	622 521	28.08914	88.82567
740	547 600	27.20294	86.02325	790	624 100	28.10694	88.88194
741	549 081	27.22132	86.08136	791	625 681	28.12472	88.93818
742	550 564	27.23968	86.13942	792	627 264	28.14249	88.99438
743	552 049	27.25803	86.20745	793	628 849	28.16026	89.05055
744	553 536	27.27636	86.25543	794	630 436	28.17801	89.10668
745	555 025	27.29469	86.31338	795	632 025	28.19574	89.16277
746	556 516	27.31300	86.37129	796	633 616	28.21347	89.21883
747	558 009	27.33130	86.42916	797	635 209	28.23119	89.27486
748	559 504	27.34959	86.48609	798	636 804	28.24889	89.33085
749	561 001	27.36786	86.54479	799	638 401	28.26659	89.38680
750	562 500	27.38613	86.60254	800	640 000	28.28427	89.44272

Appendix E (*continued*)   **Tables of squares and square roots**

N	N²	√N	√10N	N	N²	√N	√10N
800	640 000	28.28427	89.44272	850	722 500	29.15476	92.19544
801	641 601	28.30194	89.49860	851	724 201	29.17190	92.24966
802	643 204	28.31960	89.55445	852	725 904	29.18904	92.30385
803	644 809	28.33725	89.61027	853	727 609	29.20616	92.35800
804	646 416	28.35489	89.66605	854	729 316	29.22328	92.41212
805	648 025	28.37252	89.72179	855	731 025	29.24038	92.46621
806	649 636	28.39014	89.77750	856	732 736	29.25748	92.52027
807	651 249	28.40775	89.83318	857	734 449	29.27456	92.57429
808	652 864	28.42534	89.88882	858	736 164	29.29164	92.62829
809	654 481	28.44293	89.94443	859	737 881	29.30870	92.68225
810	656 100	28.46050	90.00000	860	739 600	29.32576	92.73618
811	657 721	28.47806	90.05554	861	741 321	29.34280	92.79009
812	659 344	28.49561	90.11104	862	743 044	29.35984	92.84396
813	660 969	28.51315	90.16651	863	744 769	29.37686	92.89779
814	662 596	28.53069	90.22195	864	746 496	29.39388	92.95160
815	664 225	28.54820	90.27735	865	748 225	29.41088	93.00538
816	665 856	28.56571	90.33272	866	749 956	29.42788	93.05912
817	667 489	28.58321	90.38805	867	751 689	29.44486	93.11283
818	669 124	28.60070	90.44335	868	753 424	29.46184	93.16652
819	670 761	28.61818	90.49862	869	755 161	29.47881	93.22017
820	672 400	28.63564	90.55385	870	756 900	29.49576	93.27379
821	674 041	28.65310	90.60905	871	758 641	29.51271	93.32738
822	675 684	28.67054	90.66422	872	760 384	29.52965	93.38094
823	677 329	28.68798	90.71935	873	762 129	29.54657	93.43447
824	678 976	28.70540	90.77445	874	763 876	29.56349	93.48797
825	680 625	28.72281	90.82951	875	765 625	29.58040	93.54143
826	682 276	28.74022	90.88454	876	767 376	29.59730	93.59487
827	683 929	28.75761	90.93954	877	769 129	29.61419	93.64828
828	685 584	28.77499	90.99451	878	770 884	29.63106	93.70165
829	687 241	28.79236	91.04944	879	772 641	29.64793	93.75500
830	688 900	28.80972	91.10434	880	774 400	29.66479	93.80832
831	690 561	28.82707	91.15920	881	776 161	29.68164	93.86160
832	692 224	28.84441	91.21403	882	777 924	29.69848	93.91486
833	693 889	28.86174	91.26883	883	779 689	29.71532	93.96808
834	695 556	28.87906	91.32360	884	781 456	29.73214	94.02027
835	697 225	28.89637	91.37833	885	783 225	29.74895	94.07444
836	698 896	28.91366	91.43304	886	784 996	29.76575	94.12757
837	700 569	28.93095	91.48770	887	786 769	29.78255	94.10868
838	702 244	28.94823	91.54234	888	788 544	29.79933	94.23375
839	703 921	28.96550	91.59694	889	790 321	29.81610	94.28680
840	705 600	28.98275	91.65151	890	792 100	29.83287	94.33981
841	707 281	29.00000	91.70605	891	793 881	29.84962	94.39280
842	708 964	29.01724	91.76056	892	795 664	29.86637	94.44575
843	710 649	29.03446	91.81503	893	797 449	29.88311	94.49868
844	712 336	29.05168	91.86947	894	799 236	29.89983	94.55157
845	714 025	29.06888	91.92388	895	801 025	29.91655	94.60444
846	715 716	29.08608	91.97826	896	802 816	29.93326	94.65728
847	717 409	29.10326	92.03260	897	804 609	29.94996	94.71008
848	719 104	29.12044	92.08692	898	806 404	29.96665	94.76286
849	720 801	29.13760	92.14120	899	808 201	29.98333	94.81561
850	722 500	29.15476	92.19544	900	810 000	30.00000	94.86833

Appendix E (*concluded*)   Tables of squares and square roots

N	N^2	$\sqrt{N}$	$\sqrt{10N}$	N	N^2	$\sqrt{N}$	$\sqrt{10N}$
900	810 000	30.00000	94.86833	950	902 500	30.82207	97.46794
901	811 801	30.01666	94.92102	951	904 401	30.83829	97.51923
902	813 604	30.03331	94.97368	952	906 304	30.85450	97.57049
903	815 409	30.04996	95.02631	953	908 209	30.87070	97.62172
904	817 216	30.06659	95.07891	954	910.116	30.88689	97.67292
905	819 025	30.08322	95.13149	955	912 025	30.90307	97.72410
906	820 836	30.09938	95.18403	956	913 936	30.91925	97.77525
907	822 649	30.11644	95.23655	957	915 849	30.93542	97.82638
908	824 464	30.13304	95.28903	958	917 764	30.95158	97.87747
909	826 281	30.14963	95.34149	959	919 681	30.96773	97.92855
910	828 100	30.16621	95.39392	960	921 600	30.98387	97.97959
911	829 921	30.18278	95.44632	961	923 521	31.00000	98.03061
912	831 744	30.19934	95.49869	962	925 444	31.01612	98.08160
913	833 569	30.21589	95.55103	963	927 369	31.03224	98.13256
914	835 396	30.23243	95.60335	964	929 296	31.04835	98.18350
915	837 225	30.24897	95.65563	965	931 225	31.06445	98.23441
916	839 056	30.26549	95.70789	966	933 156	31.08054	98.28530
917	840 889	30.28201	95.76012	967	935 089	31.09662	98.33616
918	842 724	30.29851	95.81232	968	937 024	31.11270	98.38699
919	844 561	30.31501	95.86449	969	938 961	31.12876	98.43780
920	846 400	30.33150	95.91663	970	940 900	31.14482	98.48858
921	848 241	30.34798	95.96874	971	942 841	31.16087	98.53933
922	850 084	30.36445	96.02083	972	944 784	31.17691	98.59006
923	851 929	30.38092	96.07289	973	946 729	31.19295	98.64076
924	853 776	30.39735	96.12492	974	948 676	31.20897	98.69144
925	855 625	30.41381	96.17692	975	950 625	31.22499	98.74209
926	857 476	30.43025	96.22889	976	952 576	31.24100	98.79271
927	859 329	30.44667	96.28084	977	954 529	31.25700	98.84331
928	861 184	30.46309	96.33276	978	956 484	31.27299	98.89388
929	863 041	30.47950	96.38465	979	958 441	31.28898	98.94443
930	864 900	30.49590	96.43651	980	960 400	31.30495	98.99495
931	866 761	30.51229	96.48834	981	962 361	31.32092	99.04544
932	868 624	30.52868	96.54015	982	964 324	31.33688	99.09591
933	870 489	30.54505	96.59193	983	966 144	31.34021	99.10321
934	872 356	30.56141	96.64368	984	968 256	31.36877	99.19677
935	874 225	30.57777	96.69540	985	970 225	31.38471	99.24717
936	876 096	30.59412	96.74709	986	972 196	31.40064	99.29753
937	877 969	30.61046	96.79876	987	974 169	31.41656	99.34787
938	879 844	30.62679	96.85040	988	976 144	31.43247	99.39819
939	881 721	30.64311	96.90201	989	978 121	31.44837	99.44848
940	883 600	30.65942	96.95360	990	980 100	31.46427	99.49874
941	885 481	30.67572	97.00515	991	982 081	31.48015	99.54898
942	887 364	30.69202	97.05668	992	984 064	31.49603	99.54920
943	889 249	30.70831	97.10819	993	986 049	31.51190	99.64939
944	891 136	30.72458	97.15966	994	988 036	31.52777	99.69955
945	893 025	30.74085	97.21111	995	990 025	31.54362	99.74969
946	894 916	30.75711	97.26253	996	992 016	31.55947	99.79980
947	896 809	30.77337	97.31393	997	994 009	31.57531	99.84989
948	898 704	30.78961	97.36529	998	996 004	31.59114	99.89995
949	900 601	30.80584	97.41663	999	998 001	31.60696	99.94999
950	902 500	30.82207	97.46794	1000	1 000 000	31.62278	100.00000

Glossary

Accelerated Cost Recovery System (ACRS) A system that specifies the allowable depreciation recovery period for different types of assets. The normal recovery period is generally shorter than that previously allowed under forms of depreciation before the passage of the 1981 Economic Recovery Tax Act.

agency securities Securities issued by federal agencies such as the Federal Land Bank and the Federal Home Loan Banks.

aging of accounts receivable Analyzing accounts by the amount of time they have been on our books.

American Depository Receipts (ADR) ADR is the acronym for American Depository Receipts. These receipts represent the ownership interest in a foreign company's common stock. The shares of the foreign company are put in trust in a New York bank. The bank, in turn, issues its depository receipts to the American stockholders of the foreign firm. Many ADRs are listed on the NYSE and many more are traded in the over-the-counter market.

annuity A series of consecutive payments or receipts of equal amount.

asset utilization ratios A group of ratios that measures the speed at which the firm is turning over or utilizing its assets. We measure inventory turnover, fixed asset turnover, total asset turnover, and the average time it takes to collect accounts receivable.

assignment The liquidation of assets without going through formal court procedures. In order to affect an assignment, creditors must agree on liquidation values and the relative priority of claims.

average collection period The average amount of time our accounts receivable have been on our books. It may be computed by dividing accounts receivable by average daily sales.

balance of payments The term refers to a system of government accounts that catalogs the flow of economic transactions between countries.

balance sheets A financial statement that indicates what assets the firm owns, and how those assets are financed in the form of liabilities or ownership interest.

banker's acceptance Short-term securities that frequently arise from foreign trade. The acceptance is a draft that is drawn on a bank for approval for future payment and is subsequently presented to the payer.

bankruptcy The market value of a firm's assets are less than its liabilities, and the firm has a negative net worth. The term is also used to describe in-court procedures associated with the reorganization or liquidation of a firm.

bear market A falling or lethargic stock market. The opposite of a bull market.

beta A measure of the volatility of returns on an individual stock relative to the market. Stocks with a beta of 1.0 are said to have risk equal to that of the market (equal volatility). Stocks with betas greater than 1.0 have more risk than the market, while those with betas of less than 1.0 have less risk than the market.

blanket inventory liens A secured borrowing arrangement in which the lender has a general claim against the inventory of the borrower.

bond ratings Bonds are rated according to risk by Standard & Poor's and Moody's Investor Service. A bond that is rated Aaa by Moody's has the lowest risk, while a bond with a C rating has the highest risk. Coupon rates are greatly influenced by a corporation's bond rating.

book value (See net worth.)

break-even analysis A numerical and graphical technique that is used to determine at what point the firm will break even (revenue = cost). To compute the break-even point, we divide fixed costs by price minus variable cost per unit.

brokers Members of organized stock exchanges who have the ability to buy and sell securities on the floor of their respective exchanges. Brokers act as agents between buyers and sellers.

bull market A rising stock market. There are many complicated interpretations of this term, usually centering on the length of time that the market should be rising in order to meet the correct criteria for classification as a bull market. For our purposes a bull market exists when stock prices are strong and rising and investors are optimistic about future market performance.

call feature Used for bonds and some preferred stock. A call allows the corporation to retire securities before maturity by forcing the bondholders to sell bonds back to it at a set price. The call provisions are included in the bond indenture.

capital Sources of the permanent financing that is available to the business firm.

capital asset pricing model A model that relates the risk-return trade-offs of individual assets to market returns. A security is presumed to receive a risk-free rate of return plus a premium for risk.

capital gains taxes Taxes on gains from holding assets. Long-term capital gains taxes apply to assets held for at least a year. The individual may exclude 60 percent of the gain from taxation and pay only the ordinary income tax rate on the remaining 40 percent.

capital lease A long-term, noncancelable lease that has many of the characteristics of debt. Under FASB *Statement No. 13*, the lease obligation must be shown directly on the balance sheet.

capital markets Competitive markets for equity securities or debt securities with maturities of more than one year. The best examples of capital market securities are common stock, bonds, and preferred stock.

capital rationing Occurs when a corporation has more dollars of capital budgeting projects with positive net present values than it has money to invest in them. Therefore, some projects that should be accepted are excluded because financial capital is rationed.

carrying costs The cost to hold an asset, usually inventory. For inventory, carrying costs include such items as interest, warehousing costs, insurance, and material handling expenses.

cash budget A series of monthly or quarterly budgets that indicate cash receipts, cash payments, and the borrowing requirements for meeting financial requirements. It is constructed from the pro forma income statement and other supportive schedules.

cash flow A value equal to income after taxes plus noncash expenses. In capital budgeting decisions, the usual noncash expense is depreciation.

certificates of deposit A certificate offered by banks, savings and loans, and other financial institutions for the deposit of funds at a given interest rate over a specified time period.

clientele effect The effect of investor preferences for dividends or capital gains. Investors tend to purchase securities that meet their needs.

coefficient of correlation The degree of associated movement between two or more variables. Variables that move in the same direction are said to be positively correlated, while negatively correlated variables move in opposite directions.

coefficient of variation A measure of risk determination that is computed by dividing the standard deviation for a series of numbers by the expected value. Generally, the larger the coefficient of variation, the greater the risk.

combined leverage The total or combined impact of operating and financial leverage.

commercial paper An unsecured promissory note that large corporations issue to investors. The minimum amount is usually $25,000.

common stock equivalent Warrants, options, and any convertible securities that pay less than two thirds of the average bond yield at the time of issue.

common stockholder Holders of common stock are the owners of the company. Common stockholders elect the members of the board of directors, who in turn help select the top management.

compensating balances A bank requirement that business customers maintain a minimum average balance. The required amount is usually computed as a percentage of customer loans outstanding or as a percentage of the future loans to which the bank has committed itself.

composition An out-of-court settlement in which creditors agree to accept a fractional settlement on their original claim.

compound sum The future value of a single amount or an annuity when compounded at a given interest rate for a specified time period.

consolidation The combination of two or more firms, generally of equal size and market power, to form an entirely new entity.

constant dollar accounting One of two methods of inflation-adjusted accounting that have been approved by the Financial Accounting Standards Board. Financial statements are adjusted to present prices, using the consumer price index. This is shown as supplemental information in the firm's annual report.

consumer price index An economic indicator published monthly by the U.S. Commerce Department. It measures the rate of inflation for consumer goods.

contribution margin The contribution to fixed costs from each unit of sales. The margin may be computed as price minus variable cost per unit.

conversion premium The market price of a convertible bond or preferred stock minus the security's conversion value.

conversion price The conversion ratio divided into the par value. The price of the common stock at which the security is convertible. An investor would usually not convert the security into common stock unless the market price were greater than the conversion price.

conversion ratio The number of shares of common stock an investor will receive if he exchanges a convertible bond or convertible preferred stock for common stock.

conversion value The conversion ratio multiplied by the market price per share of common stock.

convertible security A security that may be traded into the company for a different form or type of security. Convertible securities are usually bonds or preferred stock that may be exchanged for common stock.

corporation A form of ownership in which a separate, legal entity is created. A corporation may sue or be sued, engage in contracts and acquire property. It has a continual life and is not dependent on any one stockholder for maintaining its legal existence. A corporation is owned by stockholders who enjoy the privilege of limited liability. There is, however, the potential for double taxation in the corporate form of organization: the first time at the corporate level in the form of profits, and again at the stockholder level in the form of dividends.

cost-benefit analysis A study of the incremental costs and benefits that can be derived from a given course of action.

cost of capital The cost of alternative sources of financing to the firm. (See also weighted average cost of capital.)

cost of goods sold The cost specifically associated with units sold during the time period under study.

coupon rate The actual interest rate on the bond, usually payable in semiannual installments. The coupon rate normally stays constant during the life of the bond and indicates what the bondholder's annual dollar income will be.

credit terms The repayment provisions that are part of a credit arrangement. An example would be a 2/10, net 30 arrangement in which the customer may deduct 2 percent from the invoice price if payment takes place in the first ten days. Otherwise the full amount is due.

cumulative preferred stock If dividends from one period are not paid to the preferred stockholders, they are said to be in arrears and are then added to the next period's dividends. When dividends on preferred stock are in arrears, no dividends can legally be paid to the common stockholders. The cumulative dividend feature is very beneficial to preferred stockholders since it assures them that they will receive all dividends due before common stockholders can get any dividends.

cumulative voting Allows shareholders more than one vote per share. They are allowed to multiply their total shares by the number of directors being elected to determine their total number of votes. This system enables minority shareholders to elect directors even though they do not have 51 percent of the vote.

currency futures contract A futures contract that may be used for hedging or speculation in foreign exchange.

current cost accounting One of two methods of inflation-adjusted accounting approved by the Financial Accounting Standards Board in 1979. Financial statements are adjusted to the present, using current cost data rather than an index. This is shown as supplemental information in the firm's annual report.

current yield The yearly dollar interest payment divided by the current market price.

dealers Participants in the market who transact security trades over-the-counter from their own inventory of stocks and bonds. They are often referred to as market makers since they stand ready to buy and sell their securities at quoted prices.

debenture A long-term unsecured corporate bond. Debentures are usually issued by large, prestigious firms having excellent credit ratings in the financial community.

debt utilization ratios A group of ratios that indicates to what extent debt is being used and the prudence with which it is being managed. Calculations include debt to total assets, times interest earned, and fixed charge coverage.

decision tree A tabular or graphical analysis that lays out the sequence of decisions that are to be made and highlights the differences between choices. The presentation resembles in appearances the branches on a tree.

declaration date The day on which the board of directors officially states that a dividend will be paid.

deferred annuity An annuity that will not begin until some time period in the future.

degree of combined leverage A measure of the total combined effect of operating and financial leverage on earnings per share. The percentage change in earnings per share is divided by the percentage change in sales at a given level of operation. Other algebraic statements are also used, such as Formula 5–7 and footnote 3 in Chapter 5.

degree of financial leverage A measure of the impact of debt on the earnings capability of the firm. The percentage change in earnings per share is divided by the percentage change in earnings before interest and taxes at a given level of operation. Other algebraic statements are also used, such as Formula 5–5.

degree of operating leverage A measure of the impact of fixed costs on the operating earnings of the firm. The percentage change in operating income is divided by the percentage change in volume at a given level of operation. Other algebraic statements are also used, such as Formula 5–3 and footnote 2 in Chapter 5.

dilution of earnings This occurs when additional shares of stock are sold without creating an immediate increase in income. The result is a decline in earnings per share until earnings can be generated from the funds raised.

discount rate The interest rate at which future sums or annuities are discounted back to the present.

discounted loan A loan in which the calculated interest payment is subtracted or discounted in advance. Because this lowers the amount of available funds, the effective interest rate is increased.

disinflation A leveling off or slow down of price increases.

dividend information content This theory of dividends assumes that dividends provide information about the financial health and economic expectations of the company. If this is true, corporations must actively manage their dividends to provide the market with information.

dividend payment date The day on which a stockholder of record will receive his or her dividend.

dividend payout The percentage of dividends to earnings after taxes. It can be computed by dividing dividends per share by earnings per share.

dividend record date Stockholders owning the stock on the holder of record date are entitled to receive a dividend. In order to be listed as an owner on the corporate books, you must have bought the stock before it went ex-dividend.

dividend reinvestment plans Plans that provide the investor with an opportunity to buy additional shares of stock with the cash dividends paid by the company.

dividend valuation model A model for determining the value of a share of stock by taking the present value of an expected stream of future dividends.

dividend yield Dividends per share divided by market price per share. Dividend yield indicates the percentage return that a stockholder will receive on dividends alone.

dual trading Exists when one security such as General Motors common stock is traded on more than one stock exchange. This practice is quite common between NYSE-listed companies and regional exchanges.

Dun & Bradstreet A credit rating agency that publishes information on over 3 million business establishments through its *Reference Book*.

Du Pont System of Ratio Analysis A system of analysis that first of all breaks down return on assets between the profit margin and asset turnover. The second or modified version then goes on to show how return on assets is translated into return on equity through the amount of debt that the firm has. Actually return on assets is divided by (1 − debt/assets) to arrive at return on equity.

earnings per share The earnings available to common stockholders divided by the number of common stock shares outstanding.

economic indicators Hundreds of indicators exist. Each is a specialized series of data. The data are analyzed for their relationship to economic activity, and the indicator is classified as either a lagging indicator, a leading indicator, or a coincident indicator of economic activity.

economic ordering quantity (EOQ) The most efficient ordering quantity for the firm. The EOQ will allow the firm to minimize the total ordering and carrying costs associated with inventory.

efficient frontier A line drawn through the optimum point selections in a risk-return trade-off diagram. Each point represents the best possible trade-off between risk and return (the highest return at a given risk level or the lowest risk at a given return level).

efficient market hypothesis Hypothesis which suggests that markets adjust very quickly to new information and that it is very difficult for investors to select portfolios of securities that outperform the market. The efficient market hypothesis may be stated in many different forms as indicated in Chapter 13.

electronic funds transfer A system in which funds are moved between computer terminals without the use of checks.

Employment Act of 1946 An act which specifies that the Federal Reserve Board should strive to achieve the four goals of economic growth, stable prices, high employment, and a balance of trade.

Eurobonds Bonds payable or denominated in the borrower's currency, but sold outside the country of the borrower, usually by an international syndicate.

Eurodollar loan A loan from a foreign bank denominated in dollars.

Eurodollars U.S. dollars held on deposit by foreign banks and loaned out by those banks to anyone seeking dollars.

ex-dividend date Four business days before the holder of record date. On the ex-dividend date the purchase of the stock no longer carries with it the right to receive the dividend previously declared.

expectations theory of interest rates This theory explains the shape of the term structure relative to expectations for future short-term interest rates. It is thought that long-term rates are an average of the expected short-term rates. Therefore, an upward-sloping yield curve would indicate that short-term rates will rise.

expected value A representative value from a probability distribution arrived at by multiplying each outcome by the associated probability and summing up the values.

Export-Import Bank (Eximbank) An agency of the United States government that facilitates the financing of United States exports through its miscellaneous programs. In its direct loan program, the Eximbank lends money to foreign purchasers of U.S. products—such as aircraft, electrical equipment, heavy machinery, computers and the like. The Eximbank also purchases eligible medium-term obligations of foreign buyers of U.S. goods at a discount from face value. In this discount program, private banks and other lenders are able to rediscount (sell at a lower price) promissory notes and drafts acquired from foreign customers of U.S. firms.

expropriation The action of a country in taking away or modifying the property rights of a corporation or individual.

ex-rights The situation in which the purchase of common stock during a rights offering no longer includes rights to purchase additional shares of common stock.

extension An out-of-court settlement in which creditors agree to allow the firm more time to meet its financial obligations. A new repayment schedule will be developed subject to the acceptance of creditors.

external reorganization A reorganization under the formal bankruptcy laws in which a merger partner is found for the distressed firm. Ideally, the firm should be merged with a strong firm in its own industry, although this is not always possible.

factoring receivables Selling accounts receivable to a finance company or a bank.

federal budget deficit Government expenditures are greater than government tax revenues, and the government must borrow to balance revenues and expenditures. These deficits act as an economic stimulus.

federal budget surplus Government tax receipts are greater than government expenditures. A rarity during the last 20 years. These surpluses have a dampening effect on the economy.

Federal Reserve discount rate The rate of interest that the Fed charges on loans to the banking system. A monetary tool for management of the money supply.

field warehousing An inventory financing arrangement in which collateralized inventory is stored on the premises of the borrower but is controlled by an independent warehousing company.

FIFO A system of writing off inventory into cost of goods sold in which the items purchased first are written off first. Referred to as first-in, first out.

financial capital Common stock, preferred stock, bonds, and retained earnings. Financial capital appears on the corporate balance sheet under long-term liabilities and equity.

financial futures market A market that allows for the trading of financial instruments related to a future point in time. A purchase or sale takes place in the present, with a reversal necessitated in the future to close out the position. If a purchase (sale) takes place initially, then a sale (purchase) will be necessary in the future. The market provides for futures contracts in Treasury bonds, Treasury bills, certificates of deposits, GNMA certificates, and many other instruments. Actually, financial futures contracts may be executed on the Chicago Board of Trade, the Chicago Mercantile Exchange, the New York Futures Exchange, and other exchanges.

financial intermediary A financial institution such as a bank or a life insurance company that directs other people's money into such investments as government and corporate securities.

financial lease A long-term noncancelable lease. The financial lease has all the characteristics of long-term debt except that the lease payments are a combination of interest expense and amortization of the cost of the asset.

financial leverage A measure of the amount of debt used in the capital structure of the frim.

financial sweetener Usually refers to equity options, such as warrants or conversion privileges, attached to a debt security. The sweetener lowers the interest cost to the corporation.

fiscal policy The tax policies of the federal government and the spending associated with its tax revenues.

fixed costs Costs that remain relatively constant regardless of the volume of operations. Examples are rent, depreciation, property taxes, and executive salaries.

float The difference between the corporation's recorded cash balance on its books and the amount credited to the corporation by the bank.

floating rate bond The interest payment on the bond changes with market conditions rather than the price of the bond.

floating rate preferred stock The quarterly dividend on the preferred stock changes with market conditions. The market price is considerably less volatile than it is with regular preferred stock.

floor price Usually equal to the pure bond value. A convertible bond will not sell at less than its pure bond value even when its conversion value is below the pure bond value.

flotation cost The distribution cost of selling securities to the public. The cost includes the underwriter's spread and any associated fees.

forced conversion Occurs when a company calls a convertible security that has a conversion value greater than the call price. Investors will take the higher of the two values and convert the security to common stock rather than take a lower cash call price.

Foreign Credit Insurance Corporation (FICA) An agency established by a group of 60 U.S. insurance companies. It sells credit export insurance to interested exporters. The FICA promises to pay for the exported merchandise if the foreign importer defaults on payment.

foreign exchange rate The relationship between the value of two or more currencies. For example, the exchange rate between U.S. dollars and French francs is stated as dollars per francs or francs per dollar.

foreign exchange risk A form of risk that refers to the possibility of experiencing a drop in revenue or an increase in cost in an international transaction due to a change in foreign exchange rates. Importers, exporters, investors, and multinational firms alike are exposed to this foreign exchange risk.

fourth market A market of stock and bonds in which there is direct dealing between financial institutions such as investment bankers, insurance companies, pension funds, and mutual funds.

fronting loan A parent's loan to a foreign subsidiary is channeled through a financial intermediary, usually a large international bank. The bank fronts for the parent in extending the loan to the foreign affiliate.

fully diluted earnings per share Equals adjusted earnings after taxes divided by shares outstanding, plus common stock equivalents, plus all convertible securities.

futures contract A contract to buy or sell a commodity at some specified price in the future.

going private The process by which all publicly owned shares of common stock are repurchased or retired, thereby eliminating listing fees, annual reports, and other expenses involved with publicly owned companies.

goodwill An intangible asset that reflects value above that generally recognized in the tangible assets of the firm.

hedging To engage in a transaction that partially or fully reduces a prior risk exposure by taking a position that is the opposite of your initial position. As an example, you buy some copper now but also engage in a contract to sell copper in the future at a set price.

historical cost accounting The traditional method of accounting in which financial statements are developed based on original cost minus depreciation.

holding company A company that has voting control of one or more other companies. It often has less than a 50 percent interest in each of these other companies.

income statement A financial statement that measures the profitability of the firm over a period of time. All expenses are subtracted from sales to arrive at net income.

indenture A legal contract between the borrower and the lender that covers every detail regarding a bond issue.

indexing An adjustment for inflation incorporated into the operation of an economy. Indexing may be used to revalue assets on the balance sheet and to automatically adjust wages, tax deductions, interest payments, and a wide variety of other categories to account for inflation.

installment loan A borrowing arrangement in which a series of equal payments are used to pay off the loan.

interest factor (_IF_) The tabular value to insert into the various formulas. It is based on the number of periods (n) and the interest rate (i).

interest rate parity theory A theory based on the interplay between interest rate differentials and exchange rates. If one country has a higher interest rate than another country after adjustments for inflation, interest rates and foreign exchange rates will adjust until the foreign exchange rates and money market rates reach equilibrium (are properly balanced between the two countries).

internal rate of return (IRR) A discounted cash flow method for evaluating capital budgeting projects. The IRR is a discount rate which makes the present value of the cash inflows equal to the present value of the cash outflows.

internal reorganization A reorganization under the formal bankruptcy laws. New management may be brought in and a redesign of the capital structure may be implemented.

international diversification Achieving diversification through many different foreign investments that are influenced by a variety of factors.

International Finance Corporation (IFC) An affiliate of the World Bank established with the sole purpose of providing partial seed capital for private ventures around the world. Whenever a multinational company has difficulty raising equity capital due to lack of adequate private risk capital, the firm may explore the possibility of selling equity or debt (totaling up to 25 percent) to the International Finance Corporation.

inventory profits Profits generated as a result of an inflationary economy in which old inventory is sold at large profits because of increasing prices. This is particularly prevalent under FIFO accounting.

inverted yield curve A downward sloping yield curve. Short-term rates are higher than long-term rates.

investment banker A financial organization that specializes in selling primary offerings of securities. Investment bankers can also perform other financial functions, such as advising clients, negotiating mergers and takeovers, and selling secondary offerings.

investment tax credit (ITC) A percentage of the purchase price that may be deducted directly from tax obligations. Under the 1981 Economic Recovery Tax Act, a three-year recovery life asset is entitled to a 6 percent ITC. An asset with a life of five years or greater is entitled to an ITC of 10 percent.

leading indicators The most commonly followed series of economic indicators is the series of 12 leading indicators. These are used to help forecast economic activity.

lease A contractual arrangement between the owner of equipment (lessor) and the user of equipment (lessee) which calls for the lessee to pay the lessor an established lease payment. There are two kinds of leases, financial leases and operating leases.

letter of credit A credit letter normally issued by the importer's bank in which the bank promises to pay out the money for the merchandise when delivered.

level production Equal monthly production used to smooth out production schedules and employ manpower and equipment more efficiently and at a lower cost.

leverage The use of fixed-charge obligations with the intent of magnifying the potential returns to the firm.

life cycle curve A curve illustrating the growth phases of a firm. The dividend policy most likely to be employed during each phase is often illustrated.

LIFO A system of writing off inventory into cost of goods sold in which the items purchased last are written off first. Referred to as last-in, first-out.

limited partnership A special form of partnership to limit liability for most of the partners. Under this arrangement, one or more partners are designated as general partners and have unlimited liability for the debts of the firm, while the other partners are designated as limited partners and are only liable for their initial contribution.

liquidation A procedure that may be carried out under the formal bankruptcy laws when an internal or external reorganization does not appear to be feasible, and it appears that the assets are worth more in liquidation than through a reorganization. Priority of claims becomes extremely important in a liquidation because it is unlikely that all parties will be fully satisfied in their demands.

liquidity The relative convertibility of short-term assets to cash. Thus, marketable securities are highly liquid assets, while inventory may not be.

liquidity ratios A group of ratios that allows one to measure the firm's ability to pay off short-term obligations as they come due. Primary attention is directed to the current ratio and the quick ratio.

listing requirements Financial standards that corporations must meet before their common stock can be traded on a stock exchange. Listing requirements are not standard, but are set by each exchange. The requirements for the NYSE are the most stringent.

lockbox system A procedure used to expedite cash inflows to a business. Customers are requested to forward their checks to a post-office box in their geographic region, and a local bank picks up the checks and processes them for rapid collection. Funds are then wired to the corporate home office for immediate use.

London Interbank Offered Rate (LIBOR) An interbank rate applicable for large deposits in the Eurodollar market. It is a bench mark rate just like the prime interest rate in the United States. Interest rates on Eurodollar loans are determined by adding premiums to this basic rate. Most often LIBOR is lower than the U.S. prime rate.

majority voting All directors must be elected by a vote of more than 50 percent. Minority shareholders are unable to achieve any representation on the board of directors.

managing underwriter An investment banker who is responsible for the pricing, prospectus development, and legal work involved in the sale of a new issue of securities.

margin requirement A rule that specifies the amount of cash or equity that must be deposited with a brokerage firm or bank, with the balance of funds eligible for borrowing. Margin is set by the Board of Governors of the Federal Reserve Board. For example, margin of 60 percent would mean that a $10,000 purchase would allow the buyer to borrow $4,000 toward the purchase.

marginal corporate tax rate The rate that applies to each new dollar of taxable income. For a corporation, we use 15 percent on the first $25,000, 18 percent on the second $25,000, 30 percent on the third $25,000, 40 percent on the fourth $25,000, and 46 percent on all larger amounts.

marginal cost of capital The cost of the last dollar of funds raised. It is assumed that each dollar is financed in proportion to the firm's optimum capital structure.

marginal principle of retained earnings The corporation must be able to earn a higher return on its retained earnings than a stockholder would receive after paying taxes on the distributed dividends.

market maker (See dealers.)

market risk premium A premium over and above the risk-free rate. It is represented by the difference between the market return (K_m) and the risk-free rate (R_f), and it may be multiplied by the beta coefficient to determine additional risk-adjusted return on a security.

market stabilization Intervention in the secondary markets by an investment banker to stabilize the price of a new security offering during the offering period. Stabilization can last no more than a maximum of 30 days after the appearance of the new issue. The purpose of market stabilization is to provide an orderly market for the distribution of the new issue.

market value maximization The concept of maximizing the wealth of shareholders. This calls for a recognition not only of earnings per share but also how they will be valued in the marketplace.

maturity date The date on which the bond is retired and the principal (par value) is repaid to the lender.

merger The combination of two or more companies in which the resulting firms maintain the identity of the acquiring company.

merger arbitrageur A specialist in merger investments who attempts to capitalize on the difference between the value offered and the current market value of the acquisition candidate.

merger premium That part of a buy-out or exchange offer which represents a value over and above the market value of the acquired firm.

minimum warrant value The market value of the common stock minus the option price of the warrant multiplied by the number of shares of the common stock that each warrant entitles the holder to purchase.

monetary policy Management by the Federal Reserve Board of the money supply and the resultant interest rates.

money market accounts Accounts at banks, savings and loans, and credit unions in which the depositor receives competitive money market rates on a minimum deposit of $2,500. These accounts may have three deposits and three withdrawals per month, and are not meant to be transaction accounts, but a place to keep minimum and excess cash balances. These accounts are insured by various appropriate governmental agencies up to $100,000.

money market funds A fund in which investors may purchase shares for as little as $500 or $1,000. The fund then reinvests the proceeds in high-yielding $100,000 bank CDs, $25,000–$100,000 commercial paper, and other large-denomination, high yielding securities. The investor receives his pro rata portion of the interest proceeds daily as a credit to his shares.

money markets Competitive markets for securities with maturities of one year or less. The best example of money market instruments would be Treasury bills, commercial paper, and negotiable certificates of deposit.

mortgage agreement A loan which requires real property (plant and equipment) as collateral.

multinational corporation A firm doing business across its national borders is considered a multinational enterprise. Some definitions require a minimum percentage (often 30 percent or more) of a firm's business activities to be carried on outside its national borders.

municipal securities Securities issued by state and local government units. The income from these securities is currently exempt from federal income taxes.

mutually exclusive The selection of one choice precludes the selection of any competitive choice. For example, several machines can do an identical job in capital budgeting. If one machine is selected, the other machines will not be used.

national market system A system mandated by the Securities Acts Amendments of 1975. The national market system that is envisioned will include computer processing and computerized competitive prices for all markets trading similar stocks. The exact form of the system is yet to be determined.

net present value (NPV) The NPV equals the present value of the cash inflows minus the present value of the cash outflows with the cost of capital used as a discount rate. This method is used to evaluate capital budgeting projects. If the NPV is positive, a project should be accepted.

net trade credit A measure of the relationship between the firm's accounts receivable and accounts payable. If accounts receivable exceed accounts payable, the firm is a net provider of trade credit; otherwide, it is a net user.

net worth, or book value Stockholders' equity minus preferred stock ownership. Basically, net worth is the common stockholders' interest as represented by common stock par value, capital paid in excess of par, and retained earnings. If you take all the assets of the firm and subtract its liabilities and preferred stock, you arrive at net worth.

nominal GNP GNP (gross national product) in current dollars without any adjustments for inflation.

nominal yield A return equal to the coupon rate.

nonlinear break-even analysis Break-even analysis based on the assumption that cost and revenue relationships to quantity may vary at different levels of operation. Most of our analysis is based on *linear* break-even analysis.

normal recovery period The depreciation recovery period (3, 5, 10, 15) under the Accelerated Cost Recovery System of the 1981 Economic Recovery Tax Act.

normal yield curve An upward sloping yield curve. Long-term interest rates are higher than short-term rates.

open-market operations The purchase and sale of government securities in the open market by the Federal Reserve Board for its own account. The most common method for managing the money supply.

operating lease A short-term, nonbinding obligation that is easily cancelable.

operating leverage A reflection of the extent to which fixed assets and fixed costs are utilized in the business firm.

optimum capital structure A capital structure that has the best possible mix of debt, preferred stock, retained earnings, and new common stock. The optimum mix should provide the lowest possible cost of capital to the firm.

Overseas Private Investment Corporation (OPIC) A government agency that sells insurance policies to qualified firms. This agency insures against losses due to inconvertibility into dollars of amounts invested in a foreign country. Policies are also available from OPIC to insure against expropriation and against losses due to war or revolution.

over-the-counter markets Markets for securities (both bonds and stock) in which market makers or dealers transact purchases and sales of securities by trading from their own inventory of securities.

par value Sometimes referred to as the face value or the principal value of the bond. Most bond issues have a par value of $1,000 per bond. Common and preferred stock may also have an assigned par value.

parallel loan A U.S. firm that wishes to lend funds to a foreign affiliate (such as a Dutch affiliate) locates a foreign parent firm (such as a Dutch parent firm) that wishes to loan money to a U.S. affiliate. Avoiding the foreign exchange markets entirely, the U.S. parent lends dollars to the Dutch affiliate in the United States, while the Dutch parent lends guilders to the American affiliate in the Netherlands. At maturity, the two loans would each be repaid to the original lender. Notice that neither loan carries any foreign exchange risk in this arrangement.

participating preferred stock A small number of preferred stock issues are participating with regard to corporate earnings. For such issues, once the common stock dividend equals the preferred stock dividend, the two classes of securities may share equally (or in some ratio) in additional dividend payments.

partnership A form of ownership in which two or more partners are involved. Like the sole proprietorship, a partnership arrangement carries unlimited liability for the owners. However, there is only single taxation for the partners, an advantage over the corporate form of ownership.

payback   A value that indicates the time period required to recoup an initial investment. The payback does not include the time value of money concept.

percent-of-sales method   A method of determining future financial needs that is an alternative to the development of pro forma financial statements. We first determine the percentage relationship of various asset and liability accounts to sales, and then we show how that relationship changes as our volume of sales changes.

permanent current assets   Current assets that will not be reduced or converted to cash within the normal operating cycle of the firm. Though from a strict accounting standpoint the assets should be removed from the current assets category, they generally are not.

planning horizon   The length of time it takes to conceive, develop, and complete a project and to recover the cost of the project on a discounted cash flow basis.

pledging receivables   Using accounts receivable as collateral for a loan. The firm usually may borrow 60–80 percent of the value of acceptable collateral.

point-of-sales terminals   Computer terminals in retail stores that either allow digital input or use optical scanners. The terminals may be used for inventory control or other purposes.

pooling of interests   A method of financial recording for mergers in which the financial statements of the firms are combined subject to minor adjustments, and goodwill is not created.

portfolio effect   The impact of a given investment on the overall risk-return composition of the firm. A firm must consider not only the individual investment characteristics of a project, but also how the project relates to the entire portfolio of undertakings.

preemptive right   The right of current common stockholders to maintain their ownership percentage on new issues of common stock.

preferred stock   A hybrid security combining some of the characteristics of both common stock and debt. The dividends paid are not tax-deductible expenses for the corporation, as is true of the interest paid on debt.

present value The current or discounted value of a future sum or annuity. The value is discounted back at a given interest rate for a specified time period.

price-earnings ratio The multiplier applied to earnings per share to determine current value. The P/E ratio is influenced by the earnings and sales growth of the firm, the risk or volatility of its performance, the debt-equity structure, and other factors.

primary earnings per share Adjusted earnings after taxes divided by shares outstanding plus common stock equivalents.

prime rate The rate that the bank charges its most creditworthy customers.

private placement The sale of securities directly to a financial institution by a corporation. This eliminates the middleman and reduces the cost of issue to the corporation.

profitability ratios A group of ratios that indicates the return on sales, total assets, and invested capital. Specifically, we compute the profit margin (net income to sales), return on assets, and return on equity.

pro forma balance sheet A projection of future asset, liability, and stockholders' equity levels. Notes payable or cash is used as a plug or balancing figure for the statement.

pro forma financial statements A series of projected financial statements. Of major importance are the pro forma income statement, the balance sheet, and the cash budget.

pro forma income statement A projection of anticipated sales, expenses, and income.

public placement The sale of securities to the public through the investment banker-underwriter process. Public placements must be registered with the Securities and Exchange Commission.

public warehousing An inventory financing arrangement in which inventory, used as collateral, is stored with and controlled by an independent warehousing company.

purchase of assets A method of financial recording for mergers in which the difference between the purchase price and the adjusted book value is recognized as goodwill and amortized over a maximum time period of 40 years.

Purchasing power parity theory A theory based on the interplay between inflation and exchange rates. A parity between the purchasing powers of two countries establishes the rate of exchange between the two currencies. Currency exchange rates, therefore, tend to vary inversely with their respective purchasing powers in order to provide the same or similar purchasing power.

pure bond value   The value of the convertible bond if its present value is computed at a discount rate equal to interest rates on straight bonds of equal risk, without conversion privileges.

random walk   A term used to describe a school of thought, which believes that securities have random price movements. Therefore, stock prices cannot be predicted from past price data.

real capital   Long-term productive assets (plant and equipment).

real GNP   GNP (gross national product) in current dollars adjusted for inflation.

refunding   The process of retiring an old bond issue before maturity and replacing it with a new issue. Refunding will occur when interest rates have fallen and new bonds may be sold at lower interest rates.

reinvestment assumption   An assumption must be made concerning the rate of return that can be earned on the cash flows generated by capital budgeting projects. The NPV method assumes the rate of reinvestment to be the cost of capital, while the IRR method assumes the rate to be the actual IRR.

repatriation of earnings   returning earnings to the multinational parent company in the form of dividends.

replacement cost   The cost of replacing the existing asset base at current prices as opposed to original cost.

replacement cost accounting   Financial statements based on the present cost of replacing assets.

reserve requirements   The amount of funds that commercial banks must hold in reserve for each dollar of deposits. Reserve requirements are set by the Federal Reserve Board and are different for savings and checking accounts. Low reserve requirements are stimulating; high reserve requirements are restrictive.

residual dividends   This theory of dividend payout states that a corporation will retain as much earnings as it may profitably invest. If any income is left after investments, it will pay dividends. This theory assumes that dividends are a passive decision variable.

rights offering   A sale of new common stock through a preemptive rights offering. Usually one right will be issued for every share held. A certain number of rights may be used to buy shares of common stock from the company at a set price that is usually lower than the market price.

rights-on   The situation in which the purchase of a share of common stock includes a right attached to the stock.

risk   A measure of uncertainty about the outcome from a given event. The greater the variability of possible outcomes, on both the high side and the low side, the greater the risk.

risk-adjusted discount rate   A discount rate used in the capital budgeting process that has been adjusted upward or downward from the basic cost of capital to reflect the risk dimension of a given project.

risk averse   An aversion or dislike for risk. In order to induce most people to take larger risks, there must be an increased potential for return.

risk-free rate of interest   Rate of return on an asset that carries no risk. U.S. Treasury bills are often used to represent this measure, although longer-term government securities have also proved appropriate in some studies.

secondary offering   The sale of a large block of stock in a publicly traded company, usually by estates, foundations, or large individual stockholders. Secondary offerings must be registered with the SEC and will usually be distributed by investment bankers.

secondary trading   The buying and selling of publicly owned securities in secondary markets such as the New York Stock Exchange and the over-the-counter markets.

secured debt   A general category of debt which indicates that the loan was obtained by pledging assets as collateral. Secured debt has many forms and usually offers some protective features to a given class of bondholders.

Securities Act of 1933   An act that is sometimes referred to as the truth in securities act because it requires detailed financial disclosures before securities may be sold to the public.

Securities Acts Amendments of 1975 The major feature of this act was to mandate a national securities market. (See national market system.)

Securities Exchange Act of 1934 Legislation that established the Securities and Exchange Commission (SEC) to supervise and regulate the securities markets.

security market line A line or equation that depicts the risk-related return of a security based on a risk-free rate plus a market premium related to the beta coefficient of the security.

self-liquidating assets Assets that are converted to cash within the normal operating cycle of the firm. An example is the purchase and sell-off of seasonal inventory.

semiannual compounding A compounding period of every six months. For example, a five-year investment in which interest is compounded semiannually would indicate an n value equal to 10 and an i value at one half the annual rate.

semivariable costs Costs that are partially fixed but still change somewhat as volume changes. Examples are utilities and "repairs and maintenance."

serial bond A bond issued by one company or municipality with a series of different maturity dates and interest rates that correspond to rates on competitive bonds with the same maturity and risk.

shelf registration A process which permits large companies to file one comprehensive registration statement (under SEC Rule 415), which outlines the firm's plans for future long-term financing. Then, when market conditions appear to be appropriate, the firm can issue the securities without further SEC approval.

simulation A method of dealing with uncertainty in which future outcomes are anticipated. The model may use random variables for inputs. By programming the computer to randomly select inputs from probability distributions, the outcomes generated by a simulation are distributed about a mean and, instead of generating one return or net present value, a range of outcomes with standard deviations is provided.

sinking fund   A method for retiring bonds in an orderly process over the life of a bond. Each year or semiannually, a corporation sets aside a sum of money equal to a certain percentage of the total issue. These funds are then used by a trustee to purchase the bonds in the open market and retire them. This method will prevent the corporation from being forced to refund or raise a large amount of capital at maturity to retire the total bond issue.

sole proprietorship   A form of organization that represents single-person ownership and offers the advantages of simplicity of decision making and low organizational and operating costs.

sources and uses of funds statement   A statement of how changes in the balance sheet were financed over time. A source of funds is represented by an increase in stockholders' equity or liabilities as well as a decrease in assets. A use of funds is equated with a decrease in stockholders' equity or liabilities or an increase in assets.

speculative warrant premium   The market price of the warrant minus the warrant's intrinsic value.

spontaneous sources of funds   Funds arising through the normal course of business, such as accounts payable generated from the purchase of goods for resale.

standard deviation   A measure of the spread or dispersion of a series of numbers around the expected value. The standard deviation tells us how well the expected value represents a series of values.

step-up in conversion   A feature that is sometimes written into the contract which allows the conversion ratio to decline in steps over time. This feature encourages early conversion when the conversion value is greater than the call price.

stock dividend   A dividend paid in stock rather than cash. A book transfer equal to the market value of the stock dividend is made from retained earnings to the capital stock and paid-in-capital accounts. The stock dividend may be symbolic of corporate growth, but it does not increase the total value of the stockholders' wealth.

stock split   A division of shares by a ratio set by the board of directors—2 for 1, 3 for 1, 3 for 2, and so on. Stock splits usually indicate that the company's stock has risen in price to a level that the directors feel limits the trading appeal of the stock. The par value is divided by the ratio set, and new shares are issued to the current stockholders of record to increase their shares to the stated level. For example, a two-for-one split would increase your holdings from one share to two shares.

stockholders' equity   The total ownership position of preferred and common stockholders.

stockholder wealth maximization   Maximizing the wealth of the firm's shareholders through achieving the highest possible value for the firm in the marketplace. It is the overriding objective of the firm and should influence all decisions.

straight-line depreciation   A method of depreciation which takes the depreciable cost of an asset and divides it by the asset's useful life to determine the annual depreciation expense. Straight-line depreciation creates uniform depreciation expenses for each of the years in which an asset is depreciated.

Subchapter S corporation   A special corporate form of ownership in which profit is taxed as direct income to the stockholders and thus is only taxed once as would be true of a partnership. The stockholders still receive all the organizational benefits of a corporation, including limited liability. The Subchapter S designation can only apply to corporations with up to 35 stockholders.

subordinated debenture   An unsecured bond in which payment to the holder will take place only after designated senior debenture holders are satisfied.

synergy   The recognition that the whole may be equal to more than the sum of the parts. The "2 + 2 = 5" effect.

tax loss carry-forward   A loss that can be carried forward for a number of years to offset future taxable income and perhaps be utilized by another firm in a merger or an acquisition.

technical insolvency   A firm is unable to pay its bills as they come due.

temporary current assets   Current assets that will be reduced or converted to cash within the normal operating cycle of the firm.

tender offer takeover An unfriendly acquisition which is not initially negotiated with the management of the target firm. A tender offer is usually made directly to the stockholders of the target firm.

term loan An intermediate-length loan in which credit is generally extended from one to seven years. The loan is usually repaid in monthly or quarterly installments over its life rather than the one single period.

term structure of interest rates The relationship between interest rates and maturities for securities of equal risk. Usually government securities are used for the term structure.

terms of exchange The buy-out ratio or terms of trade in a merger or an acquisition.

third market An over-the-counter market in listed securities. This market was created in the 1970s by traders who were attempting to buy and sell listed securities at lower commissions that could be obtained on the exchanges.

tight money A term to indicate time periods in which financing may be difficult to find and interest rates may be quite high by normal standards.

trade credit Credit provided by sellers or suppliers in the normal course of business.

transaction exposure foreign exchange gains and losses resulting from *actual* international transactions. These may be hedged through the foreign exchange market, the money market, or the currency futures market.

translation exposure The foreign located assets and liabilities of a MNC, which are denominated in foreign currency units, and are exposed to losses and gains due to changing exchange rates. This is called accounting or translation exposure.

Treasury bills Short-term obligations of the federal government with maturities of up to one year.

Treasury notes Intermediate-term obligations of the federal government with maturities from three to five years.

trend analysis An analysis of performance that is made over a number of years in order to ascertain significant patterns.

trust receipt An instrument acknowledging that the borrower holds the inventory and proceeds for sale in trust for the lender.

two-step buy-out An acquisition plan in which the acquiring company attempts to gain control by offering a very high cash price for 51 percent of the shares of the target company. At the same time the acquiring company announces a second lower price that will be paid, either in cash, stock or bonds, at a subsequent point in time.

underwriting The process of selling securities and, at the same time, assuring the seller a specified price. Underwriting is done by investment bankers and represents a form of risk taking.

underwriting spread The difference between the price that a selling corporation receives for an issue of securities and the price at which the issue is sold to the public. The spread is the fee that investment bankers and others receive for selling securities.

underwriting syndicate A group of investment bankers that is formed to share the risk of a security offering and also to facilitate the distribution of the securities.

unsecured debt A loan which requires no assets as collateral, but allows the bondholder a general claim against the corporation rather than a lien against specific assets.

variable costs Costs that move directly with a change in volume. Examples are raw materials, factory labor, and sales commissions.

warrant An option to buy securities at a set price for a given period of time. Warrants commonly have a life of one to five years, but some are perpetual and others have varying time periods.

warrant intrinsic value Same as the minimum warrant value.

weighted average cost of capital The computed cost of capital determined by multiplying the cost of each item in the optimal capital structure by its weighted representation in the overall capital structure and summing up the results.

working capital management The financing and management of the current assets of the firm. The financial manager determines the mix between temporary and permanent "current assets" and the nature of the financing arrangement.

yield   The interest rate that equates a future value or an annuity to a given present value.

yield curve   A curve that shows interest rates at a specific point in time for all securities having equal risk but different maturity dates. Usually government securities are used to construct such curves. The yield curve is also referred to as the term structure of interest rates.

yield to maturity   The annualized rate of return that an investor will receive if a bond is held until its maturity date. The yield to maturity formula includes any capital gains or losses that arise because the par value is greater than or less than the market price.

zero-coupon rate bond   A bond that is sold at a deep discount from face value. The return to the investor is the difference between the investor's cost and the face value received at the end of the life of the bond.

Index